Brazil's Economy

The past century has witnessed profound transitions in Brazil's economy: from a surge of industrialization connected to export economy, to state projects of import-substitution industrialization, followed by a process of neoliberal global market integration. How have Brazilian entrepreneurs and businesses navigated these contexts?

This comprehensive text explores the institutional and sectoral structure of the Brazilian economy through a collection of new case studies, examining how key institutions work within Brazil's specific economic, political and cultural context. Offering a long-term evolutionary perspective, the book explores Brazil's economic past in order to offer insights on its present and future trajectory. The contributions gathered here offer fresh insights into representative sectors of Brazil's economy, from aerospace to software, television, music and banking, paying particular attention to sectors that are likely to drive future growth. Chapters include questions about the roles of foreign and state capital, changes in market regulation, the emergence of new technologies, the opening of markets, institutional and organizational frameworks, and changing management paradigms.

When examined together, the contributions shed light not only on Brazilian business history, but also on the country as a whole. *Brazil's Economy: An Institutional and Sectoral Approach* offers fascinating reading for anyone with an interest in: Latin American Economics; the business history of the region; and in doing business in present-day Latin America.

Werner Baer was Jorge Paulo Lemann Professor of Economics at the University of Illinois at Urbana-Champaign, USA.

Jerry Dávila is Jorge Paulo Lemann Professor of Brazilian History and Director of the Lemann Institute for Brazilian Studies at the University of Illinois at Urbana-Champaign, USA.

André de Melo Modenesi is Associate Professor at the Instituto de Economia at Universidade Federal do Rio de Janeiro, Brazil.

Maria da Graça Derengowski Fonseca is Associate Professor at the Instituto de Economia, Universidade Federal do Rio de Janeiro, Brazil.

Jaques Kerstenetzky is Associate Professor at the Instituto de Economia, Universidade Federal do Rio de Janeiro, Brazil.

Routledge Studies in the Modern World Economy

Brazil's Economy
An Institutional and Sectoral Approach

Edited by **Werner Baer, Jerry Dávila,
André de Melo Modenesi,
Maria da Graça Derengowski Fonseca
and Jaques Kerstenetzky**

Routledge
Taylor & Francis Group

LONDON AND NEW YORK

First published 2018
by Routledge
2 Park Square, Milton Park, Abingdon, Oxon OX14 4RN

and by Routledge
52 Vanderbilt Avenue, New York, NY 10017

First issued in paperback 2020

Routledge is an imprint of the Taylor & Francis Group, an informa business

British Library Cataloguing-in-Publication Data
A catalogue record for this book is available from the British Library

Library of Congress Cataloging-in-Publication Data
Title: Brazil's economy : an institutional and sectoral approach / edited by
Jerry Dávila, [and four others].
Description: Abingdon, Oxon ; New York, NY : Routledge, 2018. |
Includes bibliographical references and index.
Identifiers: LCCN 2017014353| ISBN 9781138040373 (hardback) |
ISBN 9781315175140 (ebook)
Subjects: LCSH: Economic development--Brazil. | Brazil--Economic
conditions--1945- | Brazil--Economic policy.
Classification: LCC HC187 .B8736 2018 | DDC 330.981--dc23
LC record available at https://lccn.loc.gov/2017014353

ISBN 13: 978-0-367-66765-8 (pbk)
ISBN 13: 978-1-138-04037-3 (hbk)

Typeset in Times New Roman
by Saxon Graphics Ltd, Derby

Contents

Figures

Tables

Contributors

Werner Baer held the Jorge Paulo Lemann Professorship in Economics at the University of Illinois at Urbana Champaign. Renowned economist of Brazilian economic development, he completed his PhD studies at Harvard University in 1958. He authored several books including *Industrialization and Economic Development in Brazil* (Irwin, 1965), *The Development of the Brazilian Steel Industry* (Vanderbilt, 1969), and *The Brazilian Economy: Its Growth and Development*, its most seventh revised edition published in 2014 (Lynne Rienner). He was also co-editor of several books, most recently *Energy, Bio Fuels and Development: Comparing Brazil and the United States*, with Ed Amman (Routledge, 2013).

Kamaiaji de Souza Castor is a doctoral student in Economics at Instituto de Economia, Universidade Federal do Rio de Janeiro (UFRJ). He obtained a Bachelor (2010–2013) and a Master of Arts (2014–2016) degrees in Economics from UFRJ.

Jerry Dávila is Jorge Paulo Lemann Professor of Brazilian History and Director of the Lemann Institute for Brazilian Studies at the University of Illinois at Urbana-Champaign. He is the author of several books including *Dictatorship in South America* (Wiley Blackwell, 2013); *Hotel Trópico: Brazil and the Challenge of African Decolonization* (Duke, 2010); and *Diploma of Whiteness: Race and Social Policy in Brazil, 1917-1945* (Duke, 2003). He is also a co-author of the eleventh edition of the *History of World Societies* (Macmillan, 2017).

Maria da Graça Derengowski Fonseca at Instituto de Economia, Universidade Federal do Rio de Janeiro (UFRJ), where he teaches Industrial Economics, Institutional and Evolutionary Economics and Microeconomics Fundamentals for graduate students and Industrial Economics for undergraduate students at the Instituto de Economis-UFRJ (Economics) since 1993. She also teaches Economics of Innovation at the Biotechnology Programme-UFRJ. Before that Maria also taught Brazilian Economics, Technological Economics and Agribusiness Economy at Universidade Federal Fluminense and Universidade Federal Rural do Rio de Janeiro. She is the head of the Bioeconomy Research

Group and the Infosucro Laboratory at the IE-UFRJ. Maria is member of the International Schumpeter Society being her international president from 2006 to 2008 organizing the 12th International Conference at the IE-UFRJ in Brazil at the Instituto de Economia (UFRJ). She holds a PhD in Economics (1990) at Instituto de Economia (Universidade de Campinas, São Paulo),a Masters of Sciences (1980) at the CPDA (Universidade Rural do Rio de Janeiro), and a Bachelor's degree in Economics at Faculdade de Economia e Administração (FEA-UFRJ), the former Instituto de Economia,1976). In 1999-2000 she was a honorary visiting research fellow at the Centre for Competition and Innovation of the University of Manchester, UK.

Marc Hertzman is Associate Professor of History at the University of Illinois, Urbana-Champaign. He obtained his PhD in Latin American History from the University of Wisconsin-Madison in 2008 and published his first book, *Making Samba: A New History of Race and Music in Brazil* in 2013. He has also published in *American Historical Review*, *Hispanic American Historical Review*, *Journal of Latin American Studies,* and *New York Magazine*, among others. He is currently writing a book about 300 years of memory of the death of Zumbi dos Palmares.

Jaques Kerstenetzky is Associate Professor at Instituto de Economia, Universidade Federal do Rio de Janeiro (UFRJ). He was a visiting scholar at MIT and New York University. His research interests are Firms and Markets from the perspective of Business History and History of the Economic Thought.

George Kornis is Associate Professor of Institute for Social Medicine Studies (IMS)/Rio de Janeiro State University (UERJ), Brazil, and is Associate to the Research Group of Economics of the Entertainment Industry (GENT/UFRJ). He is author of circa 40 articles and co-author of A Economia da Cadeia Produtiva do Livro, with Fabio Sá-Earp (BNDES, 2005). He holds a DSc. Degree in Economics (UFRJ).

Ronaldo Lemos is Professor of Law & Technology at the Rio de Janeiro State University (UERJ), Brazil and a visiting professor at Columbia University's School of International Public Affairs. He obtained his LL.D. in Philosophy and General Theory of Law from the University of Sao Paulo in 2004, and his LL. M. from Harvard Law School in 2002. He has published articles and books in Portuguese and English on law, technology, and intellectual property. His research interests include copyright, music and other cultural industries, and Internet regulation.

Joseph L. Love is Professor Emeritus of History at the University of Illinois at Urbana-Champaign. He was formerly director of the Lemann Institute of Brazilian Studies at the University, where he had previously been director of the Center for Latin American and Caribbean Studies. In addition to having published some 70 journal articles and book chapters, he is the author of *The Revolt of the Whip* (Stanford UP, 2012); *Crafting the Third World: Theorizing,*

Underdevelopment in Rumania and Brazil (Stanford UP, 1996); *São Paulo in the Brazilian Federation, 1889-1937* (Stanford UP, 1980); and *Rio Grande do Sul and Brazilian Regionalism, 1882-1930* (Stanford UP, 1971). He is also co-editor of several books, most recently *Brazil under Lula: Economy, Society, and Politics under the Worker-President*, with Werner Baer (Palgrave Macmillan, 2009).

André de Melo Modenesi is Associate Professor at the Instituto de Economia, Universidade Federal do Rio de Janeiro, Brazil and CNPq Research Fellow. He obtained his PhD in Economics from the Universidade Federal do Rio de Janeiro in 2008. His research interests include Macroeconomic Theory, Monetary Theory and Policy and Brazilian Studies. In addition to having published some 35 journal articles and book chapters, he is the author of the text book *Regimes Monetários: Teoria e a Experiência do Real* (Manole, 2005). He was also co-author of chapters in: *The Brazilian Economy Today: Towards a New Socio-Economic Model?* (Palgrave Macmillan, 2016); *The Global South after the Crisis: Growth, Inequality and Development in the Aftermath of the Great Recession* (Edward Elgar, 2016); and *The New Brazilian Economy: Dynamic Transitions into the Future* (Palgrave Macmillan, 2017). He was the Deputy Executive Secretary of the Associação Nacional dos Centros de Pós-Graduação em Economia (2014–2016) and was Director of Associação Keynesiana Brasileira (2012–14). In 2007 he was a visiting scholar at the University of Illinois in Urbana-Champaign. He was also a Visiting Research Fellow at Instituto de Pesquisa Econômica Aplicada (IPEA), during 2007–09 and 2012–13.

Rui Lyrio Modenesi is economist (retired) at Banco Nacional de Desenvolvimento Econômico e Social (BNDES), Rio de Janeiro, Brazil. He was Under Secretary of Economic Policy and of the Tariff Policy Commission, at the Finance Minister. He also held senior positions at BNDES, and worked at the Instituto de Pesquisa Econômica Aplicada. Associate Professor at the Universidade Federal Fluminense and Visiting Professor at PUC-Rio, he co-authored books and articles mostly on the Brazilian Economy.

Luiz Carlos Delorme Prado is Associate Professor at the Instituto de Economia, Universidade Federal do Rio de Janeiro, Brazil. He is also a member of the Research Group on Law, Economics and Competition of the Institute of Economics, UFRJ. Prado holds a B.Sc degree on Economics and, also, a degree on Law, by Federal University of Rio de Janeiro. He obtained his PhD in Economics from the University of London, Queen Mary College (1991) and his M.Sc from the Federal University of Rio de Janeiro. He was a commissioner at Council for Economic Defense (CADE), the Brazilian competition authority (2004–2008) and he was, also, President of the Federal Council of Economics (Conselho Federal de Economia). He has done commissioned work for International Organizations, such as ECLAC (Economic Commission of Latin American and Caribbean – United Nations),

PNUD, UNDP (United Nations Developed Program), Mercosur Audiovisual Program (Cooperación Mercosur – Union Europeia), to Regulatory Agencies, such as ANATEL and, also, to public and private firms. His research interests include: competition and regulation policies, law and economics, trade policy and developing economics. He is the author of more than forty articles, books and monographs on those areas.

Leonardo Fernandes Moutinho Rocha is a PhD candidate at the Instituto de Economia, Universidade Federal do Rio de Janeiro (UFRJ). He holds an MA Degree (2011–2013) in Economics at UFRJ. He is a researcher of the Beyond the Technological Revolution Project. His research interests include Information and Communication Technology Industry, Neo-Schumpeterian Evolutionary Economics, Complexity Economics, Agent-Based Modeling, Development and Public Policy.

Eduardo Pontual Ribeiro is Associate Professor at the Instituto de Economia, Universidade Federal do Rio de Janeiro, Brazil and CNPq Research Fellow. He obtained his PhD from the University of Illinois at Urbana-Champaign. His research interests include Microeconometrics, Antitrust and Labor Economics.

Tarciso Gouveia da Silva is PhD candidate at Instituto de Economia, Universidade Federal do Rio de Janeiro (UFRJ) and Researcher at the Money and Financial System Study Group at the UFRJ. He holds MA Degree in Economics at the UFRJ. He has a career centered on economics, financial systems and capital markets. His research areas are Macroeconomics and Monetary Economics. He is currently working in the pension fund industry as an Investment Analysis and Economic Research Manager with expertise in Macroeconomic Analysis.

Fábio Sá-Earp is Associate Professor at the Instituto de Economia, Universidade Federal do Rio de Janeiro, Brazil. His research area is the economics of entertainment industry. He is Coordinator of the Research Group of the Entertainment Industry (GENT/UFRJ). He is co-author of A Economia da Cadeia Produtiva do Livro, with George Kornis (BNDES, 2005) and editor of Pão e Circo: Limites e Perspectivas da Economia do Entretenimento (Palavra e Imagem, 2002). He is also co-editor of Como Vai o Brasil, with André de Melo Modenesi e Eduardo Bastian (Imã editorial, 2014). He holds a DSc. Degree in Economics (UFRJ).

Paulo Bastos Tigre is full professor at Instituto de Economia, Universidade Federal do Rio de Janeiro (UFRJ). He earned his PhD in Science and Technology Policy at the University of Sussex, UK in 1982 and is author of several books and articles on Innovation, Information and Telecommunication Technologies, and Industrial Economics. He was visiting research fellow in University of Brighton (1994), University of Paris XIII (1996) and University of California Berkeley (1997) and served as consultant and advisor to several national and international organizations.

Acknowledgements

We wish to thank the contributors to this volume for their original contributions to our understanding of the institutional and entrepreneurial effects of economic factors and policies. As a project built out of collaboration between two institutions, one in Brazil and one in the United States, we thank our colleagues at the Federal University of Rio de Janeiro Department of Economics, and the University of Illinois Departments of Economics, History and Lemann Institute for Brazilian Studies. We offer our enthusiastic thanks to Kelly Senters who read and edited the chapters from Brazil, as well as the research work conducted by Bárbara Costa e Silva, Lucas Bressan de Andrade and Mattheus Vianna. Finally, we are grateful to Emily Kindleysides and Elanor Best at Routledge for the ways they helped us bring the volume forward amid the loss of our co-editor, Werner Baer, to whom we owe this book's inspiration.

Introduction

Case studies in Brazil's economy

Jerry Dávila, André de Melo Modenesi, Maria da Graça Derengowski Fonseca and Jaques Kerstenetzky

When Werner Baer convened the economists and historians who have collaborated in this volume, he had the intention of bringing new focus to the granularity of economic and entrepreneurial experiences. Long critical of "aggregate" approaches to the study of economics, he sought to combine a series of lenses that could raise new questions about the Brazilian economy. We can see these lenses line up in the following way: first, this is a study of Brazil as an example of the experiences of emerging economies; second, it is an effort to think about how key institutions work within Brazil's economic, political, and cultural contexts. To accomplish this, the authors have focused on case studies of businesses, entrepreneurs and institutions. These case studies reveal particularities about Brazil's economy, interpreted through the ways in which individuals and enterprises have recognized and navigated them.

The studies bound in this volume are the product of a collaboration between faculty in economics and history at the University of Illinois at Urbana-Champaign and at the Federal University of Rio de Janeiro. Responding to Baer's challenge that we think about Brazil's economy through the specific contexts reflected in a series of case studies, we have developed a book that is grounded in business history and is attuned to the significance of political, social and cultural factors. We work with the premise that economics and history mutually benefit from the recognition of national, local and sectorial contexts. In other words, it matters that these case studies are about Brazil, and in turn, we see these case studies as not just informing business history, but helping us understand and interpret Brazil.

Though some of the chapters of this book reach back to the era of import substitution industrialization in the 1930s and even as far back as the early formative experiences with industrialization, the approach here is to explore how Brazilian firms and sectors of the Brazilian economy experienced the great changes that occurred in the business environment in the context of globalization and liberalization. Globalization brought with it competitive challenges, but also brought opportunities such as new technologies, trade opening, increased presence of foreign capital, changes in market regulations, institutional and organizational frameworks, and changed management paradigms.

The cases that make up the book must each be understood on their own terms, rather than as simple expressions of a single phenomenon. Circumstances, capabilities and strategies evolved differently in particular firms and sectors, giving rise to distinct trajectories of development. As for their circumstances, experiences with globalization had different effects on different sectors and firms. In some sectors, regulatory change was of paramount importance; in others, the impact of competition from transnational companies and trade liberalization was far greater. Capabilities and strategies are just as idiosyncratic as are the historical particularities under study.

As each case reflects different institutionalities, problems, challenges and opportunities, different analytical tools and conceptual frameworks are used. Choosing theories and analytical instruments according to the problems at hand has the advantage of preventing theory from overriding the historical content of the cases. In the end, the pluralistic and prominently historical approach of the chapters maintains conceptual frameworks at the background and is meant to deliver nuanced explanations of successful cases (and also of an unsuccessful one).

The first chapter, by André de Melo Modenesi, Tarcisio Gouveia, Kamaiaji de Souza Castor and Rui Lyrio Modenesi traces the trajectory of Brazilian banking since the watershed 1995 Real Plan. The authors look at the fragility of the banking system, despite its periods of high profitability. Banks – especially state owned ones – were highly dependent on floating revenue. The authors examine the succession of fusions, mergers, and privatizations that this fragility induced, which had the effect of significantly reducing the number of banking institutions. The authors see Brazil's high banking spreads as a likely result of the concentration of market and low competition between banks that emerged from this cycle of mergers. Exploring in particular the 2008 merger between two large national banks, Itaú and Unibanco, they estimate the degree of competition through the Panzar-Rosse Index and, in line with the literature, they argue that the emergent Brazilian banking system can be understood as one that functions through monopolistic competition.

In Chapter 2, Eduardo Pontual Ribeiro explores the explosive growth of the private higher education sector in Brazil. Since the regulatory change allowing institutions of higher education to be maintained by for profit corporations in 1997, the size of the private higher education market grew more than four-fold. It also became a significant business market with a market capitalization of almost USD $1 billion in 2014 for the four largest firms. The sector also received extensive foreign direct investment in equity form. Pontual explores the growth patterns and business strategies of these firms, focusing on their firm dynamics as well as patterns of mergers and acquisitions. Pontual sees that for profit higher education institutions focus on mass education with lower quality than public universities. The sector exploited scale economies through standardization and distance learning. He further finds significant price differentiation across majors and institutions. He focuses on one of the firms, Anhanguera Educational, as a detailed example of this model. Controlled by Brazilians, it was able to grow significantly through mergers and acquisition, financed by equity and direct investors, as the founders let go of managerial control while maintaining financial control.

In Chapter 3, Fabio Sá-Earp, George Kornis, and Luiz Carlos Delorme Prado examine the patterns of Brazil's television sector through a focus on regulatory and technological changes. In particular they examine the experience of Globo Network, whose history reflects the most important changes in Brazil's television market (both, broadcast and pay TV) over the last thirty years. Brazil's television broadcast is a 65 year-old business, which began as a network that was restricted to a few large cities. By the end of the century, it reached the whole country: by the beginning of the twenty-first century, nearly all Brazilian homes had access to TV. Most program content was produced in Rio de Janeiro and São Paulo, the headquarters of the four largest networks, which broadcast their programs to a territory of about 8,5 million square kilometers. Brazil is peculiar among developing countries in that most television content is domestically produced and the country has been able to project a coherent national identity through that content. Nonetheless, Brazil's television market has been changing fast over the last decade due to the commercial and political impact of paid television. The authors trace recent trends in television framed by legal and regulatory changes, along with the recent growth of internet television channels.

In Chapter 4, Jaques Kerstenetzky traces the life cycle of Metal Leve (ML), the automotive parts manufacturer, from its creation in the beginning of the 1950s, examining the patterns of its growth, success and leadership in the Brazilian auto parts industry, exercised until the end of the 1980s. In the 1990s, problems related to competition from multinationals and changes in external trade policy brought about the denationalization of ML. The chapter offers a counterpoint to the other business case studies in this volume, as Metal Leve was unsuccessful at navigating the fallout of liberalizaton. Metal Leve's case is emblematic of business in a peripheral country in the era of globalization. During the decades of import substitution industrialization, ML was recognized for its national business excellence, achieving international recognition in the 1980s as a supplier to foreign companies through its exports. But with the onset of denationalization, ownership and control were relinquished to a large German auto parts firm that had already participated in the early phases of ML's history. Though the ML case contains nuances that give it marked characteristics and interest in its own right, it is also broadly representative of the development and transformation of the auto parts manufacturing sector and automobile industry both in Brazil and the world.

In Chapter 5, Paulo Bastos Tigre and Leonardo Moutinho examine the unique case of TOTVS, a Brazilian supplier of Enterprise Resource Planning (ERP), a software tool designed to automate business processes. TOTVS has adopted a fast growth strategy based on mergers and acquisitions, aiming at acquiring technology, market and specific business processes expertise in different industrial sectors. The world ERP market is very competitive and TOTVS occupies the market niche of small and medium size firms, a low end of the ERP market relatively neglected by industry leaders like SAP and Oracle. As technology moves from products to services and from on-premise systems to cloud computing, new business models are being developed based on the potential of networking. Despite its past success, TOTVS faces the challenge of becoming more international and entering in major markets where customers are already locked-in by competing firms.

In Chapter 6, "Brazil's Embraer: Institutional Entrepreneurship," Werner Baer and Joseph Love trace the creation and evolution of Brazil's aircraft manufacturer from a small government-owned enterprise to a privately-owned world leader in the production of regional jets. Emphasis is placed in various strategic alliances with foreign aircraft designers and aircraft producers which resulted in a continuous transfer and adaptation of new technologies. The emergence of *Embraer* was largely the product of "institutional entrepreneurship." But the rise of Brazil's aircraft manufacturer, Embraer, was not the result of the efforts of one *entrepreneur*. Instead, Embraer resulted from institutional developments which brought forth entrepreneurial efforts. Yet one person stands out in the development of Embraer, so this case shows the significance of the combined importance of institutions and individual leadership.

In Chapter 7, Marc Adam Hertzman and Ronaldo Lemos explore two of this volume's central concerns – entrepreneurship and competitive markets. Music requires one to revisit standard definitions and basic assumption of entrepreneurial endeavors and competition. What is a music entrepreneur, and how does s/he compare to industrialists, business magnates, and technology innovators? How does a musician's relationship to his/her means and fruits of production compare to that of other figures studied in this volume? What does competition mean in music? Is the Brazilian music market a competitive one? Hertzman and Lemos show how the answers to these questions change when studied across time.

In Chapter 8, Jerry Dávila revisits Werner Baer's classic study *The Development of the Brazilian Steel Industry* to consider the kinds of analytical pathways Baer's approach pursued. Baer's study interlaced thick readings of Brazilian history and of the technical and engineering dimensions of steel manufacturing in order to interpret the experience with economic development as one that is locally grounded and dependent on a convergence of political, economic and technological factors. Dávila suggests that this approach opens new interpretive directions. In particular, he considers the role of nationalist thought and ideology in framing the perceptions of opportunities and constraints that shaped the emergence of Brazil's steel sector. In this case, nationalist ideology is understood as a combination of factors ranging from the thinking of jurist Alberto Torres, who advocated the creation of a strong central state capable of implementing solutions to perceived national problems; the influence of European and, in particular, French nationalism in the aftermath of the First World War in conceptualizing the integration of industries; and the strain of nationalism and regionalism among Brazilian political leaders who were wary of foreign ownership of mineral resources and major industries. The chapter focuses in particular on the role of a central actor in the planning and implementation of Brazil's national steel complex in Volta Redonda, Edmundo de Macedo Soares.

Unfortunately, Werner Baer left us before the work went to press. Still, his presence is felt not only in this book and in his lifetime of work on the Brazilian economy, but also in the minds and feelings of all of us who benefitted from his company, gentleness and brilliance. The chapters that follow reflect the influence of his thought, and we dedicate this work to his memory.

1 The Brazilian banking industry

Evolution, concentration, and competition after the 1990s

André de Melo Modenesi, Tarciso Gouveia da Silva, Kamaiaji de Souza Castor and Rui Lyrio Modenesi

Introduction

The aim of this chapter is to analyze the Brazilian banking industry's competitive regime from the Real Price Stabilization Plan in 1995 to 2015.

In the aftermath of the Washington Consensus, the Brazilian banking industry experienced a period of substantial structural change beginning at the end of the 1980s and continuing in the decade that followed. This process can be divided into two periods: i) the first of which lasted from 1987 to 1993 and exhibited a macroeconomic scenario dominated by chronically high inflation; and ii) the second of which took place between 1994 and 1998 and witnessed a coupling of the liberalization process with the price stabilization measures in the Real Plan.

During the first phase, the 1988 Banking Reform authorized the creation of multiple banks as well as unified commercial banking and credit activities with investment activities in a single institution. The new legislation streamlined the process and bureaucratic requirements involved in opening new banks. In addition, Brazil adopted a set of regulatory rules designed under the Basel Accord.

Notably, the reform substantially benefited large financial conglomerates, allowing these groups to operate as universal banks since the reform. Indeed, the reform had a profound impact on the market structure, and it helps to explain the current high levels of concentration in the Brazilian banking industry.

During the second phase, in the aftermath of the Real Plan in 1994, price stabilization proved challenging for the Brazilian banking and financial system. Indeed, the banking industry experienced profound changes in adapting to the new macroeconomic environment. Price stabilization put a sudden end to one of the most important sources of revenue for Brazilian banks – the so-called "inflationary revenues" earned from inflationary floating. Thus, the fragility of the balance sheets of many banks was revealed.

To compensate for this revenue loss, banks increased loans and credit concessions. On the one hand, inflationary controls encouraged families to seek credit and financing; on the other hand, banks became more confident in engaging in lending. Notwithstanding, the rapid expansion of banking credit, coupled with very high interest rates, resulted in sharp growth in non-performing loans.

Consequently, the risk of a banking crisis rose dramatically after the Real Plan's implementation. To manage this looming risk, the Brazilian government established a set of measures to facilitate bank acquisitions. The most relevant of these measures was the Program of Incentives for the Restructuring and Strengthening of the National Financial System (PROER). Additionally, some measures encouraging the entry of foreign banks were adopted in 1995.

To address the solvency problems of state-owned public banks, the federal government implemented the Program for the Reduction of the State Public Banking Sector (PROES) in 1996. As a result, the number of banks was reduced, as was state participation in the banking industry, and industry internationalization was promoted.

The evolution of the number of commercial banks in Brazil shows a sharp reduction from 1995 to 2014. This period can be divided into two paradigmatic moments. In the aftermath of the Real Plan, the reduction of the numbers of banks can largely be explained by the end of the inflationary revenue. As a result, many banks became insolvent and/or went bankrupt, and the PROER and PROES promoted the restructuring of the banking industry. After 2000, the reduced number of banks is a result of the process of banking industry consolidation.

The Brazilian banking industry has two characteristics: it has one of the highest bank spreads in the world; and it still experiences substantial participation by public banks.

Despite a decrease in the net interest margin of the banking industry after the implementation of the Real Plan, Brazil continues to have one of the largest banking spreads in the world. As a result, Brazil also stands out with high market interest rates. Indeed, the lending rates in Brazil are considerably higher than those in many less-developed economies with almost nonexistent financial systems (such as the economies in Uganda, Tajikistan, Mongolia, and Honduras). This is evidence that Brazilian banks have substantial market power and, thus, charge high prices (through interest rates) for loan concessions.

The Brazilian banking industry is also characterized by significant participation of public banks. For instance, in 2015, the federal-owned *Banco do Brasil* (BB) and *Caixa Econômica Federal* (CEF) ranked first and third, respectively, in size by total assets. Regarding loan portfolios, BB and CEF rank first and second with 25.2 percent and 23.3 percent of total loans (including the BNDES) outstanding in the country, respectively. In relation to total deposits, BB and CEF account for 48.7 percent of the total market.

Public banks' market share rose significantly following the 2008 subprime crisis. Indeed, public banks played a major role in avoiding a credit crunch and, thus, in smoothing the sharp decline in private banks' credit supply. Private banks drastically reduced the rhythm of their loan concessions. However, public commercial and development banks immediately and aggressively expanded the pace of their lending. In the aftermath of the Euro Crisis (2011–2012), private and public banks once again maintained an uneven path. As a result, public banks' market share has increased substantially, from 34.4 percent in 2008, to

55.0 percent in 2015. Private banks' market share fell from a peak of 65.6 percent to a low of 44.9 percent over the same period.

This chapter presents a comprehensive analysis of the market structure and competitive regime of the Brazilian banking industry and, in doing so, seeks to meaningfully contribute to the inconclusive literature in the field. We propose that after the 1990s, the Brazilian banking industry exhibits two stylized facts: it is highly concentrated (showing a growing trend in all the concentration measures), and there is little to no price competition. The high spread charged by Brazilian banks (a measure of mark-up) is, to a large extent, explained by those two stylized facts.

Currently, the banking industry is more concentrated in Brazil than it is in Chile, Argentina, Colombia, Korea, and India. The market participation of the four largest institutions – considering total deposits, demand deposits, and total assets – shows a clear growing trend. Notably, there are high levels of concentration in the demand deposit market. After 2002, these levels surpassed 70 percent, which was twice the level of concentration in the US in 2014. The ten biggest Brazilian banks received almost all of the demand deposits; this is an outstanding number indicating that the market is highly concentrated.

We have also calculated the H index, a standard index estimating the level of competition in a given market (Panzar and Rosse, 1987), for the Brazilian banking industry. According to our estimation, the banking sector follows monopolistic competition.

Accompanying this introduction and brief conclusion, this chapter has three sections. The first section provides a brief overview of the Brazilian banking industry after price stabilization in the aftermath of the Real Plan. The second section focuses on two main characteristics – high bank spread and involvement of public banks – of the Brazilian banking industry. The Brazilian banking industry exhibits one of the highest bank spreads in the world, and it features substantial participation by public banks. The third section contains the core of our contribution – an analysis of the Brazilian banking industry market structure. First we explore concentration indexes and then we analyze the competitive regime.

In conclusion, the empirical evidence presented here, coupled with the fact that the Brazilian economy presents one of the highest bank spreads in the world, indicates that the Brazilian banks do not compete through prices and that the level of competition in the banking industry is low.

The Brazilian banking industry after price stabilization: an overview

In the aftermath of the Washington Consensus, Brazil engaged in a broad process of economic liberalization (including trade and financial liberalization). In particular, the Brazilian banking industry pursued a transformation that resulted in substantial structural change at the end of the 1980s. This process can be divided into two periods: i) the first of which lasted from 1987 to 1993 and exhibited a macroeconomic scenario dominated by chronically high inflation; and ii) the second of which took place between 1994 and 1998 and witnessed a coupling of the liberalization process with the price stabilization measures in the Real Plan.

During the first phase, the 1988 Banking Reform is particularly notable. This reform authorized the creation of multiple banks and unified commercial banking and credit activities with investment activities in a single institution. The new legislation streamlined the process and bureaucratic requirements involved in opening new banks. In addition, a set of regulatory rules under the Basel Accord were adopted. These rules were based on the following features: i) minimum capital requirements; ii) leverage limitations; iii) operational and financial capacities; and iv) stringent qualification of board members. Notably, the reform substantially benefited large financial conglomerates – and their subsidiaries – that have operated as universal banks since the reform. Indeed, the reform had a profound impact on the market structure, and it helps in explaining the current high levels of concentration in the Brazilian banking industry (as analyzed in section 3).

During the second phase, in the aftermath of the Real Plan in 1994, price stabilization has proved a challenge for the Brazilian banking and financial system.[1] Indeed, the banking industry has experienced profound changes in adapting to the new macroeconomic environment. Price stabilization put a sudden end to one of the most important sources of revenue for Brazilian bank – the so-called "inflationary revenues" earned from inflationary floating.[2] These measures revealed the fragility of the balance sheets of many banks – particularly small and medium ones but also some state-owned (nonfederal) banks.[3]

Indeed, the banking industry's inflationary (floating) revenue fell from an average of approximately 4 percent of GDP, during the early 1990s, to 2 percent of GDP in 1994. In 1995, it was eliminated altogether (see Table 1.1). Regarding the imputed value of bank output, inflationary revenue – which represented 41.9 percent of bank output in 1992 – dropped to 20.4 percent of bank output in 1994 and to 0.6 percent of bank output in 1995. The end of inflationary revenue has negatively affected smaller banks, in particular, which had become highly dependent on this revenue in the 1970s and 1980s (Hermann, 2002).[4]

To compensate for this huge revenue loss, banks have increased loans and credit concessions. On the one hand, the inflationary controls have encouraged families to seek credit and financing, and on the other hand, banks have felt more confident to engage in more lending when presented with a more stable and, thus, less risky macroeconomic scenario. Indeed, there was an increase in the average banking service revenues. Service revenues jumped from an average 8.4 percent

Table 1.1 Inflationary revenues: 1990–1995

	1990	1991	1992	1993	1994	1995
Inflationary Revenue/GDP	4.0	3.9	4.0	4.2	2.0	0.0
Inflationary Revenue/Valeu of Production Imputed	35.7	41.3	41.9	35.3	20.4	0.6

Source: IBGE

of the value added by private banking industry to 15.6 percent of the value added between 1994 and 1995. Public banks followed the same trend: Service revenues (as a proportion of the value added by public banks) rose from 13.1 percent to 20.1 percent over the same period (IBGE, 1997; Hermann, 2002).

The rapid expansion of banking credit, coupled with very high interest rates – one of the hallmarks of the Brazilian economy after the Real Plan – resulted in sharp growth in non-performing loans. Indeed, the delinquency rates rose from an average of 7.7 percent in 1994 to 12.6 percent at the end of 1995 (BCB, 1996).

Although the fragility of the banking sector has been associated with the new macroeconomic scenario, some microeconomic and/or idiosyncratic factors have also played an important role in explaining the liquidity problems (or financial fragility) of several individual banks and of some niche markets. Many problem-prone banks (such as *Banco do Brasil* (BB) and *Caixa Econômica Federal* (CEF)) were federal-owned. However, the state government banks suffered the greatest setbacks. The state government banks of the State of São Paulo and the State of Rio de Janeiro (*Banespa* and *BANERJ*, respectively) were among those experiencing severe tribulations; consequently, many of these institutions endured interventions by the Brazilian Central Bank (BCB).

The low inflation scenario also proved challenging for privately owned banks. Two large private banks with national capillarity, *Banco Econômico* and *Banco Nacional*, experienced substantial difficulties in adjusting to the new macroeconomic scenario marked by low inflation and tight monetary policy. In the end, these two banks were also subject to interventions by the BCB.

In summary, Brazilian banks' risks of experiencing banking crises rose dramatically after the adoption of the Real Plan. To manage this risk and/or to maintain the soundness of the banking sector, the Brazilian government established a set of measures to facilitate bank acquisitions. The most relevant of these measures was the Program of Incentives for the Restructuring and Strengthening of the National Financial System (PROER – *Programa de Estímulo à Reestruturação e ao Fortalecimento do Sistema Financeiro Nacional*). Additionally, the Brazilian banking market was opened to foreign competitors, and a measure encouraging the entry of foreign banks was adopted in 1995.

The BCB launched PROER in 1995. PROER consisted of a special line of credit (at low, or even subsidized, rates). It amounted to a large sum of money (approximately 2.5 percent of GDP) funded by the reserve requirements. Additionally, the BCB eased regulatory rules (Basel) to permit the purchase of insolvent banks and equity issues by other banks considered under better market conditions. In addition, the minimum capital required for foreign banks to enter the Brazilian market was reduced in an effort to foster financial stability. As a result, banks from other countries have entered the Brazilian market by acquiring local banks; HSBC's acquisition of Banco *Bamerindus* in 1997 exemplifies this practice.

To address the solvency problems of state-owned public banks, the federal government implemented the Program for the Reduction of the State Public Banking Sector (PROES – *Programa de Redução do Setor Público Estatal na Atividade Bancária*) in 1996. The program's main objectives were to reduce the presence of the public sector in the banking industry (in line with the goals of the Washington Consensus) and, thus, to ensure financial stability and/or reduce the risk of systemic crisis. Moreover, the government also sought to prevent the expansion of fiscal deficits. Throughout this multiple-year process, 12 major banks were privatized and 22 ceased operations.

In conclusion, PROER and PROES played an important role in defining the new structure of the Brazilian banking industry. Under these programs, the number of Brazilian banks was reduced. The government succeeded in reducing state participation in the banking industry and also promoted the internationalization of the industry by encouraging the entry of foreign banks.

Indeed, the number of banks operating in Brazil has dropped substantially since the 1990s (Table 1.2). For instance, there was a decrease of 50 banks between

Table 1.2 Brazilian banking industry evolution: 1994–2015

Banking Industry						
Commercial/Multiple Banks				Others		
Year	Total[1]	Private	Public[2]	Investment Banks	Federal Develop. Banks	Regional Develop. Banks
1994	244	219	25	17	1	5
1995	240	215	25	17	1	5
1996	229	203	26	23	1	5
1997	217	190	27	22	1	5
1998	203	180	23	22	1	4
1999	194	175	19	21	1	4
2000	192	175	17	19	1	4
2001	182	167	15	20	1	3
2002	167	152	15	23	1	3
2003	165	150	15	21	1	3
2004	164	150	14	21	1	3
2005	161	147	14	20	1	3
2006	159	146	13	18	1	3
2007	156	143	13	17	1	3
2008	159	147	12	17	1	3
2009	158	148	10	16	1	3
2010	157	148	9	15	1	3
2011	160	151	9	14	1	3
2012	160	151	9	14	1	3
2013	155	146	9	14	1	3
2014	153	143	10	14	1	3
2015	154	144	10	13	1	3

Source: BCB

1 Including investment banks
2 Including the State Savings Bank (CEF - Caixa Econômica Federal)

1994 and 1999. Whether this process resulted in a more concentrated market structure is a question that we address below in Section 3. Before addressing this question, however, we will briefly describe some peculiarities of the Brazilian banking industry.

Brazilian banking industry and its current characteristics: an overview

The Brazilian banking industry features three distinct characteristics: i) it practices one of the highest bank spreads in the world; ii) it has substantial participation by public banks; and iii) it is one of the most strictly regulated banking industries in the world[5] (Hermann, 2002; De Paula and Sobreira, 2010; BCBS, 2013; and Gouveia da Silva et al., 2016). At this juncture, we will focus on the first two characteristics.

Despite a decrease in the net interest margin of the banking industry after implementing the Real Plan, Brazil continues to have one of the largest banking spreads in the world, even in comparison with developing countries (Figure 1.1).

We do not attempt to analyze the bank spread composition and/or its determinants. Other scholars have addressed these topics, and their work has given rise to an intense debate on why Brazilian bank spreads have remained so high for such a long period. Some such studies seeking to explain bank spreads focus on microeconomic and institutional determinants whereas others focus on macroeconomic determinants (Gouveia da Silva, 2011).[6]

Although understanding the determinants is not critical for the purposes of this review, it is important to note that the bank spread, also referred to as the interest margin, is a measure of the mark-up. Accordingly, the Brazilian banking industry practices high markup, which points to the conclusion that banks have enough market power and/or they do not compete through price (this issue is explored in the following sections).

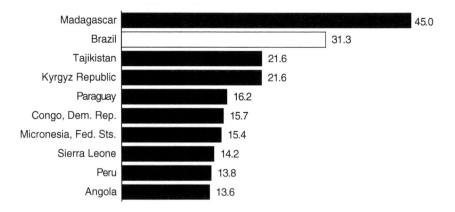

Figure 1.1 Top 10 highest banking spreads in the world: 2015 (p.p.)

Source: World Bank.

As a result, Brazil also stands out due to its high market interest rates (Figure 1.2). Indeed, the lending rates in Brazil are considerably higher than those in many less-developed economies with almost nonexistent financial systems (such as Uganda's, Tajikistan's, Mongolia's, and Honduras's). Brazil's high market interest rates provide another piece of evidence that Brazilian banks have substantial market power.

The Brazilian banking industry is also characterized by large participation by federal-owned banks. For instance, in 2015, BB and CEF ranked first and third, respectively, in size by total assets. Regarding loan portfolios, BB and CEF rank first and second with 25.2 percent and 23.3 percent of total loans (including BNDES) outstanding in the country, respectively. In relation to total deposits, BB and CEF account for 48.7 percent of the total market (more details in next section).

Notably, public banks' market share rose significantly after 2009. According to De Paula et al. (2015), in the aftermath of the subprime crisis (2008–2009), the banking sector has dramatically increased its liquidity preference due to strong agents' deteriorating expectations. The result was a deep pooling of liquidity in the banking reserves market. In addition, Brazil also faced a sudden cessation of external credit inflow both to banks and firms.

In the face of this drastic credit conditions deterioration, the BCB engaged in substantial relevant liquidity-enhancing measures for the banking industry.[7] In short, the BCB has promptly and successfully acted as a lender of last resort through the use of both conventional and non-conventional tools. Although a credit crunch was avoided, there was a sharp decline in credit supply, led mainly by private banks.

Total domestic credit growth rate reached a peak of 34.2 percent p.a. in October 2008 and fell sharply over the next 14 months, reaching a low of 14.6 percent p.a. in November 2009. Public banks played a major role in avoiding a credit crunch and thus smoothing the sharp decline in private banks' credit supply (Figure 1.3). Private banks drastically reduced the rhythm of their loan concessions (dotted line). However, public commercial and development banks (bold line) immediately and aggressively expanded the pace of their lending. In the second half of 2009, while private credit was growing at a rate of approximately 5 percent over 12 months, public credit was increasing at a 34–41 percent rate.

In the aftermath of the Euro crisis (2011–2012), private and public banks once again maintained an uneven path. As a result, public banks' market share has increased substantially, from 34.4 percent of GDP in 2008, to 55.0 percent of GDP in 2015 (Table 1.3). Private banks' market share fell from a peak of 65.6 percent to a low of 44.9 percent over the same period.

According to De Paula et al. (2015), the expansionary strategy of the public banks and, specifically, of the three federal 'giants' (BNDES, BB and CEF) was a political decision made by the Brazilian government to combat the contagion of the subprime and Euro crises. Accordingly, public banks played a major counter-cyclical role (both during the subprime and the Euro crises) in the credit market and contributed to avoiding a sharper decline in the total credit supply.

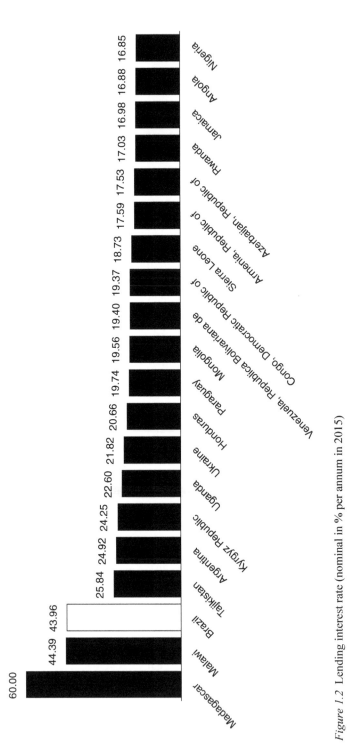

Figure 1.2 Lending interest rate (nominal in % per annum in 2015)

Source: IMF.

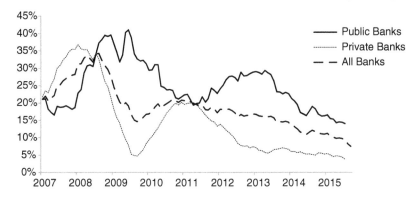

Figure 1.3 Overall outstanding credit operation (all banks %): March 2007–December 2015

Source: BCB.

Table 1.3 Credit/GDP and market share: 2007–2015

	2007	2008	2009	2010	2011	2012	2013	2014	2015
Total Credit/ GDP (%)	32.28	37.23	40.84	42.84	44.64	47.35	49.76	51.26	53.50
Public Banks (market share %)	35.03	34.42	39.05	41.70	42.28	45.55	49.91	52.86	55.06
Private Banks (market share %)	64.97	65.58	60.95	58.30	57.72	54.45	50.09	47.14	44.94
BNDES Loans/ GDP (%)	5.42	5.98	7.39	8.77	9.13	9.50	10.07	10.58	11.35

Source: BCB.

In addition to BB and CEF, the BNDES (the main long-term credit institution) has played a prominent role in counterbalancing the effects of the global financial and debt crises (Table 1.3). Although they concentrated on manufacturing, the BNDES credit concessions also substantially benefited agriculture, infrastructure, and the trade and services sector. Established in 1952, the BNDES is the main long-term financing agent of the Brazilian economy. The BNDES also significantly increased its market share (measured by the BNDES credit/GDP ratio) from 5.4 percent to 11.4 percent in 2015 (credit/GDP ratio) over the 2007–2015 period.

Finally, Table 1.4 shows the banking industry income share in 2015. Loan income represents only 47 percent of the total banking industry income. The second highest revenue share, 27 percent, results from treasury operations. Notably, the high share of banking services income, and fees and charge income, amounts to almost 11 percent of the total banking industry income.

In the next section, we analyze the Brazilian banking industry's market structure. First, we explore concentration indices. Then, the competitive regime will be analyzed.

Table 1.4 Banks' income share (% of total): 2015

Loan Income	47.04%
Treasury Income	27.09%
Derivatives and Exchange Income	3.51%
Banking Services Income	7.28%
Fees and Charges Income	3.52%
Others	11.56%

Source: BCB. Note: Only banks with commercial banking activities.

Market structure: concentration and competition

Concentration in the brazilian banking industry: 1995–2014

The literature analyzing the concentration level in the Brazilian commercial banking industry is inconclusive. For instance, Nakane and Rocha (2010) emphasize the stability of concentration indicators. Rondon (2011), by contrast, highlights a growing concentration trend.

Nakane and Rocha (2010) investigate the impact of two major M&As in the aftermath of the 2008 subprime crisis – the cases of *Itau Holding Financeira* and *Unibanco* and the acquisition of *Banco Real* by *Santander*. Their study covers the 2001–2008 period and uses data from BCB's Accounting Plan for Institutions of the National Financial System (COSIF) for the commercial banking industry. They calculated the concentration coefficient for the top three institutions C *(3)*[8] and the Herfindahl Hirschman Index (*HHI*)[9] using three variables – total loans, total credit and leasing operations, and total assets. According to these authors, there is a "(…) **relative stability** in the **degree** of **banking concentration** between June **2001** and June **2008**" (Nakane and Rocha, 2010, p. 16).

Rondon (2011) covers the longer 1995–2008 period. In calculating the *CR* (5) and the *HHI* for loans, securities stock, total deposits, and services revenue, he concludes the following: "Between 2001 and 2008, *HHI* and *CR5* indicators point to a **clear trend** of **concentration** in the **credit market**" (Rondon, 2011, p. 118).

Araújo, Neto, and Ponce (2006) cover the period from December/1995 to June/2004 and focus on the evolution of *CR* (3), *CR* (5) and *CR* (10) and the *HHI* for total deposits, loans, and total assets. According to these authors: "(…) the concentration indices for deposits, loans and assets shows that there was a movement of concentration among the top ten banks (and / or groups) of the Brazilian banking market in deposits and assets. (...) The other indicators of concentration in deposits remain relatively stable, indicating that mergers and liquidations experienced in the Brazilian banking industry had little effect on deposits" (Araujo, Neto and Ponce, 2006, pp. 565–566).

In considering international experience, Nakane and Rocha (2010) conclude that, in general, the Brazilian market cannot be considered more concentrated than other countries' banking markets: "Despite its increase in 2007, the level of concentration shows no major discrepancies in relation to that practiced in other countries. In that year, the high-income countries and middle income had *CR (3)* coefficient[s], respectively, [of] 73.6 percent and 66.2 percent" (Nakane and Rocha, 2010, p. 17).

Nevertheless, it should be noted that the banking industry is more concentrated in Brazil than in Chile, Argentina, Colombia, Korea and India, but less concentrated than it is in China: "In summary, the international data seem to indicate that the banking sector is characterized by a reasonable market concentration and this is not exclusive to the segment in the country. Although there is no more updated data, by 2007, the market share of the three largest institutions in total assets in Brazil does not stand out against to that registered in countries of the same level of development" (Nakane and Rocha, 2010, p. 18).

Indeed, the number of commercial banks in Brazil presented a sharp reduction from 1995 to 2014. In 1995, the country had 144 banks, and in 2014, there were only 96 banks. This process can be divided into two paradigmatic moments. In the aftermath of the Real Plan, the reduction of the numbers of banks is largely explained by the end of the inflationary revenue (as explained above). As a result, many banks became insolvent and/or went bankrupt, and the PROER and PROES promoted the restructuring of the banking industry. After 2000, the reduced number of banks is the result of the process of banking industry consolidation.

It should be noted that although the number of commercial banks has fallen, the sector has expanded. Indeed, the number of branches across the country has increased. The growth trend begins in 1998 and was interrupted only during the crisis of 2008, which is notable because the banking growth (the expansion of the number of current accounts and loans) is directly related to structural changes in the economy over this period, notably economic and social expansion.

Here, we analyze the evolution of concentration indices during the two paradigmatic moments of banking industry consolidation, ranging from December 1995 to December 2014. To construct these indices, we use data from the *Top 50 Banks in Brazil* (from the BCB); this database provides information for each bank on a quarterly basis. We considered only commercial banks and calculated *CR (4)*, *CR (10)* and *HHI*. These computations encompassed total assets (capturing the size of the institution), total deposits (both demand, time, and savings), loan and leasing operations, and net income.

Figure 1.4 shows the market participation (calculated by considering total deposits, demand deposits, and total assets) of the four largest institutions. Indeed, the *C (4)* shows a clear growing trend. Notably, there are high levels of concentration in the demand deposit market: *C (4)* remained above 70 percent after 2002 (for comparison, the same index in the US was approximately 35 percent in 2014, according to the Federal Deposit Insurance Corporation).

Figure 1.5 shows the market share of the top ten banks, *C(10)*, in terms of total deposits, demand deposits, and total assets. This figure also depicts a clear growing trend in all the calculated measures. For instance, in 1994, the *C (10)* for total deposits was 84.94 percent. In 2014, it approaches 96 percent. This means that the ten biggest banks received almost all of the demand deposits; this is an outstanding number that indicates that the market is highly concentrated.[10]

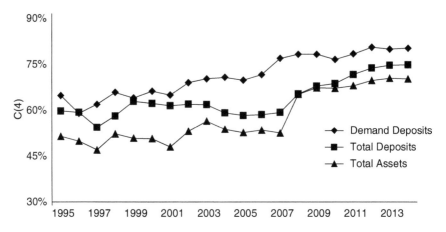

Figure 1.4 C(4) Index: 1995–2014

Source: Author's elaboration based on BCB (2016).

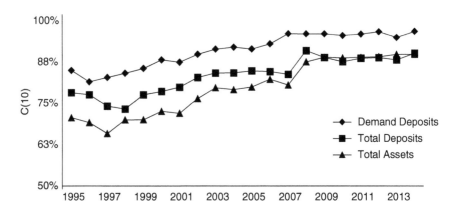

Figure 1.5 C(10) Index: 1995–2014

Source: Author's elaboration based on BCB (2016).

Figure 1.6 shows the evolution of another concentration index, the Herfindahl Hirschman Index (*HHI*). Again, this index clearly depicts increasing market concentration especially from 1995 to 2013. In addition to this trend of growing concentration, two breaks in the series should be noted – the breaks in December 2007 and December 2008.

Notably, in November 2008, two major banks, *Itaú* and *Unibanco*, announced a merger. The two banks were controlled by the Setubal and Moreira Salles families, respectively, and the merger was an important strategic move for both banks to maintain their competitiveness. Itaú maintained its branches and brand whereas Unibanco's branches were replaced.

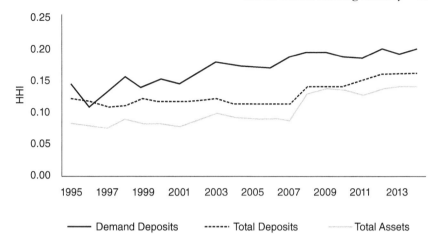

Figure 1.6 Herfindahl Hirschman Index (*HHI*): 1995–2014

Source: Author's elaboration based on BCB (2016).

According to the BCB Merger Guide, it is important to analyze the change in the *HHI* in the pre- and post-merger period of an M&A. Following the Itaú-Unibanco merger, there was an increase of more than 200 points in the *HHI* (calculated by considering total deposits and total credit operations). Given this fact, a merger's anticompetitive impact was a real possibility. Table 1.5 depicts the evolution in *HHI* over time.

Nevertheless, this merger was approved by the antitrust agency (*Conselho de Administração Econômica*, CADE). CADE's argument basically centered on the fact that the market share accumulated was less than 20 p.p. in most of the relevant markets considered, and there was not a reasonable chance of market power exercise. The BCB also approved such operation. Although BCB's decision reports are not public, the press has reported that the BCB required the two institutions to reduce their tariffs; this suggests that there was at least some possibility of damage to competition.[11]

Table 1.6 shows two snapshots of the market performance between September and December 2008, the period encompassing the merger between Itaú and Unibanco. We note that in loan operations, Itaú expanded its market share by 7 p.p.

Table 1.5 Herfindahl Hirschman Index (*HHI*): September 2008–December 2008

	September/2008	*December/2008*	*Variation*
Total Deposits	1174.72	1390.78	216.07
Demand Deposits	1690.6	1837.57	146.97
Total Credit Operations	1093.96	1315.07	221.11

Note: *HHI* was multiplied by 10,000.

Source: Author's elaboration based on BCB (2016).

Table 1.6 Market share: September 2008–December 2008

Total Deposits

September 2008				December 2008		
	Bank	Share			Bank	Share
1	ITAU	21.26%		1	BB	22.58%
2	CEF	14.55%		2	ITAU	18.54%
3	BRADESCO	12.97%		3	BRADESCO	13.88%
4	BB	11.56%		4	CEF	13.78%
5	SANTANDER	11.29%		5	SANTANDER	10.38%
6	VOTORANTIM	5.80%		6	HSBC	5.45%
7	HSBC	5.31%		7	NOSSA CAIXA	3.10%
8	CITIBANK	3.14%		8	VOTORANTIM	1.58%
9	SAFRA	2.16%		9	SAFRA	1.23%
10	CREDIT SUISSE	1.26%		10	BANRISUL	1.20%

Demand Deposits

September 2008				December 2008		
	Bank	Share			Bank	Share
1	BB	29.92%		1	BB	31.62%
2	BRADESCO	19.46%		2	ITAU	18.30%
3	ITAU	14.50%		3	BRADESCO	17.64%
4	SANTANDER	9.80%		4	SANTANDER	9.42%
5	CEF	8.33%		5	CEF	8.44%
6	HSBC	4.82%		6	HSBC	4.41%
7	NOSSA CAIXA	2.45%		7	NOSSA CAIXA	2.63%
8	UNIBANCO	2.45%		8	CITIBANK	1.39%
9	CITIBANK	1.50%		9	BANRISUL	1.20%
10	BANRISUL	1.08%		10	SAFRA	0.99%

Total Credit Operations

September 2008				December 2008		
	Bank	Share			Bank	Share
1	BB	20.95%		1	BB	21.86%
2	BRADESCO	15.08%		2	ITAU	18.57%
3	SANTANDER	12.27%		3	BRADESCO	15.01%
4	ITAU	11.30%		4	SANTANDER	12.46%
5	CEF	7.77%		5	CEF	8.57%
6	UNIBANCO	6.66%		6	VOTORANTIM	3.82%
7	VOTORANTIM	4.04%		7	HSBC	3.52%
8	HSBC	3.65%		8	SAFRA	1.75%
9	SAFRA	2.45%		9	NOSSA CAIXA	1.37%
10	NOSSA CAIXA	1.27%		10	BANRISUL	1.17%

Source: Author's elaboration based on BCB (2016).

after the merger, making it the second largest bank in the country. Itaú expanded its participation in the demand deposit market by 4 p.p.

Competition in the Brazilian banking industry: 2002–2014

Panzar and Rosse (1987) present a methodology to estimate the level of competition in a given market. Their basic idea is to estimate how a change in the price of inputs is reflected in income earned by a firm. Accordingly, the market power of a firm can be measured by the effect on the revenue resulting from a change in input prices. In other words, the question of market power depends on the elasticities of revenue relative to input prices. The so-called H index is given by the sum of revenue elasticities with respect to the price of each of the (j) inputs used:

$$H - \sum \frac{\partial Total\ Revenue}{\partial p_j} \frac{p_j}{Total\ Revenue}$$

If $H \leq 0$, the analyzed market is considered a monopoly (or a cartel). In this case, an increase in input price will cause a reduction in production and an increase in the price of the product. Thus, total revenue will remain the same or will be reduced given that monopolists operate on the elastic point of the demand curve.

If $H = 1$, the market structure approaches perfect completion. In this case, an increase in the input price will result in a proportional increase in firm total revenue; the price will increase by the same proportion.

Finally, if $0 < H < 1$, the market structure approaches monopolistic competition with firms competing through product differentiation.

According to our estimations of the H index (ranging from June 2002 to December 2014), the Brazilian banking market structure may be characterized neither as a monopoly (or cartel equilibrium) nor as perfect competition (for more details, see Appendix A). Thus, evidence indicates that the banking industry follows monopolistic competition. The statistic H averages approximately 0.7 (close to the findings of reviewed literature).

In summary, our results suggest that banks compete through product differentiation and not through price. Unfortunately, the literature does not offer a more precise definition/characterization of this type of competition regarding the banking sector. Anecdotal evidence suggests that advertising, branch density, and internet banking are used as competition strategies by banks in a highly concentrated structure.

Nevertheless, it should be noted that the H index shows a decreasing trend: it ranges from a peak of 0.84 (December 2002) to a low of 0.64 (December 2011).[12] Since December/2012 it has stabilized at 0.68. This trend is in line with the larger and growing trend of the concentration indexes (presented in previous item) and indicates that the degree of competition in the Brazilian banking industry has fallen. Accordingly, one can say that we are moving further away from a perfect competition market structure.

In conclusion, the empirical evidence presented here, coupled with the fact that the Brazilian economy presents one of the highest bank spreads in the world, indicates that the Brazilian banks do not compete through prices and/or that the level of competition in the banking industry is low.

Concluding remarks

Summing up, the post-1990s Brazilian banking industry exhibits two stylized facts: 1) it is highly concentrated and shows a growing trend in all concentration measures; and 2) there is little (or no) price competition. The high spread charged by Brazilian banks is explained to a great extent by those two stylized facts. In conclusion, the Brazilian banking industry is characterized by a highly concentrated market in which a few large banks have sufficient market power to charge a high mark-up, measured by the bank spread (or interest margin).

Notes

1 The Real Plan was a stabilization plan based on an exchange rate anchor (see Baer (2003) and Giambiagi et al. (2011)).
2 Inflationary floating refers to the revenue earned by banks through funds held by customers on demand deposit (current account). Prior to 1994, banks experienced high gains resulting from the loss of real value of demand deposits and/or the adjustment of bank deposits to values below inflation.
3 Before the banking industry restructuring, each state of the federation owned its own state bank.
4 According to the Central Bank, 32 banks of this type were closed between 1994 and 1998.
5 For details on the regulatory characteristics of the Brazilian banking industry, see Hermann (2002) and ANBIMA (2010).
6 According to many studies, the high level of bank spreads may be explained by the profile of public debt. Indeed, Brazilian public debt maturity is short (approximately 36 months). In addition, a significant portion of public debt is indexed to both the Selic (basic interest) rate (LFT) and to inflation (NTN-B). As a result, banks portfolios are dominated by liquid and low-risk short-term securities. As a consequence, the Brazilian yield curve exists only for short maturities (Carvalho (2005), Hermann (2013) and Almeida (2014)).
7 According to De Paula et al. (2015), the BCB adopted the following measures: (i) a reduction in reserve requirements that resulted in an expansion of liquidity of approximately 3.3 percent of GDP in the money market; (ii) the creation of incentives for larger financial institutions to purchase the loan portfolios of small and medium-sized banks; and (iii) an additional insurance deposit for small and medium-sized banks.
8 $C(k) = \sum_{i=1}^{k} s_i$, where s_i is firm i's market share. $C(k)$ is the concentration index that sums the market share for the top k firms.
9 The Herfindahl Hirschman Index is given by: $HHi = \sum_{i=1}^{n} s_i^2$, where s_i is firm i market share and n is the number of firms in the relevant market. This index measures how concentrated a market is and takes into account the market share variance given that greater s_i means greater weight.
10 Notably, the high level of concentration is convenient for the regulatory agencies as it makes the supervision process easier and less costly. See De Paula and Marques (2006), Araújo and Neto (2007) and Pinto (2011).

11 http://g1.globo.com/Noticias/Economia_Negocios/0,,MUL1008304-9356,00-BANCO
+CENTRAL+APROVA+FUSAO+DO+ITAU+COM+O+UNIBANCO.html
12 Statistical significance of this decreasing trend should be addressed more carefully in
future work.

References

Almeida, L.F.C.R. A Política Monetária e a Curva de Rendimentos dos Títulos Públicos
Federais: A Atuação do Banco Central do Brasil no período 2003–2012, Dissertação de
Mestrado em Economia. Instituto de Economia da Universidade Federal do Rio de
Janeiro, 2014.

ANBIMA (Associação Brasileira das Entidades do Mercado Financeiro e de Capitais).
Basileia III: novos desafios para adequação da regulação bancária, 2010. Available on:
http://portal.anbima.com.br/informacoes-tecnicas/estudos/perspectivas/Documents/
Perspectivas%20ANBIMA%20Basileia%20III.pdf

Araújo, L. A., D'ávila De, Jorge Neto, P. M., Ponce, D.A. S. Competição e Concentração
entre os Bancos Brasileiros. *Economia, Brasília*, v. 7, n. 3, pp. 561–586, Sep./Dec.
2006.

Baer, W. *Economia Brasileira*, 2 ed., Nobel, 2002.

BCB (Brazilian Central Bank). Relatório de Economia Bancária e Crédito, 1999. Available
on: www.bcb.gov.br/?SPREAD.

——. Relatório de Economia Bancária e Crédito, 2000. Available on: www.bcb.gov.
br/?SPREAD.

——. Relatório de Economia Bancária e Crédito, 2001. Available on: www.bcb.gov.
br/?SPREAD.

——. Relatório de Economia Bancária e Crédito, 2002. Available on: www.bcb.gov.
br/?SPREAD.

——. Relatório de Economia Bancária e Crédito, 2003. Available on: www.bcb.gov.
br/?SPREAD.

——. Relatório de Economia Bancária e Crédito, 2004. Available on: www.bcb.gov.
br/?SPREAD.

——. Relatório de Economia Bancária e Crédito, 2005. Available on: www.bcb.gov.
br/?SPREAD.

——. Relatório de Economia Bancária e Crédito, 2006. Available on: www.bcb.gov.
br/?SPREAD.

——. Relatório de Economia Bancária e Crédito, 2007. Available on: www.bcb.gov.
br/?SPREAD.

——. Relatório de Economia Bancária e Crédito, 2008. Available on: www.bcb.gov.
br/?SPREAD.

——. Relatório de Economia Bancária e Crédito, 2009. Available on: www.bcb.gov.
br/?SPREAD.

——. Relatório de Economia Bancária e Crédito, 2010. Available on: www.bcb.gov.
br/?SPREAD.

——. Relatório de Economia Bancária e Crédito, 2011. Available on: www.bcb.gov.
br/?SPREAD.

——. Relatório de Economia Bancária e Crédito, 2012. Available on: www.bcb.gov.
br/?SPREAD.

——. Relatório de Economia Bancária e Crédito, 2013. Available on: www.bcb.gov.
br/?SPREAD.

——. Relatório de Economia Bancária e Crédito, 2014. Available on: www.bcb.gov. br/?SPREAD.

BCBS (2013). Regulatory Consistency Assessment Programme (RCAP) Assessment of Basel III regulations in Brazil. Available on www.bis.org/bcbs/implementation/ l2_br.pdf.

Carvalho, F. J. C. Uma Contribuição ao Debate em torno da Eficácia da Política Monetária e Algumas Implicações para o Caso do Brasil. *Revista de Economia Política*, v. 25, pp. 323–336, 2005.

Giambiagi, F.;, Villela, A., Castro, L.B., Hermann, J. Economia Brasileira Contemporânea [1945-2010], 2 ed., Elsevier, 2011.

Gouveia Da Silva, T., Política monetária e sistema bancário: o papel das expectativas na determinação do spread brasileiro (2003-2011), Dissertação de Mestrado em Economia. Instituto de Economia da Universidade Federal do Rio de Janeiro, 2012.

Gouveia Da Silva, T., Ribeiro, E.P, MODENESI, A.M. Determinantes Macroeconômicos e o papel das expectativas: uma análise do spread bancário no Brasil 2003–2011. *Estudos Econômicos*, v.46, n.3, pp. 643–673, 2016.

Hermann, J. Liberalização e Crises Financeiras: o Debate Teórico e a Experiência Brasileira nos Anos 1990. Tese de Doutoramento. Rio de Janeiro: IE/UFRJ, 2002.

Hermann, J. Curva de Rendimentos: crítica aos enfoques convencionais e uma proposta de interpretação pós-keynesiana, VI Encontro Internacional da Associação Keynesiana Brasileira, 2013.

IBGE (Instituto Brasileiro de Geografia e Estatística). "Sistema Financeiro, uma Análise a partir das Contas Nacionais 1990–1995." Rio de Janeiro, IBGE, Departamento de Contas Nacionais, 1997.

Nakane, M. I., Rocha, B. Concentração, concorrência e rentabilidade no setor bancário brasileiro: uma visão atualizada. Tendências Consultoria Integrada, BACEN, 2010.

Panzar, J., Rosse, J. Testing for monopoly equilibrium. *Journal of Industrial Economics*. v 3, n.37, pp. 443–446, 1987

Paula, L.F., Modenesi, A. M., Pires, M. C. C. "The tale of the contagion of two crises and policy responses in Brazil: a case of (Keynesian) policy coordination?". *Journal of Post Keynesian Economics*, v. 37, pp. 408–435, 2015.

Rondon, L.V. *Competitividade e Eficiência do Sistema Financeiro Nacional: 1995–2008.* 2011. 207. Doctoral dissertation. Cedeplar, Universidade Federal de Minas Gerais, Minas Gerais, 2011.

Sobreira, R.; De Paula, L.F. The 2008 financial crisis and banking behavior in Brazil: the role of financial regulation. *Journal of Innovation Economics* (2), pp. 73–93, 2010.

Appendix A: methodology: the *H* index

Here, we present the methodology used to estimate the *H* index presented above. Following Rondon (2011), Nakane and Rocha (2010) and Araújo, Neto and Ponce (2006), the *H* statistic was estimated using the following equations:

$$logR_i = \beta + \Sigma_{j=1}^q \theta_j \, logP_{i,j} + \Sigma_{k=1}^q \gamma_k X_{i,k} + \varepsilon_i \tag{1}$$
$$E(\varepsilon_i | P_{i,j}, X_{i,k}) = 0 \tag{2}$$

In equation (1), we have for bank *i*: log of total revenue (R_i), log of price of input *j* ($P_{i,j}$), control variables (X_i) and an error term (ε_i). Finally, we consider the mean independence condition described in equation (2). We can obtain the *H* statistics from:

$$H = \Sigma_j \theta_j \tag{3}$$

Using data from the COSIF (from the BCB), we estimate the Panzar and Rosse index (*H*) from June/2002 to December/2014. We consider the following variables (Table 1A.1): personnel expenses divided by number of employees (*P1*); financial expenses divided by the sum of deposits; borrowing; Liabilities for Acceptances and debentures (*P2*); and operational expenditures divided by current, long term and permanent assets (*P3*). *X* is a matrix that includes total assets (*X1*); net worth (*X2*); Basel index (*X3*); and the sum of securities, total deposits and borrowed funds (*X4*).

Table 1A.1 Estimation input

Dependent Variable: Operating Revenue								
Variables	Constant	P1	P2	P3	X1	X2	X3	X4
Date								
Jun–02	0.73	0	–0.0426	0.8123	0.9884	0.1568	–0.13	0.0234
	–0.4345	–0.0218	–0.0296	–0.00294	–0.0159	–0.00291	–0.0542	–0.0392
Dec–02	0.7648	0.0399	–0.0431	0.8408	0.9918	0.1638	–0.2222	–0.0388
	–0.4619	–0.0292	–0.041	–0.029	–0.0185	–0.0362	–0.0534	–0.0403
Jun–03	0.5169	–0.0228	0.0311	0.7494	0.9981	0.1218	–0.1498	0.1228
	–0.4609	–0.0352	–0.0646	–0.0384	–0.0175	–0.0326	–0.0533	–0.0496
Dec–03	0.5855	–0.0025	0.0267	0.7647	1.0003	0.1366	–0.195	0.1211
	–0.4288	–0.0323	–0.0616	–0.0363	–0.0169	–0.0324	–0.0553	–0.0477
Jun–04	1.9572	–0.0276	0.0798	0.8113	0.9553	0.0889	–0.2293	0.1053
	–0.5487	–0.0284	–0.0467	–0.00303	–0.0175	–0.0409	–0.0813	–0.0661
Dec–04	0.0625	–0.0403	0.0655	0.7096	0.9901	0.056	0.1304	–0.2066
	–0.5918	–0.042	–0.0778	–0.00604	–0.0234	–0.00498	–0.0428	–0.0622
Jun–05	0.026	0.0543	0.1186	0.6112	0.9873	0.0895	0.027	–0.1184
	–0.6909	–0.0481	–0.0772	–0.0571	–0.0236	–0.044	–0.0404	–0.054

(*Continued*)

Table 1A.1 continued

Dependent Variable: Operating Revenue

Variables	Constant	P1	P2	P3	X1	X2	X3	X4
Date								
Dec–05	1.0536	–0.0517	0.0287	0.7391	0.9586	0.047	0.0024	–0.1054
	–0.6365	–0.0471	–0.0519	–0.0622	–0.0221	–0.0352	–0.0361	–0.0649
Jun–06	1.2057	–0.1235	0.0298	0.711	0.9556	0.0613	0.0748	–0.1812
	–0.6396	–0.0513	–0.0194	–0.0554	–0.0208	–0.0338	–0.0481	–0.0624
Dec–06	1.9197	–0.049	–0.001	0.737	0.9221	0.024	–0.0551	–0.1352
	–0.6374	–0.0532	–0.0552	–0.0667	–0.0208	–0.0336	–0.0496	–0.0652
Jun–07	0.8249	–0.0808	0.0075	0.7511	0.9699	0.1277	0.0704	–0.1132
	–0.5603	–0.0467	–0.033	–0.0472	–0.0186	–0.0301	–0.0432	–0.0499
Dec–07	2.1094	0.0082	0.054	0.7281	0.9342	0.067	–0.2071	–0.1399
	–0.5987	–0.0424	–0.035	–0.0492	–0.0174	–0.00315	–0.0665	–0.0566
Jun–08	0.802	–0.0534	0.0334	0.7302	0.973	0.151	0.0386	–0.2657
	–0.5191	–0.0494	–0.0318	–0.0431	–0.0182	–0.00399	–0.0644	–0.00776
Dec–08	1.2674	–0.0064	0.0651	0.7739	0.9603	0.0621	–0.0715	–0.1548
	–0.549	–0.0326	–0.0284	–0.0414	–0.0161	–0.0279	–0.059	–0.0648
Jun–09	1.0668	–0.0103	0.0525	0.7576	0.9605	0.055	–0.0254	0.1669
	–0.5068	–0.0401	–0.0309	–0.0416	–0.0161	–0.0324	–0.0692	–0.0686
Dec–09	1.6826	–0.0239	0.0615	0.7625	0.9547	0.08	–0.1459	–0.1835
	–0.5935	–0.0362	–0.029	–0.0407	–0.0159	–0.032	–0.0777	–0.0659
Jun–10	–0.0103	–0.024	0.0744	0.5739	1.0218	0.3007	–0.1339	–0.1022
	–0.6709	–0.0448	–0.0369	–0.0435	–0.0204	–0.0553	–0.0925	–0.0916
Dec–10	1.5661	–0.0583	0.0004	0.7781	0.9452	0.0044	–0.078	–0.1187
	–0.605	–0.0604	–0.0591	–0.0536	–0.0173	–0.0324	–0.0774	–0.0839
Jun–11	1.3351	0.0531	–0.0684	0.7095	0.917	–0.0503	–0.1927	0.0354
	–0.605	–0.0604	–0.0591	–0.0536	–0.0173	–0.0324	–0.0774	–0.0839
Dec–11	0.6297	–0.0606	–0.1186	0.817	0.9728	0.0607	–0.0602	–0.0156
	–0.529	–0.0318	–0.0357	–0.0389	–0.0149	–0.0234	–0.0805	–0.0632
Jun–12	–0.2803	–0.0262	–0.02	0.7549	0.9961	0.1353	0.0859	0.1024
	–0.5732	–0.0437	–0.0273	–0.0454	–0.0168	–0.0299	–0.0795	–0.0676
Dec–12	0.56	–0.01	–0.07	0.76	0.96	0.05	–0.06	0.04
	–0.2978	–0.0046	–0.04491	–0.05925	–0.0216	–0.0679	–0.0501	–0.0196
Jun–13	0.23	–0.03	–0.07	0.78	0.98	0.08	–0.01	0.04
	–0.0803	–0.0338	–0.0208	–0.0587	–0.01843	–0.03142	–0.01335	–0.1722
Dec–13	0.16964	–0.02	–0.05	0.76	0.98	0.09	0.01	0.06
	–0.04755	–0.02404	–0.03086	–0.00285	–0.01792	–0.04069	–0.0023	–0.0388
Jun–14	0.31962	–0.02	–0.06	0.77	0.97	0.07	–0.02	0.05
	–0.11273	–0.01986	–0.04142	–0.07169	–0.02324	–0.03581	–0.0293	–0.02206
Dec–14	0.63	–0.03	–0.06	0.77	0.98	0.08	–0.01	0.05
	–0.562718	–0.04038	–0.12849	–0.0394	–0.0171	–0.0216	–0.002713	–0.02056

Source: Author's elaboration based on BCB (2016)

Note: p-value in parentheses.

Table 1A.2 presents calculated *H* index for the sample period ranging from June/2002 to December/2014.

Table 1A.2 *H* Index: June 2002–December 2014

Date	H
Jun–02	0.77
Dec–02	0.84
Jun–03	0.76
Dec–03	0.79
Jun–04	0.86
Dec–04	0.73
Jun–05	0.78
Dec–05	0.72
Jun–06	0.62
Dec–06	0.69
Jun–07	0.68
Dec–07	0.79
Jun–08	0.71
Dec–08	0.83
Jun–09	0.8
Dec–09	0.8
Jun–10	0.69
Dec–10	0.68
Jun–11	0.69
Dec–11	0.64
Jun–12	0.71
Dec–12	0.68
Jun–13	0.68
Dec–13	0.69
Jun–14	0.69
Dec–14	0.74

2 Private higher education expansion in Brazil

A case study[1]

Eduardo Pontual Ribeiro

Introduction

Two structural changes are common in the development process: the expansion of a country's service sector and the increase in its schooling levels. The Brazilian case is no different. Services account for the largest share in GDP since the 1990s (Baer, 2011), and the average schooling level increased from 3.8 years in 1981 to 7.8 in 2014 for those aged 25 and older. The share of (male) adults with a college degree increased from 1.7 percent in 1982 to 10.3 percent in 2010, with a sharp increase in the last 15 years.

Higher education systems are configured differently around the world. Brazil employs a dual system, meaning that tax-funded, tuition-free public universities and tuition-funded private institutions coexist. Access to public universities is rationed by student admission exams that almost always have excess demand. Private universities, on the other hand, are responsible for about 75 percent of national enrollment and may not fill all positions.

The higher education system in Brazil is heavily regulated with government control over entry, quantity, and quality. Degree quality is evaluated by the Education Ministry in three-year cycles. Tuition is unregulated and there is ample public student funding, either through federally funded loans or tax breaks to universities. Recently (1997) for profit private higher education institutions (HEI) were allowed and mergers could be carried out between HEI. Following a surge in private equity funding and foreign institutional investors (IFC, BlackRock, Advent and others, e.g., Economist, 2012), a small group of firms started a sector consolidation. More than forty mergers were registered at the competition authority from 2009 to 2014.

Sector growth has been impressive. Enrollment almost doubled from 1980–2000 and nearly tripled in the following fourteen years. The number of HEIs rose from 1,180 in 2000 to 2,368 in 2014. From 2000–2014, private enrollment increased more than threefold. In the United States, Kwoka and Snyder (2004) indicate that it took approximately forty years (1955–1997) for enrollment to increase fivefold.

In this chapter, we study the recent growth of the private higher education sector in Brazil. The private education sector is key to the future development of Brazil.

Public policy master documents, such as the National Education Plan ('*Plano Nacional de Educação*') highlight the significant role of this private sector to increase education levels throughout Brazil, contrary to basic education where public education is the driver for universal coverage. The sector is an interesting example of structural transformation after regulatory reform both at the firm organization level (for profit institutions) and the product supply dimension (distance learning). After a regulatory overview and the presentation of the sector dynamics, we cover the antitrust stand on the sector. In just three years, the antitrust standing changed radically in response to an extremely high merger wave (central to firm expansion strategy in the sector). We conclude with a case study of the radical changes in the sector. We consider Anhanguera Educational in an effort to understand the roles of external financing and internal organization in firm growth. In twenty years, Anhanguera grew from just four local colleges to a half-million student giant, the second largest higher education group in the country.

The Anhanguera story is an interesting case in firm growth where equity funds and the separation of ownership and control were central to its survival and growth in key stages of its evolution. Anhanguera's trajectory is also interesting given its USD$6 billion merger with the largest higher education group in Brazil, an event that made headlines overseas (Economist, 2013).

This chapter is organized as follows. The section following this introduction summarizes the relevant regulatory framework on higher education in Brazil. The second section provides an overview of market structure, growth, demographics, and concentration of private higher education in Brazil using recent available microdata. The next section summarizes the antitrust response to the significant mergers in the industry, and the case study of Anhanguera follows. The last section concludes.

Regulatory highlights

Higher education is an extensively regulated industry in Brazil. The Education Ministry (*Ministério da Educação*) and other regulatory bodies, such as the National Education Council (*Conselho Nacional de Educação*), oversee and write legislation pertaining to the sector. Non-public, non-religious higher education institutions (HEIs) have been permitted in Brazil since the 1950s. The Education Ministry oversees HEI entry, degree/course openings, maximum enrollment levels, and quality. HEI quality is evaluated constantly with overlapping, three-year degree evaluation cycles, carried out by the Education Ministry. The evaluation cycles include graduates and students national tests by degree/major as well as local infrastructure evaluation (see, e.g., Rezende 2010 for an overview of the exam-emphasized quality evaluation methodology). Throughout this chapter, we consider a *degree* a major such as Economics or Mechanical Engineering. It ought to be noted that students enroll in a specific degree upon admission. Changing majors generally requires taking a new entry exam (see e.g., Machado and Szerman (2015) for an overview of entry exams with an emphasis on exams given at public institutions).

There are three types of HEIs: *Faculdade, Universidade,* and *Centro Universitário*. These HEIs correspond to small colleges, universities, and colleges, in the US denomination, respectively. *Faculdades* typically offer one or two degrees/majors. The primary differences between colleges and universities are the ranges of majors offered and the research requirements associated with the latter. Product-wise, there are three types of HEI degrees: *Bacharelado* (B.A., taking four to five years); *Tecnólogo* (two-year degrees with a practical approach), and *Licenciatura* (three–four year Basic Education Teacher training).[2] Two-year degrees were introduced in the late 1990s/early 2000s. In contrast to the US, Brazilian HEIs are not sharply segregated by degree types. A single HEI may offer all three degree types, even though some colleges specialize in certain degree types, such as *Tecnólogo*.

The Education Law (*Lei de Diretrizes e Bases da Educação – LDB*, 1996) consolidated a coexistence of public and private institutions. Decree 2307/1997 allows for-profit firms to control HEIs. To segregate financial assets and liabilities from educational assets, HEIs are required to be funded by an institution called *Mantenedora*. The previously mentioned decree allowed these *Mantenedora* to be private for-profit firms.

A HEI is seen by the regulator as a sum of its degrees intertwined with shared infrastructure across degrees. So a degree or group of courses cannot be transferred between HEIs or *Mantenedoras*. A College may be accredited and degrees may be offered only if basic infrastructure (including a library with a minimum book–student ratio, teaching labs, classroom infrastructure, and dedicated faculty) is provided.

Regulators have partial control over course/degree openings. Their leverage varies as a function of the size and quality of the HEI. Universities and *Centro Universitário* may offer a new course without requesting permission from the Ministry of Education. Halfway through the course duration (say, two years in a four-year degree program), the course receives an *in loco* evaluation. These evaluations either approve degree granting or rule that enrolled students must transfer to another HEI and that no new admissions can be made to the course. Small colleges (*Faculdades*) operate slightly differently in that they are required to receive an authorization by the Ministry of Education before starting enrollment in new courses (see e.g., Octaviani, 2013).

In the late 1990s, the National Education Council allowed higher education degrees to be awarded through Distance Learning (DL). Distance Learning started in an effort to improve the geographic outreach to basic education teachers in all corners of the country (Chaves, 2010). The 1996 Education Law (LDB) set the goal to have all basic education teachers obtain at least a four-year degree. Over time, regulation evolved, and since 2005 (Decree 5622/2005), Distance Learning majors require the support from a local base ("polo") and that students attend online classes with a tutor on the premises and take examinations.[3] Local bases are often based in commercial property in office buildings, or in (private) high school buildings, for the night shift. Regulatory local base infrastructure requirements are lower than that of a full college. Also note that Distance Learning/online courses as a teaching technique may be used in up to 25 percent of non-distance learning degrees, generating economies of scope across distance- and in-person learning courses (Octaviani, 2013, *inter alia*).

Private HEIs use two primary distance-learning models: streaming and live feed. Streaming involves the student choosing the time and date to watch previously recorded lectures, completing exercises, and using additional material available online. Live feed (*teleaula*) involves students gathering at the local base to watch a live feed. This live feed is generally a class taught by a single faculty and transmitted to all Brazil. Students can interact with the faculty through *tutores/* teaching assistants in the local base (see also, Economist, 2014).

Industry growth and dynamics

The higher private education sector grew quickly over the last ten to fifteen years as evidenced in Table 2.1. From 2004–2014, enrollments almost doubled, reaching about 8 million students (many of whom are 25 or older). However, the number of students receiving private higher education is still shy of the national goal of 50 percent of all 18–24 year olds (in absolute and relative terms). The share of enrollments in public HEI has hovered around the 25 percent mark since 2007, decreasing slightly from a 30 percent share in 2003.

Distance learning experienced very rapid growth with a marked change in 2008. Currently, 17 percent of students enrolled in private higher education institutions are in distance learning courses. Interestingly, while distance learning degrees started at the public universities, private universities have embraced this teaching mode with *gusto*. In 2014, 90 percent of distance learning students attended private universities. Economies of scale may explain this shift. Distance learning reduces labor costs and increases accessibility (Economist, 2014). The savings accumulated through distance learning are passed on to students, as the

Table 2.1 Higher education in Brazil – enrollment: 2003–2014

Year	Total Enrollment	Public Share	DL Share	Public Share on DL
2003	3,936,933	30%	1.3%	80%
2004	4,223,344	29%	1.4%	60%
2005	4,567,798	27%	2.5%	48%
2006	4,883,852	26%	4.2%	20%
2007	5,250,147	25%	7.0%	25%
2008	5,808,017	27%	12.5%	38%
2009	5,954,021	26%	14.1%	21%
2010	6,379,299	26%	14.6%	20%
2011	6,739,689	26%	14.7%	18%
2012	7,037,688	27%	15.8%	16%
2013	7,305,977	26%	15.8%	13%
2014	7,839,731	25%	17.1%	10%

prices associated with degrees offered via distance learning are 20–50 percent cheaper than the same major non-distance learning degrees (based on 2013 data).

Regarding degree types, Table 2.2 indicates that private universities have expanded their BA/four-year enrollments from 2009 to 2014 at the expense of teacher degrees (*Licenciatura*). Breaking up these figures by teaching method (distance and non-distance learning), Table 2.3 suggests that BA and two-year degrees have been pursued more frequently through distance learning. Firms are moving away from teacher education in distance learning programs and are, instead, focusing on professional and other majors.

Firm (i.e., HEI) size grew over time. From 2010–2014, the average HEI size increased from 2,863 students to 3,312.1 students. Given stability in HEI numbers, overall expansion can be attributed solely to growth in the average firm size. Public HEI institutions tend to be larger than private institutions.

Firm dynamics can be measured looking at entry and exit and mergers by HEI. Our dataset is well suited to perform these tasks. The Higher Education Census by the Ministry of Education/INEP is a census of all HEIs. Firms receive unique identifiers that persist over their lifetimes. There are also unique, different controller (*Mantenedora*) identifiers. Entry is recorded as a new identifier in the database and exit as a disappearance of an identifier in the data. The asynchronous evaluation cycle for degrees in the institutions and information requirements for funding from the government guarantee that firms file the Census information every year. Mergers are identified as change in *Mantenedora* code for a given HEI, whose code does not change ever. This allows us to track mergers.

Table 2.2 Higher education enrollment in private institutions: 2009–2014

Year	Total	NDL	DL	DL/Total
2009	4,428,084	3,762,655	665,429	15.0%
2010	4,735,946	3,987,369	748,577	15.8%
2011	4,966,293	4,151,290	815,003	16.4%
2012	5,197,088	4,251,263	945,825	18.2%
2013	5,437,373	4,424,440	1,012,933	18.6%
2014	5,903,351	4,698,666	1,204,685	20.4%

Table 2.3 Higher education enrollment in private institutions – by teaching method and degree type: 2009–2014

	NDL				DL		
Ano	4Yr	Licentienship	2Yr		4Yr	Licentienship	2Yr
2009	75%	14%	11%		24%	50%	26%
2010	77%	12%	11%		28%	43%	28%
2011	77%	11%	12%		30%	40%	30%
2012	78%	10%	12%		33%	37%	31%
2013	78%	10%	12%		32%	35%	33%
2014	80%	9%	11%		32%	37%	31%

Table 2.4 Higher education institution firm dynamics: unweighted (top) and enrollment weighted (bottom): Brazil 2010–2014

Year	Entry	Merger	Exit
2010	7%	5%	5%
2011	3%	5%	4%
2012	4%	3%	2%
2013	2%	2%	3%
2014	2%	1%	3%

Year	New public	New private	Merged
2010	0.17%	0.74%	4.97%
2011	0.05%	0.14%	10.88%
2012	0.03%	0.26%	4.24%
2013	0.09%	0.06%	2.32%
2014	0.14%	0.14%	1.65%

In comparison to other industries, entry and exit rates are relatively small in higher private education institutions. Compared to nationwide entry and exit rates of 12–18 percent in service (OECD, 2014) and 15–20 percent in manufacturing (Rezende, Ribeiro and Zaidan, 2015), churning is much lower in the higher education sector. At the same time, mergers are quite common in higher education. In 2011 the merger rate was higher than the entry or exit rates (see Table 2.4).

Weighted by enrollments, the firm entry, exit and merger rates are even more impressive (see bottom part of Table 2.4). In 2010, 5 percent of all enrollments were in acquired firms. In the same year, the enrollment in new firms was only 0.2 percent of total enrollment. This difference is partly influenced by firm sizes (entrants are generally smaller) but nevertheless highlights the relevance of mergers in this industry. Large groups use mergers as entry strategies in new (local) markets. Out of the 348 local market mergers, 85 percent were in markets where the acquirer did not operate previously.

Regarding HEI educational quality, we use two indicators. First, we use the HEI overall evaluation rate (IGC) published by INEP/Ministry of Education. It is based on tri-annual, major-rotating student graduation national exams, *in loco* assessments and permanent evaluations of each degree in the HEI. IGC range from 1 (lowest) to 5 (highest). HEIs receiving scores of 1 cannot contract new students, and HEIs receiving a score of 2 require *in loco* regulator visits and improvement agreements.

As Figure 2.1 demonstrates, in 2013 38.1 percent of public universities received a general ICG score of "4" or "5," and 15.1 percent of private universities received these scores. The majority (64 percent) of private HEIs received a score of "3." Relatively more private universities obtained "2" or "1" grades than public universities. The lower grades for private universities are not a surprise. According to the financial statement of one of the largest educational groups:

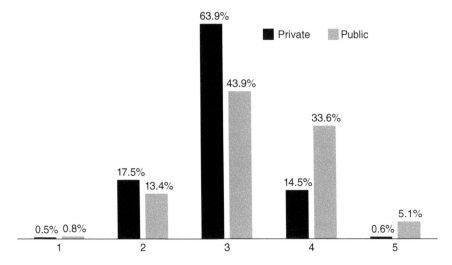

Figure 2.1 HEI course evaluation grades (IGC) – 2013

While the public higher education institutions are directed to serve as centers of excellence and research, with extremely competitive admissions standards and a limited capacity for expansion, the private higher education institutions are focusing their attention on the professional requirements imposed by the labor market and they develop flexible programs to meet the needs of the working population.

(Anima 2015)

Comparing HEI productivity and quality production in Brazil, Zoghbi et al. (2013) argued that once student characteristics are accounted for, private HEIs appear more productive than public HEIs regarding student quality growth over the college years (as measured by standardized student exams).

Another approach to measure HEI quality considers faculty skill level. Table 2.6 presents the evolution of faculty quality in the HEIs, highlighting the share of faculty holding PhD (Doctorate) degrees at public and private institutions. From 2003 to 2014, the number of faculty numbers at HEIs increased by 56 percent, and the number of faculty with a PhD increased by 152 percent. It is important to note that there was a significant expansion in the number of PhD/Doctorate programs offered in the country, growing out of MA programs in the mid- and late-1990s. The share of faculty with PhDs increased from 21 percent to 35 percent in HEIs overall.

Regarding private institutions, the relative share of faculty in private institutions decreased from 65 percent to 57 percent. In private HEIs, there was a 37 percent increase in the number of faculty members. Given the near doubling of enrollments in these institutions, enrollment/faculty ratio increased from 16 percent to more than 25 percent. Part of this more intense use of labor inputs can be associated with the shift towards distance learning. Nevertheless, the *relative* share of PhDs

Table 2.5 Faculty numbers and share of PhDs – public and private HEI: 2003–2014

Year	Total	PhD/ Doctorate	Share PhD	Private's Faculty Share	Private's PhD Share
2003	254,153	54,487	21%	65%	12%
2004	279,058	58,431	21%	66%	12%
2005	292,504	63,294	22%	66%	12%
2006	302,006	67,583	22%	67%	12%
2007	317,041	72,931	23%	66%	12%
2008	321,493	77,164	24%	65%	13%
2009	340,817	89,850	26%	64%	14%
2010	345,335	98,195	28%	62%	15%
2011	357,418	107,013	30%	61%	17%
2012	362,732	115,087	32%	59%	18%
2013	367,282	121,190	33%	58%	18%
2014	396,595	137,554	35%	57%	20%

in the number of private faculty members actually increased (from 12 percent in 2003 to 20 percent in 2014), following the trend in public universities.

To close this section, we present information on market structure. Generally, market competition exists at the local level, as students do not traditionally move to pursue their education (in contrast with the US experience). As discussed in detail in the next section on the antitrust response to the higher education growth strategy through mergers, market studies point to catchment areas about the size of a municipality. The sector can be characterized as monopolistic competition/oligopoly with relatively small entry rates, significant product variety (in degrees and quality, as discussed above), and having very different firm sizes. The five largest groups control about 25 percent of all enrollment considering Brazil as a whole (Anima, 2014). In local markets, concentration may vary significantly. Some of the concentration levels depend on market size, as the possibility that significant economies of scale allow the largest firms to thrive in larger markets. On the other hand, smaller markets may not financially sustain many firms. Figure 2.2 below presents a general view of the local market concentration. We calculated the Hirschman-Herfindahl Index (HHI) for each municipality and plotted this figure over the (log) market size (number of enrollments).

Figure 2.2 indicates that both very small and very large municipalities have small HHI indices. Mid-sized municipalities may be very concentrated (defined as above the 1800 level used as standard by the US Federal Trade Commission) (FTC, 2010). A non-parametric conditional mean estimator (loess) suggests that there is a negative relationship between size and concentration for medium and large municipalities, although the relationship is clearly driven by some very high HHI indices on medium markets. There are 3,315 municipalities with at least one HEI (out of 5,570). The average HHI is 475, and the median HHI 313.

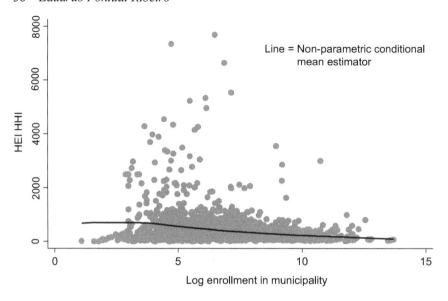

Figure 2.2 Market concentration across 'municípios' enrollment size – 2013

Source: Censo Ensino Superio/INEP 2013.

Antitrust evaluation of higher education mergers in Brazil

As discussed above, mergers are important characteristics of HEI growth in Brazil. Mergers are subject to antitrust scrutiny if firms have revenues above a certain level. The Brazilian Antitrust Authority – CADE in the Portuguese acronym – evaluated the first merger in 2007 under the 1994 antitrust law which required firms with more than BRL400 million (USD 100 million in 2010) in revenues to file (Teodorovicz et al. 2015). This is indirect evidence that the market was very fragmented in medium and small *mantenedoras*.

Up to 2011, relevant markets were defined broadly at CADE: higher education was considered a product market and a state as geographical markets. CADE believed that assets could be deployed from one course or major to another except for very specific courses. In addition, it was argued that students could move from smaller cities to larger cities (or state capitals which generally correspond with the largest cities in the state) to pursue their degrees. Private HEIs did not compete directly with public institutions given that the latter were tuition free and selective on the basis of student performance in entry exams. Given this broad market definition, concentration was minimal, and all cases were cleared without much regard to entry and rivalry.

Since 2011, there has been a significant change in market definition. Using a demand-based relevant market definition in the Plinio Leite case, Commissioner Elvino Mendonça argued and provided evidence to suggest that there was minimal degree substitution (i.e., less than 5 percent of students substituted one major for another). In addition, note that in Brazil students must decide which major to pursue when registering for the entry exams, and these exams are HEI specific for private higher education. Despite possible supply-side substitution, he argued that degrees/majors did not compete against one other and that each degree (such as Economics, or Accounting), should be considered as a product-relevant market. Regarding geographical markets and using actual student data, he noticed that there was a visible discontinuity in the cumulative distribution of student residency distance from the HEI. In general, this discontinuity was at the 80th distance from the HEI percentile. Catchment areas from the *acquired* institution were defined as geographical markets. This new conception was quickly adopted by the CADE Tribunal, and by 2013, all relevant markets in HEI were defined as such. There are, however, small adaptabilities for specific degrees: for *Tecnologo* (two-year degrees), product markets are defined as degree groups (e.g. "*business*," including hospital management, logistics management, human resources management), as defined by regulation. Graduate degrees (MBA, MA and PhD) are taken as separate product market, and their geographical markets are state-wide.

The new relevant market definition increased the task for parties and authorities. Large mergers, such as Kroton-Anhanguera required the analysis of more than 400 different markets. Concentration filters have been used to conclude for the likelihood of a significant loss of competition, before considering entry and rivalry (and efficiency) effects. For example, in the previously mentioned Kroton-Anhanguera case, markets were cleared if post-merger concentration was 30 percent or concentration share increased by less than 5 percentage points.

Concentration arose when an acquiring institution was located within the catchment area of an acquired institution. Concentration rates started to increase in specific locations, such as São Paulo and other metropolitan areas. This required the Authority to describe entry and rivalry in detail. We take two merges analysis as examples of the analysis: Kroton-Anhanguera (Frazão 2014), a USD 4 billion merger between the two largest HEI private *Mantenedoras* and Anhanguera-Anchieta (Octaviani, 2013), where extensive remedies were enacted. Teodorivcs et al. (2014) and Garcia and Azevedo (2015) provide an extensive list of additional mergers.

The Kroton-Anhanguera and Anhanguera-Anchieta cases analysis at CADE concluded that entry is not effective to contest mergers. Firm entry may take more than two years due to regulation requirements even if with small start-up sizes (this is particularly acute in distance learning). Entrants start too small to effectively compete in this sector. Regarding rivalry, the market seems segmented in two dimensions. First, from a quality x price perspective, prices vary significantly according to quality, such that there is limited substitution between majors across HEIs. Second, brands are important (marketing is usually the largest expense of the largest firm, after labor), so national, marketing-intense brands compete with each other and are mostly isolated from a fringe of small, 'faculdade' local institutions.

Firms recognize synergies from elimination of staff redundancies and administrative costs (markedly on marketing and class sizes), but they do not suffice to clear a merger (Frazão, 2014). As of 2015, merger remedies[4] have been imposed on at least four mergers.[5] There is a significant regulatory restriction regarding remedies in this market. Generally, degrees/majors cannot be transferred. However, a set of degrees/majors organized and accredited by the Ministry of Education as a unique HEI may be transferred. There is a difference between the relevant market definition and the remedy minimum scope that influences the decision. Often, non-concentrated markets (courses) have to be included to allow concentrated markets with a significant loss of competition problem to be addressed. This problem was particularly acute in the Kroton-Anhanguera merger.

All remedies in higher education cases were determined with an agreement (i.e., were not imposed unilaterally by the Authority). Remedies are often structural (Anhanguera-Anchieta, Kroton-Unirondon, Kroton-Anhanguera) with the transferring of a HEI to another *Mantenedora*. Quantity (enrollment) restrictions have been imposed (Estácio-UniSEB) to allow smaller rivals and entrants to grow over time, particularly in cases in which a structural solution was seen as non-proportional given the entire HEI transferring restriction. Last, but not least, quality remedies were imposed (Kroton-Anhanguera). Given that private HEIs have lower quality as measured by the regulator quality index (IGC; see Figure 2.2 above), conduct much less research, have fewer PhDs on their faculty (see Table 2.4 above) in comparison to public HEIs, and a widespread view in the Education literature (Chaves, 2010, e.g.) that for-profit firms would trade quality for quantity to reduce prices, a quality target was agreed to for merged parties HEIs. Quality is measured using the regulator quality indicator (IGC), regularly carried out by the Ministry of Education, as seen in Figure 2.2 above.

For-profit higher education growth: a case study

Anhanguera started in the mid-1990s as did many other private HEI institutions (particularly those outside major cities). A few faculty members took control of a non-profit HEI and started managing it under a new name, focusing on business, social science, education and law degrees. The owners (the Carbonaris and Polis) had a business plan that was based on giving reasonable quality and medium prices for working students. This business plan came from the realization that the increase in enrollment figures would come from lower income families that did not have the opportunity to attend tuition-free public higher education institutions as a consequence of receiving lower quality public basic education. Clearly, this would prove a successful business strategy only if costs were lower (to correspond with lower tuition fees) and if quality were measured relative to students' initial skills. The students' degrees offered 'quality' perception would come from (i) employability and/or (ii) empowerment (having the opportunity of a better life with a university degree, after being deemed not good enough for public universities). Thus, management techniques and working capital for investments were key to exploring economies of scale and modularity (Anhanguera, 2009). Economies of scale came from the centralization and standardization of courses.

Table 2.6 Anhanguera timeline

Year	Highlights	Size
1994	Founded in 1994 under the name *Faculdades Integradas Anhanguera* by Antonio Carbonari Netto, Maria Elisa Carbonari and José Luis Poli.	2 HEI
2001	Anhanguera Educacional Participações S/A (AEPSA) created as financial controller of HEIs.	
2003	Higher Education Institutions 'Mantenedora' as Anhanguera Educacional S/A (AESA). Partial aquisition by Anhembi Morumbi 'Mantenedora' (ISCP), controlled by Gabriel Rodrigues and Family.	8,800
2005	ISCP control acquires by Laureate International. ICSP shares at AESA replaced by FEBR equity fund, managed by Pátria Bank and controlled by the Rodrigues Family. FEBR receives funding from IFC (USD12million) . FEBR acquires control of AESA. Aporte de novos recursos do Pátria.	17,600
2006	Internal structuring for IPO. Starts its acquisitions using FEBR funds. FEBR holds 59% shares, Carbonaris and Poli 19% and others 28%.	24,500
2007	IPO at Bovespa at USD 250 million. Expands its acquisitions and start distance learning courses using one of acquired HEI.	56,700
2008	Further shares issued at USD 350million. Ventures into prep exam courses business (LFG) and vocational training (Microlins). 15 aquisitions. FEBR holds 49,8% shares; Carbonaris and Poli, 10,2%; float and others 40%.	157,200
2009	FEBR confirms its control over AESA. Further funding from IFC, Proparco and DEG. Addition shares issues raising USD350million.	253,576
2010	AESA enters the Bovespa new Market. Additional shares issued raising USD 420million. Expands mergers	300,959
2011	Closes largest HEI merger to date (Uniban). Debt issued at USD200million. Investment from US pension funds	358,346
2012	Consolidation and incorporation of previous mergers	421,779
2013	Kroton-AESA merger, reducing its leverage. FEBR holds 4,4% of the merged firm equity; Kroton controllers 19,7%, and others 75,9%. Shared control with Kroton. Starts purely distance learning courses.	428,779

Source: Anhanguera annual reports and presentations taken from http://www.anhanguera.com/ri/. Size: enrollment.

Course materials, for example, are purchased in bulk from editors for all units.[6] Course programs are standardized across majors. A relevant share (usually up to 30 percent of course work) of course hours in non-distance learning courses consists of online (distance learning) work to reduce faculty hours. Part-time professionals are preferred as faculty, rather than full-time (PhD) researchers.

After the 1997 regulatory reform, Anhanguera changed its status to for-profit and sought funding from equity funds to support organic expansion. First, funding came from BBA bank and Mehir Holdings started working with Anhanguera, which organized itself under the *Mantenedora* Anhanguera Educational Participações S.A.

Second, and key to the firm trajectory, Gabriel Rodrigues (an important entrepreneur in the industry and controller of Anhembi-Morumbi University,

ICSP) and his family acquired part of Anhanguera from the Mehir Holdings in 2003. At the time, ICSP was already influenced by FEBR (Fundo Educação para o Brasil) and by the equity fund for higher education. These equity funds usually exert direct influence on company business strategies and activities, pushing for results-based management (lower costs, higher revenues) (see DeMaria, 2013).

By 2003, private for profit higher education was attracting attention from investors. The 2001 National Education Plan proposed a target enrollment of 30 percent of all 18–24 year-olds, despite the fact that, at that time, the enrollment figure was much lower and still lingered at 20 percent in 2007. It is important to note that the private higher education expansion of the late-1990s (following the Plano Real income increase) was dwindling as a result of pressure from high unemployment and slower economic growth.

Then, by 2005, Gabriel Rodrigues and his family sold ownership control of ICSP to the Laureate International Group and used the funds to expand its control over Anhanguera. He saw Anhanguera as a complement to Anhembi-Morumbi, where the former focused on C-D-class working students paying low tuition and enrolling in night classes and the latter focused on upper-class students paying higher tuition and pursuing "innovative" courses (fashion design, gastronomy and others). In these two cases, we see the co-existence of sector entrepreneurs (with both a better view of the business and of the meaning of teaching and learning means) and equity fund personnel (with a business management focus on financial results). Gabriel Rodrigues stayed as President of Anhembi-Morumbi, even with 51 percent of shares at Laureate hands. On the other hand, at Anhanguera, he did not participate directly on the Board of Executive Directors but had de facto control through FEBR (possibly to avoid conflict of interest under Brazilian regulation). FEBR personnel, the founders Carbonaris and Poli, and one of Rodrigues's daughters participated on the Anhanguera Board (Oscar, 2012).

In 2006, FEBR made headlines for received funding from the IFC, the financial investment arm of the World Bank (Oliveira, 2009). At the time Brazil did not hold an Investment Grade from international rating agencies. But anticipating the effects of the sharp decrease in inequality and increase in the income of the poor in the second half of the 2000s, Anhanguera's business model started to attract more attention.

By 2007, Anhanguera started its expansion through mergers. The controllers' argument published in financial prospects and presentations was that economies of scale could be attained through standardizing books and materials across courses, optimizing classroom use, extending the use of online courses, and hiring professionally-oriented part-time faculty (instead of MA or PhD academics). Controllers also argued that there was also a large untapped demand from working students (Anhanguera 2008 CVM report). It is important to note that the 1990s were characterized by an expansion in basic (up to ninth grade, or 'educação fundamental') public education. In the 2000s, this more educated generation was reaching college age (even if taking a bit longer due to work during and after high school). Anhanguera's view was that smaller institutions were unable to weather outstanding tuition rates and cash flow losses, so mergers provided a sound business strategy to increase size rapidly.

The merger strategy momentum was impressive. In three years, Anhanguera acquired nineteen HEI *Mantenedoras* and more than tripled its enrollment by 2010 (making enrollment thirty times larger than in 1997).

The previously described strategy led Anhanguera to pursue other educational services. In 2007, it expanded from higher education to vocational training (involving computer use, English classes, basic accounting, etc.), acquiring Microlins. It also acquired LFG, a preparatory course for civil servant entry and bar exams franchise with extensive expertise in distance learning (via satellite feeds) and, later, another franchise, Praetorium. Microlins appeared as an early entry for future Higher Education students. LFG, in addition to its technical resources, maintained its graduates within Anhanguera reach, as they prepared for civil servant entry exams. The Microlins merger was short-lived, as technical developments and increasing computer popularity made basic computer training (using spreadsheets, using a web browser, etc.) obsolete. By 2011, Anhanguera sold Microlins and focused purely on higher education and graduate education.

The 2007 IPO was considered a financial success, with further share issues over the next four years. It is interesting to note the fast growth using shares led to relatively diminishing control of the founders and the increased professional management of the company in this same time period. While Anhanguera stopped short of entering the Bovespa New Market (with no separation between preferential and ordinary shares), the issue of control appeared to become secondary to the founders and majority holders (e.g. Gabriel Rodrigues's family), at least in public information.

Most of the mergers were used as means to enter in new markets (an industry characteristic as seen in the previous sections of this chapter). Other mergers were used to consolidate a footprint in the São Paulo metropolitan area – the largest in the country. The UNIDERP merger allowed them to enter the distance learning market. The Central West region's UNIDERP had a highly regarded asset, namely many local 'polos' that allowed Anhanguera to expand rapidly into distance learning. These 'polos' were authorized by MEC at the start of the distance learning regulation in the early 2000s. By 2010, the perceived restriction (or diminishing regulatory clearance for) on new 'polos' by MEC made the UNIDERP distance learning 'polos' a valued asset.

Cost reductions in distance learning are significant as one can infer from the difference in distance learning and non-distance learning tuition prices. By 2014, the average revenue per student was USD 200,00 for non-distance learning and USD 85,00 for distance learning approximately, according to Anhanguera financial statements.

In most mergers conducted by Anhanguera, the acquired HEI (family) owners either received cash and severed ties with the acquired entity or they maintained the university buildings property and were paid as a stream of long-term rental payments from the corporation. In other cases, the buildings were acquired by FEBR directly and rented to Anhanguera. This generated a long-term income flow to the Rodrigues family (see CVM Anhanguera reports – relational obligations). It is important to note the interest in the maintenance of a secure revenue stream for the Anhanguera de facto family owners while leaving the management of the universities themselves to market professionals.

Interestingly, by 2009, the sector was viewed in an accommodation mode (Valor, 2012). The 2009 economic crisis hit the HEIs significantly, and many (small) HEIs were experiencing financial difficulties. Outstanding (unpaid) tuition rates increased from the historical level of 20 percent to 25 percent. There was an excess supply of new courses opened by small- and medium-sized universities (similar to the 1995–1997 expansion that generated excess supply by the 1999–2001 crisis). The expansion in two-year courses (*tecnólogo*), permitted since 2006, started to mature, increasing supply. Public funding was limited to tax breaks with requirements to give tuition waivers to low-income students (PROUNI). Although the funds for this program were increasing, they did not generate new revenues.

Then, by 2010, the federal student loan system (FIES) started to receive massive funding from the federal government. In this form of student loans, the federal government used very low interest rates and long grace periods to induce students to contract. The HEIs would receive the tuition contracted in the loan directly. Default by the student was supported only 15 percent by the HEI. While the official discourse for allocating massive revenues was a response to the difficulties in reaching the PNE goals, it provided a significant boost to (large) private HEIs.

The FIES expansion was exponential and generated a secure income stream for HEI institutions. Reports suggest that by 2014, 44 percent of all Anhanguera students held a FIES loan. From 2009 to 2014, three more HEI 'Mantenedoras' issued IPOs, and the sector experienced a significant increase. FIES outlays became impressive, reaching USD 6.5 billion by 2014. By comparison, Bolsa Família expenditures in 2014 were approximately USD 12.5 billion (Estadão).[7]

The last step in Anhanguera's history came in 2014, the year it merged with Kroton. Speculation of a large merger was not new in the market. The merged firms believe that there are extensive synergies to be exploited from economies of scale and scope. The movement for the merger can be traced to Gabriel Rodrigues's selling of the remaining 49 percent held at Anhembi-Morumbi to Laureate a little earlier, in 2013. At about this same time, some board members exited and the Patria/FEBR fund started reducing its exposure to Anhanguera. A week after the Laurate-Anhembi operation was cleared at CADE, Anhanguera's merger with Kroton was announced. Oliveira (2012) claims that the lack of interest of the younger Rodrigues to take the father's role could have induced him to concentrate efforts. Severing ties with Anhembi allowed Rodrigues to adopt a more eminent role in Anhanguera business affairs without risking antitrust opposition. With the merger, the younger Rodrigues became president of the Kroton Board. Formally, Anhanguera will cease to exist as a holding firm. Its stock is traded under Kroton, but its brand name and business model and market position focus will continue.

Concluding comments

Human capital accumulation has been a key input for Brazilian growth, development, and inequality reduction since the 1950s (Baer, 2014). Public policy goals aim for 50 percent higher education enrollment rates among 18–24 year olds (MEC, 2014). Such ambitious goals were followed by public policies that promoted the expansion of public as well as private higher education, deepening the dual characteristic of this market, with the coexistence of public (no-tuition) and private (tuition funded) higher education institutions (HEIs). In the mid-1990s, regulatory changes allowed higher education institutions to be run by for-profit enterprises. This opened the scope for funding and expansion, both organically with new firms and through mergers and acquisitions.

This chapter pursued two goals. First, it sought to provide an economic overview of the private higher education sector expansion and business demographics given the described institutional, regulatory setting, background. Second, given the significant role of mergers and acquisitions to the sector dynamics, the chapter presented the antitrust evaluation of these mergers and a case study of the main sector expansion strategy, namely mergers. The analysis of the Anhanguera Educacional case provides an excellent opportunity to examine the required changes the firm took to guarantee its expansion.

In the case study, two dimensions stand out: one, related to market positioning in the face of regulatory and consumer profile and another related to command and control choices of founding and controlling entrepreneurs.

First, Anhanguera correctly positioned itself in the face of regulatory change. Anhanguera would not have the funding to grow if private education for profit had not been allowed in Brazil. With the onset of regulatory changes, Anhanguera changed its business model to offer short, two-year courses with a focus on market skills rather than technical academic knowledge building, reaching the influx of high school students from the 1990s basic education expansion and tapping on a stock of high-schoolers that were not able to enter the public, tuition-free higher education institutions. Anhanguera was able to expand its course portfolio targeted at its main consumer group (work-study young adults with average or low quality high school education). With regulatory changes pertaining to distance learning, Anhanguera expanded its teaching method to explore extensive economies of scale. Last, but not least on regulatory changes, it benefitted disproportionally from the public college credit expansion (FIES) after 2010.

Second, its evolution across the lines of a modern corporation, transitioning from a family-controlled, closed firm to an equity traded, command-control separated entity appeared central to its merger growth strategy. This merger growth strategy was advantageous for Anhanguera given (i) regulatory entry barriers that contributed to long delays for new HEI authorizations, (ii) the local market knowledge required for success, and (iii) a fragmented/non-concentrated market with many local firms selling differentiated products with significant economies of scope and some local economies of scale across majors.

A merger growth strategy requires significant funding. This funding is not generally available from bank loans and requires debentures and other papers or equity investment. Equity investors are certainly concerned with placing significant funds in family firms given their lack of influence on the firm management. Family firms may place too much weight on firm size (prestige) and less on profits in comparison to equity funds that have a focus on return on its invested capital. Tapping the equity market requires giving up control or management of the firm. Anhanguera seemed to follow this path at two significant points in time – first, when the founders Carbonaris and Polis sold its control to the Rodrigues family; and second when the Rodrigues family used financial vehicles to exert control. The lack of absolute control of the Board and the use of professionals from equity firms to run the business signaled to funding suppliers a commitment to return on equity as a central goal. When a firm becomes publicly traded enhances this separation of management and control and increases the role of minority investors to the protection of its investment in a virtuous circle of more funding, further growth, and higher returns.

In addition to these two dimensions, economic long run and business cycles cannot be taken for granted. The change in demographics from the 1980s (where family size decreased), the expansion of basic education in the 1990s, and the pro-poor growth cycle in the 2000s created the opportunity for HEI growth. Given the arguable end of the latter factor by 2017, it remains to be seen how the firm sectors will progress.

Notes

1 Financial support from CNPq, excellent research assistance from Gabrielle Leite (PIBIC), Lucas Carvalho (PIBIC) and Rafael Xavier (PPGE/IE), and comments/suggestions from Maria Graça Derengowski, Werner Baer, Luis Carlos Prado, and workshop participants is gratefully acknowledged. A reference exchange rate of BRL2.00=USD1.00 is used everywhere in the chapter. The author participated in the antitrust approval of mergers in the sector, from 2012–2014 as Commissioner at CADE. Only public information is used in this chapter. Data estimates and analysis is solely our responsibility and should not be associated with the official view of UFRJ, INEP, CADE or CNPq. Contact author: eribeiro@ie.ufrj.br
2 Although some summaries of the Brazilian education system equate *Tecnólogo* with vocational/training courses (such as WENR 2012), tecnólogo should not be confused with technical or vocational training that may be part of a high school curriculum. These two-year courses were regulated in 1997 ('Decreto 2208/1997') and 2001 ('Parecer CNE/CES 436/2001').
3 Regulation requires HEIs to offer majors available in in-person teaching modes in distance learning. In practice, this requirement is loosely adhered to as the presence learning major may have a hundred students in the university campus and ten thousand students spread across 'polos' over the country.
4 Merger remedies refer to authority-imposed obligations on merging firms to conditionally clear a merger. This may include selling assets or following a specific business practice (such as non-discrimination of vertically related competitors). See e.g. Soares et al. (2015).

5 Many cases had to adjust their non-competing clauses to the changing market definitions by CADE (Teodorovicz et al. 2015). This is often carried out in a fix-it-first move by merging parties. These remedies are not considered here.
6 Suppose introductory economics for business and accounting courses use nine chapters from a twenty-chapter textbook, as, say Stiglitz's Econ101 text. Anhanguera would contact the publisher and produce an excerpt of the book with these nine chapters, sold to the students with an Anhanguera cover. See e.g. www.dandc.eu/en/article/why-many-brazilian-students-choose-go-night-school-after-work
7 The actual effect of FIES on graduation rates is unknown. As an unseen negative consequence, Ferreira-Duarte and Pinho de Melo (2015) show that FIES contributed to large tuition increases.

References

Anhanguera (2007) *Reunião APIMEC com investidores e analistas*. Presentation – Investors Relations.

Anhanguera Educacional (many years). Investors Relations presentations and reports

Anima (2015) The Brazilian Market. *Financial statements. Investors Relations*. http://ri.animaeducacao.com.br/anima/web/conteudo_en.asp?idioma=1&conta=44&tipo=49122

Baer, W. (2011) *The Brazilian Economy: its growth and development*, 6th Edition. Lynn.

Baer, W. (2014) *Higher Education in Brazil.* Presentation at Lehman Institute – Stanford University.

Chaves, V.L. (2010) The expansion of privatization and mercantilization of Brazilian higher education: the formation of oligopolies. *Educação e Sociedade*, 31(111), pp. 481–500.

DeMaria, C. (2013) *Introduction to Private Equity: Venture, Growth, LBO and Turn-Around Capital*, 2nd Edition. New York: Wiley.

Economist (2012) The mortarboard boom. *The Economist*, September 15, 2012.

Economist (2014) A Winning recipe. *The Economist*, June 28, 2014.

Ferreira Duarte, I. and Pinho De Melho, J.M. (2015) Student Loans Impacts on Tuition Costs – Consequences of FIES. Lacea Meetings 2015.

Frazão, A. (2014) Voto Ato de Concentração Kroton Anhanguera. CADE.

Garcia, C. and Azevedo, P.F. (2015) Impacto de fusões e aquisições sobre a qualidade do ensino superior. ANPEC Meetings 2015.

Kwoka, J. and Snyder, C. (2004) Dynamic Adjustment in the U.S. Higher Education Industry, 1955–1997. *Review of Industrial Organization* 24(4), pp. 355–378.

MEC (2014) "Planejando a Próxima Década Conhecendo as 20 Metas do Plano Nacional de Educação." Brasília: MEC.

Moita, R. et al. (2015) Permanent demand excess as business strategy: an analysis of the Brazilian higher-education market. Revista de Administração (São Paulo) – RAUSP v.50(1).

Motis, J. (2007) Mergers and Acquisitions Motives. *Mimeo.*

Machado, C. and Szerman, C. (2015) The Effects of a Centralized College Admission Mechanism on Migration and College Enrollment: Evidence from Brazil?. SBE Meetings.

Octaviani, A. (2013) Voto Ato de Concentração Anhanguera-Anchieta. CADE.

OECD (2014) Unleashing innovation in firms – Entry and exit. Mimeo.

Oliveira, R (2012) A transformação da educação em mercadoria no Brasil. *Educação e Sociedade*, 30(108), 729–760.

Oscar, N. (2012) Duas concorrentes e um professor em comum. *O Estado de São Paulo*, June 11, 2012 edition.

Rezende, M. (2010) The effects of accountability on higher education. *Economics of Education Review*, 29, 842–856.

Resende, M., Ribeiro, E. and Zeidan, R. (2015) Dynamic Entry and Exit Linkages in the Brazilian Manufacturing Industry: an Econometric Investigation. *International Journal of the Economics of Business*, 22(3), 279–292.

Schwartzman, S. (1990) The Future of Higher Education in Brazil. *Mimeo*.

Soares, M. Zuccolo, R. and Lima, J. (2015) Remedies in merger cases: Brazil´s recent experience. In INSTITUTO BRASILEIRO DE ESTUDOS DE CONCORRÊNCIA; *Overview of Competition Law in Brazil*. São Paulo: Singular.

Teodorovicz et al. (2014) The evolution of a methodology for relevant market definition: an analysis of CADE's jurisprudence on private higher educational markets. *Economic Analysis of Law Review*, v. 6 (2), 246–268.

Valor Economico (2009). *Análise Setorial – Ensino Superior*. São Paulo:Valor.

Wenr. (2012) Evaluating academic credentials from Brazil. *World Education News and Reports*, March 1, 2012.

Zoghbi, A.C. et al. (2013) Education production efficiency: Evidence from Brazilian universities. *Economic Modelling*, v. 31, p. 94–103.

3 A short economic history of the television industry in Brazil

Fábio Sá-Earp, George Kornis and
Luiz Carlos Delorme Prado

Introduction

Television broadcasting emerged in Brazil during the 1950s, when the country was building its manufacturing industry of durable consumer goods. During this decade, the first TV channels and the TV appliance industry were both created. Originally, television broadcasting was restricted to only a few major cities, but a half-century later, the TV was present in all households in the country. Nevertheless, this remarkable growth was a highly-concentrated process. Specifically, the content production was (and still is) mostly developed in Rio de Janeiro and São Paulo, the two largest Brazilian cities. These two cities host the four major networks and distribute most of the programming, which now extends to include a territory with an area of 8.5 million km².

The television broadcasting industry in Brazil showed very early on that it was able to produce the content of a large part of its domestic programming. Television's transformation of programs originally created by the radio such as shows, news forecasts, comedies and mainly soap operas – the so called "*novelas*" – facilitated the native supply of domestic programing. On the other hand, imported productions – mainly from the US – have also attracted the attention of many Brazilians.

After more than six decades, Brazil's TV market could reach almost all Brazilian homes and has become more complex and sophisticated. In the last decade, this market has experienced major changes due to competition with Pay-TV. In recent years, it is also possible to notice the changes resulting from the different types of programs on demand – available through Pay TV and internet streaming services. The latter service is still very small, but it is growing rapidly. In addition, changes in the regulatory framework (especially with the promulgation of the Audiovisual Act (Law 12,485/2011) which established rules for the production and distribution of pay-TV content) have led to large changes in the supply of domestic production content.

This chapter offers a short economic history of Brazil's television industry with an emphasis on the observed industry-related technological and regulatory changes. This work argues that:

- Content production and TV operations in Brazil were characterized by very few regulations from the foundation of the television industry until the 2010s. Throughout this period, political influence was required to obtain concessions to operate TV channels. Therefore, the foundation and ownership of television networks were the result of the media entrepreneurs' abilities to combine economic capacity with the appropriate political connections. However, the financing of these activities depended on the audience share – meaning that business continuity depended on the technical and artistic ability to gain and maintain an audience capable of attracting private funding through advertising.
- From the establishment of the first channels in the 1950s to the creation of national networks, the relevant geographic markets for content production, as well as for the broadcast, were all local. The relevant product market included not only broadcast television but also the radio. Therefore, although television advertising was sold at a higher insertion price than that of the radio, the low TV penetration rate meant that advertising was also mainly aimed at the radio. Therefore, the radio and TV from the 1950s up to the 1960s were competitors over audiences and advertising – as they were not perceived as being two clearly distinct markets under the advertiser's point of view.
- Since the 1970s, locally produced content was distributed nationally. Therefore, the national networks have unified their schedule programming. Since the 1970s, competition in production and transmission has occurred between networks and not exclusively via local channels. From this decade, TV and Radio did not belong to the same relevant market. An oligopolistic competitive structure was formed between networks based on in-house content production.
- Despite the oligopolistic market structure, there is always a group with greater market power. This group has a majority audience stake and is able to get a disproportionate share (i.e. higher than its market share) in advertising revenues. As a result, the dominant group has market power to impose a high advertising price on its network.
- Since 2005, and especially after 2011, the dominant group has experienced increased competition due to technical and market changes, regulatory changes (through the Audiovisual Act of 2011), and particularly due to the growing importance of pay TV.

This chapter is organized into three sections, besides the introduction and the conclusion. The first section presents the evolution and transformation of the broadcasting TV market from the 1950s until the end of the century. In essence, it gives a brief overview of the first 50 years of television in Brazil. The second section discusses the emergence of Pay TV in the 1990s and its operation until the present day. The third section looks at the changes in broadcast and pay television markets over the last five years as well as the impact of new technologies.

Broadcasting television in Brazil

The business

Broadcast television signal is a public good.[1] There are two ways of financing broadcast TV: private financing and public funding. Private financing involves a two-sided market where viewers have access to free contents, and broadcasters obtain financial compensation by selling advertising proportionally to the size of the audience obtained.[2] Public funding requires institutional arrangements: government funds or via payments made by the consumers (through compulsory subscriptions paid by the owners of TV receivers).

The US is a paradigmatic case of the private financing model. The public financing model, however, originated in Western Europe and is native of the region. As such, the British model requires licenses to access television (in the case of the BBC, for example), and the French model is based on public money funding. The Brazilian case resembles the US model in that Brazilian television channels are financed by advertising in a classic two-sided market structure. However, in Brazil's case, there is no regulatory body (such as the FCC in the case of the US) for broadcasting television. According to Brazilian legislation, broadcasting Television is a public service granted to the private sector by the federal government and is historically highly dependent on political influence.

The era of live television

The television was a curiosity and an unviable economic activity in practically the entire world until the end of World War II. The only exception was the US which set up its first networks during the war.[3] In the 1950s, several precarious TV channels were created in Europe, the Americas, and in parts of Asia. Brazil was one of the first countries to create a regular broadcasting TV service.[4] The Diários Associados, Brazil's largest media group owned by the entrepreneur Assis Chateaubriand, founded Brazil's first television channel. This channel was created in Sao Paulo in September of 1950.

In order to establish the first television channels in Brazil, Assis Chateuabriand needed to overcome many problems. Firstly, obtaining receptor equipment was challenging. Since the country did not yet have an electronics industry (though it produced some radio sets), this needed to be imported. In fact, all material needed for the generation and image distribution had to be imported. Additionally, the human resources required to provide technical support were nonexistent. Therefore, it was necessary to work closely with international companies to train the local workforce and/or supply technicians when necessary. In sum, the first Brazilian television channel had to import all equipment (from the transmission antennas to the cameras) and to sign contracts with suppliers to design technical solutions to broadcast television signals in Brazilian cities, install equipment, and train operational and maintenance technicians.

Secondly, all the required production and receptor equipments were very expensive. Consequently, the audience was restricted, and only few could buy a TV receiver, which at the time had a very high cost value.[5] The high prices of imported equipment and the vast size of the country (comprised of a predominantly rural population) hindered the popularization of the media.[6] Brazil was a country with low per capita income, and its population was mostly concentrated in the countryside and spread over a large territory. Even the metropolitan areas were far apart. In fact, the Brazilian state capitals could be more distant from each other than those of American states – a more populous country than Brazil but of a similar size.

Thirdly, it was challenging to convince companies to invest in this new form of media advertising given accompanying low audience ratings. Fourth, in addition to having international contacts and financial capacity, the industry entrepreneur needed to have the right political connections to obtain a channel license from the President of the Republic authorizing its operation. Finally, obtaining access to foreign currency (or authorization to exchange the Cruzeiro, the Brazilian currency at that time, to international currencies – e.g. the dollar) to pay for imports and technical services was difficult given that the country was facing a severe shortage of foreign funds during this period.

In Brazil, as in the US, the pioneering entrepreneurs investing in television had experience with the radio and other media businesses. For example, one pioneer, Assis Chateaubriand, controlled a large number of radio stations and newspapers in some of the most important Brazilian cities before investing in the television industry. Training and technical support for Brazil's first television channel, TV Tupy São Paulo, was carried out by RCA. Prior to investing in TV Tupy São Paulo, RCA had commercial ties in the country as a supplier for radio equipment with offices in São Paulo, Rio de Janeiro, and Recife.[7]

TV Tupy São Paulo began on September 18, 1950, just 18 days after the opening of Channel 4 in Mexico City, Latin America's first TV station. Rio de Janeiro's first channel, TV Tupy Rio, began its activities several months later on January 20, 1951. The technology was not the same for the two Brazilian television channels. Tupy TV Sao Paulo operated according to the US standard (525 lines, 30 frames, 6 channel-mc, FM sound). By contrast, TV Tupy Rio operated according to the European standard (625 lines, 25 frames, 6-mc channel FM sound). The diversity in transmission made it difficult for São Paulo and Rio to exchange material. Consequently, programming was generally produced locally and transmitted to local publics. By the mid-1950s, there were six TV stations in Brazil – three in São Paulo, two in Rio de Janeiro, and one in Belo Horizonte.

Although the country only had a small number of channels the television business was fairly competitive during this period. This was because the relevant market also included radio broadcasting, an already consolidated media. In this two-sided market, the new television channels had to compete with radio for advertising investments. The relevant market for TV production and distribution was local, as far as the audience was restricted to the metropolitan area where it was located. The product market was composed of television and radio stations operating in the city of its concession.

The growth of the television market depended on the emergence of mass consumption defined by a substantial portion of the population acquiring a television set. At the time of live programming (1950–1961), TV program consumption was restricted to middle and high-income families that had the resources and capacity to obtain the credit required to purchase the receptors. When the TV Tupi started broadcasting in 1950, there were only 200 TV receivers in the country, all of which were imported by Assis Chateaubriand at very elevated prices.[8] In 1951, a domestic manufacturing firm, Invictus, began to produce television sets in the country. Consequently, prices fell, and the number of households with television sets slowly increased, reaching just over 140,000 in 1956 and surpassing one million in 1962.[9]

During the 1950s, up to the beginning of the 1960s, in spite of the increased accessibility, access was still notably limited. Restricted access to television sets and limited transmission area coverage made it an unattractive market for advertising. In addition, costs were high since all the programming was broadcasted live and only reached local audiences. Therefore, business was only made possible with the exploitation of economies of scope by media groups (which replicated both the entertainment and journalistic programming of its radio stations and its newspapers). There were only stations located in the three major cities of the country, and programming consisted of a mix of local content produced live and imported movies series. Without exception, their equipment was precarious and included only a few cameras, improvised studios, and rare and obsolete external trucks for live transmission outside the studios.

The programs with the largest audience and highest cost were made by advertising agencies that rented broadcasters' timeslots and produced content according to the advertisers' tastes. Advertising agencies that hired several programs ended up buying packages with substantial discounts. By outsourcing part of the production and renting display time (for reduced prices due to discount given to the annual contract customers), TV stations lost access to commercial breaks during these programs. Therefore, market power was transferred to the sponsors. Broadcasters could sell the intervals between programs for low prices given that they were less valued.

The precarious management of the first Brazilian television stations and the informality in business conduct made it near impossible to determine the expected earned rate of return. Sale prices of commercialized hours were not based on any cost study. In fact, there were no price tables, and the sale of these timeslots were not dictated by detailed business calculations. Therefore, advertising revenues oftentimes failed to cover production costs. This can be attributed to the lack of joint planning activity between the departments of production and commercialization. Agency problems arose due to executives' disinterest in rationalizing activities given that they were paid a fixed salary and a percentage over sales as opposed to being paid in accordance with the profits obtained.

The poor management and, in particular, the absence of an effective control contributed to widespread agency problems that reached even the lower levels of the corporate hierarchy.[10] The cheap commercial intervals sold outnumbered the timeslots available. This resulted in approximately 20-minute commercial intervals that deterred viewers from watching. Walter Clark mentioned a time when a commercial break lasted for 63 minutes. Therefore, although the audience increased dramatically following the very rapid growth of the country, most of the television channels lost money. Reversing this trend and increasing revenue only became possible by replacing the sale of airtime with the sale of isolated commercials and with higher control over corruption and the introduction of the concept of control per second. In spite of these developments, there was still much to do in order to start controlling costs and making profits.[11]

The first TV station to adopt professional management was the Excelsior. The Excelsior began its operations at São Paulo in 1960 and arrived in Rio de Janeiro in 1963. Excelsior belonged to coffee exporter Mario Wallace Simonsen (who also owned 30 other companies). The Excelsior revolutionized programming aimed at the most demanding public. It transmitted films of the Nouvelle Vague as well as opinionated news programs that supported João Goulart's government reforms. Despite its pioneering in these areas, the Excelsior was unable to cope with the changes made to the television market and the hostility of the military government that came to rule the country after the overthrow of Goulart in 1964.

The videotape era

Since programming was broadcasted live, the possibility of showing the same program in multiple cities required sending the cast by train or plane to the location of the next day's presentation or to show the same program with different cast members. This approach yielded a relatively small cost savings compared to the norm of having completely different programs in each city.

Videotape equipment arrived in Brazil in 1961. Until then, each station would produce all their programs live with their own casts, and the programs would only be broadcasted in the city in which they were recorded. With the introduction of videotape equipment, programs produced in one place could be displayed in other locations as long as the tapes were sent by air or land. This development led to economies of scale where companies that owned stations in more than one place acquired a significant competitive advantage. Programs generated in companies' main locations were later sold to the companies' smaller markets, yielding a process similar to that of the film distribution system.

During the same year, the introduction of a regulatory change had a revolutionary impact. This regulatory change involved the government limiting the maximum commercial break time. As a result, it became possible to create vertical programming grids; if the programming was good, it would attract a certain type of viewer and retain the attention of this type of viewer between programs. Thus, minimal commercial intervals contributed both to the development of a loyal audience and to sponsors increasingly valuing television time.[12]

With grid stabilization and the dissemination of the videotape, Excelsior began investing heavily in programming. This was particularly the case in São Paulo in 1961, when Excelsior overtook massive contracts from its competitor, Tupi São

Paulo. This same practice occurred when Excelsior started its activities in Rio de Janeiro in 1963.[13] The reign of Excelsior would, however, be ephemeral. In 1964, the Goulart government was overthrown by a military coup as Simonsen, the owner of Excelsion, was seen as an enemy of the regime. Its ability to retrieve loans decreased and made room for the entry of a new competitor at each local market. Competitors TV Record and TV Globo emerged in São Paulo and Rio de Janeiro, respectively.

São Paulo's TV Record belonged to businessman Paulo Machado de Carvalho, an owner of various radio stations with strong links to football. TV Record's programming included popular music and comedy shows during the week and, above all, football on Sundays (likely due to Carvalho's strong interest and connection in the sport). The absence of a broadcasting rights fee for the football matches initially compensated the company for the high cost of transporting all the camera equipment to the stadium and contributed to TV Record's initial success.[14] However, after some time, TV Record was threatened by football clubs refusing to continue allowing free broadcast of football matches. With no funds to pay for rights, the station changed its Sunday schedule to include popular music as opposed to football matches. TV Record quickly won audience leadership in São Paulo as well as in other cities repeating its programming.[15]

TV Globo was the newest station of the country as of 1965, and had two competitive advantages over other stations. The first advantage was an agreement with Time-Life group, which, at the time, was investing in partnerships with several television stations in Latin America (see below). The second advantage involved TV Globo following the example of the now decadent Excelsior in the sense that it was managed by a team of professional executives specializing in television and without any interference by the owner.[16] The agreement between TV Globo and Time-Life was important for the creation of a television station with transmission technology and modern management quality in Brazil. When the regulation for television was established, it did not explicitly prohibit this type of agreement. Later, with the Decree Law No. 236 of February 28, 1967, this kind of joint venture was prohibited. However, the law had no retroactive effect and, therefore, the Globo agreement remained legal. On July 8, 1971, the end of the Globo and Time-Life agreement was publicly announced in an editorial signed by Roberto Marinho.[17] At the time, TV Globo had become the audience leader in the country and, as later acknowledged by the journalist, the agreement with Time-Life produced the expected effect by contributing to the construction of the business model and the technical quality of the station.

The period of rapid growth of the Brazilian economy between 1968 and 1973, which became known as the "economic miracle," increased income and consumer access to TV sets. As a result, TV penetration doubled between 1968 and 1974, reaching 40 percent of households – as shown in Table 3.1. In 1974, broadcasting TV began to receive more than half of the country's advertising investment. In the mid-1970s, TV receivers' sales (then fully manufactured in Brazil by transnational companies that controlled the product's world market) became part of the standard household consumption package of middle-income families.

54 Sá-Earp et al.

Table 3.1 Brazil: households with TV sets, advertising investment in free-to-air TV and coverage density – selected years

Year	Number of households with TV sets	% advertising investment in broadcast TV	Number of households	Coverage density
1950	200	Nd	10,046,199	0.0
1956	141,000	Nd	11,994,313	1.2
1962	1,056,000	24.7%	14,238,198	7.4
1968	3,276,000	44.5%	16,712,020	19.6
1974	8,171,000	51.1%	20,367,377	40.1
1980	14,192,424	57.8%	25,293,411	56.1
1991	27,650,179	55.4%*	33,747,409	88.9
2000	38,906,707	72.7%**	44,795,101	86.9
2010	54,457,800	64.5%	57,324,000	95.0
2014	65,094,869	58.5%	67,039,000	97.1

Sources: Authors' elaboration based on data provided by Mattos (1990), IPEADATA, Alves (2004), Alves & Cavenaghi (2012); IBGE Census of 1980 and 1991, and IBGE/PNAD. Projeto Inter-meios – Meio e Mensagem Magazine (several issues).

(*) – value for 1989.
(**) – Data for year 2002. Number of households in the period between censuses calculated by geometric interpolation.

The national networks era

In the late 1960s, another innovation emerged that made an even greater impact than the videotape. This development was the long-distance communication system through satellite networks and microwaves via the state-owned company Embratel. This new communication system was developed as a part of a military project linked to national security with the goal of unifying Brazil through radio, telex and telephone. The transmission of television signals was not viewed as strategic by the military. At that time, the military did not attempt to convey a unified Brazilian culture through national programming. This effort was a typical Schumpetarian, private innovation which involved the use of a new technology to increase the innovative company's, in this case the main television channels, market power.

Globo was the first company with a corporate organization capable of meeting the needs of its domestic market. It structured network affiliates through an offline programming distribution line via Embratel that allowed the same programming to be seen in the entire country, at the same time. Embratel's system also allowed real-time transmission of the news. Therefore, as a result of their business efficiency and technical quality, the Globo network became a national leader in the production and distribution of national programs and in integrating the entire Brazilian territory.

At the same time, the military government changed the regulations of the industry. For the first time, legislation was created to regulate the broadcast television activity in Brazil. Decree-Law 236 of 02/28/1967, which amended the

Brazilian Telecommunications Code (Law 4177 of 27/8/1962), substantially increased the control of the federal government over radio channels and broadcast TV licensees. Per these pieces of legislation, the President acquired the power to grant and renew concessions for such services. The government was able to (and did) dictate that only native Brazilians could hold director and chief positions and that each entrepreneurial group could only have 10 TV stations, 10 local radio stations, six regional (two per state) and four national. The legislation restricted people from acting as cross-director (in different entrepreneurial groups) in broadcasting companies. The legislation required that the transfer of concessions be approved in advance and established strict rules to prevent a group's excessive control over all the stations.

The national television networks were established as a radical innovation. At the moment of their installation, no one understood or imagined the cultural and economic impact that unifying customs would have nor the ensuing impact of creating a domestic market for consumer goods. The system was perceived as important only after it was implemented.[18]

In practice, the creation of television networks allowed greater control of one station (head of the network) over a series of stations (affiliates) than was intended in Decree-Law 236 of 02/28/1967. In order to benefit from economies of scale (producing national content) and economies of scope (sharing costs between different media outlets including newspapers, the radio, and television), the networks substantially reduced competition within means of communication media in Brazil. In other words, the networks created large national media groups, restricting the competitive capacity between local companies, which began relying on programming content produced by national groups.

The impact of this legislation on the television station's economy was even greater. When it became possible to transmit images over long distances (initially possible only between the states within the Southeast Region, which were already the country's largest consumer markets), the price of television advertising increased considerably. Broadcasters with an early start in content production became network leaders of retransmission, initially reaching regional audiences but, later, extending their influence to include national audiences. These broadcasters multiplied the economies of scale without the cost of air or ground transportation.

This change occurred at exactly the time in which the number of households with TV sets had expanded substantially, reaching a broad middle class market spread throughout large and medium-sized cities. The price of advertising time on TV Globo, a pioneer in national programming, became much higher than that of its competitors. This, in turn, allowed TV Globo to consolidate their leadership by hiring a more expensive cast and investing in the quality of the programs and to acquire a competitive advantage that it has retained over time. As a result, the market power of the network heads increased substantially. Among these, TV Globo, as an audience leader, had the greatest market power. This meant that its ability to impose a higher price for the placement of advertising was more than proportional to its market share.

Globo's leadership generated an immediate reaction from its competitors. Unable to pay the high salaries of the leading company (Globo), the other stations began to appeal to a more popular programming. Globo also showcased these types of programs at certain times (such as on Sundays). This provoked a negative reaction from the military, as they realized that censoring news transmitted on the television was insufficient to generate "good citizens." In early 1970, the Ministry of Communications, Hygino Caetano Corsetti began to interfere in the content and the production structure of entertainment programming. A campaign against the low quality of popular programming began in 1971. Hygino Caetano Corsetti, the minister heading this campaign made threats and demanded immediate changes. At the same time, Hygino Corsetti demanded the introduction of color transmission to symbolize the country's progress. This did not interest broadcasters who needed to simultaneously invest in new equipments and change their routine in order to make color transmission a reality.[19] In addition, families would need to change their TV receivers (which the vast majority acquired only just recently) to make them compatible with color transmission.[20] Both requirements were a result of a tense negotiation.

The color transmission was introduced gradually, starting with the transmission of the Grape Festival. This festival occurred in the native state of the minister, on the day of the eighth anniversary of the military coup.[21] It was a symbolic gesture that pleased the ministry. Only during the following year was the first color program produced. This production was made by possible by ABINEE's (the Brazilian association of electrical and electronic producers) subsidy. At this slow pace, Globo took five years to showcase all its programming in color; its competitors took even more time. This transition to the color phase consolidated a new aesthetic to the leading station. This "Globo Quality Standard" combined with a carefully understand of the market segmentation, allowed for the station's lasting competitive advantage.

In the mid-1970s, approximately 40 percent of households (encompassing more than eight million middle class families) owned television sets and broadcasting television had a share of more than half of the country's advertising investment. In this period of time, one of the Globo directors said, "*money began to go out the window.*"[22] The substitution process of the imported TV receptors and content was complete. After five years, more than 18 million homes were covered, reaching more than two-thirds of the population.

The creation of national networks led to fierce competition and with it, the dismantling of groups that could not match the speed of technological, artistic and managerial innovations. Only networks that had economic and artistic capacity to produce content capable of attracting a national public could consolidate themselves. This led to the bankruptcy of some of the television pioneers in Brazil, such as TV Tupy, the founder of the first television channels in Brazil. Subsequently, TV Globo's leadership consolidated the market. Under this scenario, new groups, such as the presently existing TV Manchete network and the STB, were formed.

In 1985, the first Brazilian satellite, BRASILSAT, went into orbit. BRASILSAT allowed for the transmission of real time broadcasts nationwide without the need of sending videos overnight. The low costs and space availability of BRASILSAT made the business more lucrative, especially for the leading company, Globo.

The rise of the Globo

After receiving a favorable assessment from the Radios Technical Commission, Roberto Marinho's Globo group requested a TV channel concession in Rio de Janeiro at the end of the Dutra government in 1951. However, President Getúlio Vargas did not authorize the concession. It was only in 1957 that President Juscelino Kubitschek authorized the channel to operate in Rio de Janeiro. During 1962, President João Goulart authorized another channel in Brasilia.[23] TV Globo's operations only began a decade after it was first awarded. The first transmission took place in January 1965.

In the 1960s, several US television groups started to expand into Latin America. This approach began during the radio period, with the creation of AIR – *Asociación Interamericana de Radiodifusión* (Interamerican Broadcasting Association) in 1945. The association's objective was to diffuse the broadcasting business model within the region and to tackle statist tendencies. In the beginning, the relationship between the North Americans and the local entrepreneurs was limited to the supply of equipment (especially RCA) and programming and technical assistance (CBS and NBC). The arrangement initially adopted this form because the market was too small to attract investment. As of 1960, however, the situation began to change. Although the markets continued modestly, major North American television advertisers were creating subsidiaries in Latin America and their advertising agencies accompanied them. ABC was the most prominent network in international direct investment. The ABC network invested in Mexico, Chile, Argentina and the five Central American countries through its international division, Worldvision.[24] Time-Life was a smaller participant in the expansion movement. It had investments in Argentina, Venezuela, and partnered with TV Globo in Brazil.[25]

Time-Life Broadcasting was a subsidiary of the group Time-Life established in 1952, through partnership with the former chairman of the FCC, Wayne Coy, to buy the KOB-TV in Albuquerque, New Mexico. Subsequently, Time-Life Broadcasting acquired new channels in medium-sized cities in the United States including Denver, Colorado and Indianapolis, Indiana. The group was never strong in broadcast TV, but in 1972, it became very successful in pay-TV as a subsidiary of Sterling Information Services Group, Ltd (founder of HBO (Home Box Office).[26] It entered the TV business with the goal of achieving economies of scope through news production despite the fact that then the group did not have the entertainment programming tradition of the large North American television groups, such as ABC and NBC. This international expansion lasted for a decade but was eventually reverted due to low profitability and changes made to the North American regulation.[27]

In 1965, soon after its inauguration, TV Globo in Rio de Janeiro had modern studios and the best equipment.[28] In spite of this, they remained the city's fourth audience ratings station; their losses amounted to $250,000 dollars leading the North American company to claim it "had no idea what was going on."[29] Survival was only possible due to the modernization of their administration and the injection of new money from other companies within the Globo group and from its North American partner.[30]

The new Globo executive professionals incited an administrative revolution in Brazilian television. Two of these professionals, the CEO Walter Clark and production manager Jose Bonifacio 'Boni' de Oliveira Sobrinho, had histories linked to advertising agencies and television administration. A third professional, Joe Wallach, was responsible for the financial administration and mediation of conflicts between the company and the North American partner.

Wallach's mission was to transform Globo into a lucrative business. However, this was made difficult given that the North American partner never received the dividends from its investment. At first, it was difficult to accept the rationalization of its activities, and the station had accumulated losses. Progressively, Wallach began convincing his peers that there was no solution other than to operate with strong cost control.

Soon after its emergence, Globo suffered a terrible threat. The former governor of Rio de Janeiro, Carlos Lacerda, sent the Minister of Justice a complaint regarding Globo's contract with Time-Life. This complaint was supported and amplified by Senator John Calmon, the president of ABERT – Brazilian Radio and Television Stations Association (*Associação Brasileira de Emissoras de Rádio e Televisão)* – and head of TV Tupy, Globo's biggest competitor.[31] The Congress set up a Parliamentary Commission of Inquiry (*Comissão Parlamentar de Inquérito* – CPI) to inquire whether the agreement violated the Constitution which prohibited foreign participation in the country's communication companies. The CPI's final report considered the contracts between TV Globo and Time Life to be unconstitutional.[32]

This incident united conservative congressmen (some of whom were known for their strong, business-driven right-wing positions) and liberal congressmen (who saw the participation of Time-Life as a threat to the independence of the Brazilian media in an alliance against the Rede Globo). Although Time-Life and Globo partnership has often been intensively treated (with a bias either against or in favor of Globo), there is consensus that this was a controversial issue. In 1967, the government clarified the legislation in order to avoid any misunderstandings. This legislation created restrictions for contracts with foreign companies. However, the contract with Globo was predated and regulation had no retroactive effect. In September 1967 the Republic General Attorney decided in favor of Globo, concluding that "... *everything indicates that there is currently no interference from TIME-LIFE in the management and intellectual guidance of TV.*"[33]

The incident also reveals that the quality of management was a problem within the Brazilian communication networks during that period. The operating sector regulation (which was based solely on the exclusion of foreign capital and individual ownership of native Brazilians) controlled traditional business sector executives, who used to have little concern for professional management and were late to follow modern management systems. At the time, various business segments in the country – but not the media businesses – were experiencing important changes in quality management. These changes were partly due to the rapid economic growth, which began in 1967, and partly due to the emergence of a new generation of professional managers from technical fields including engineering and economics. Therefore, its possible that the nature of the contract between TV Globo and Time-Life can explain why this network would come to be the first to have a professional administration and some autonomy with respect to its shareholders.[34]

Globo's relationship with Time-Life ended in 1970. The American group asked for USD 6.3 million for its share of the business. Globo's Roberto Marinho paid the group 60 percent of the requested amount in installments. He took a long-term loan from a local state-owned bank and offered his personal assets as collateral.[35] Globo would start to make profits right after that.

The company's success was exhibited in its real-time news coverage of the floods and the Carnival of 1966 in Rio de Janeiro. However, the main catalyst of Globo TV's ascendency to power was not its news coverage but, rather, the success of its "novelas." Its "novelas" gradually differentiated themselves from early radio drama serials. They had more modern plots that were better suited to large Brazilian cities; they were much different from the old serial melodramas typical of Spanish-speaking countries.

Effective budget management enabled the company to make notable changes in the aesthetics of television broadcasting. The changing aesthetics started with hiring costume designers experienced in the "Escolas de Samba." This yielded significant changes in costumes and scenography design.[36] Subsequently, improvements were made with the hiring of extremely sophisticated German designer Hans Donner. All of these came together with new hires and best plots that contributed to improvements in the quality of TV scripts and the in-house production.

The "Globo Quality Standard," though, was not superior purely as a product of its appealing aesthetics but also due to the successful application marketing skills that enabled the network to target specific audiences. In general, programming was enhanced with an intensive use of audience measurement techniques, just like in advertising. All TV channels used audience data collected by IBOPE, but they all lacked assessment tools. Globo TV created the Department of Audience Survey and Analysis to fill this gap and hired Argentinean sociologist Homero Icaza Sanches to run it. "The Wizard," as Sanches came to be known, implemented an analytical model that classified the network's audience according to geographic residence, sociodemographic profile (based on income level), and sociocultural profile (based on consumption patterns of cultural goods and services).[37] Qualitative and quantitative research methods were then combined to study the way in which the audience interacted with or responded to network content. Small groups of viewers with given profiles were gathered so that the department could investigate the reasons motivating fluctuation of audience rates of given TV shows. This information facilitated, for instance, the changing of soap opera scripts to better peak the interest of particular audiences.

As a result of the application of these marketing techniques, audience rates grew to record levels. This directly impacted revenues. At the beginning of the 1970s, Globo became the dominant firm in the oligopolistic broadcasting television market in Brazil. Its flagship products were the news show Jornal Nacional and the high-cost "novelas" authored by Brazilian writers. According to the established pattern of competition, rivals' products were low-cost imitations of Globo's products. These satisfied less demanding audiences and were cheaper for advertisers. In spite of the creation of these imitations, Globo was able to absorb around 75 percent of the country's TV advertising revenues.

It is important to address the role of the military regime in, allegedly, favoring Globo. That is a common sense idea when it comes to the assessment of its rise as the dominant firm in the broadcasting business – where the lack of evidence is replaced with the product of fertile imagination. It is now well established that Globo was not granted any new broadcasting licenses during that period. Actually, the company had two concession bids denied (in Curitiba and João Pessoa) and could only expand by means of acquisitions of local TV channels (in São Paulo, Belo Horizonte and Recife). All the other stations that are part of the Globo network are affiliates. Even though the owners of Globo were strongly sympathetic to the military rule, there is no evidence that its competitors, who share the same view, were entitled any special treatment (except for the case of Excelsior in the 1960s).

The issue of great concern during military rule was censorship, and censorship affected all networks equally. Globo programming was no less subject to censorship than any other broadcasters' were. The fact that news shows were censored on a daily basis (for political reasons) was worrisome. Any news report could be censored just before being aired. When the censorship revealed an 'unacceptable' content, the television producers were challenging to find a replacement to this content Though less common, sometimes networks could be prohibited from airing TV shows that had already been recorded. In such situations, networks incurred huge financial losses.[38] The heaviest penalty for networks failing to comply with the government-imposed rules was the non-renewal of their broadcasting licenses. All television and radio broadcasting companies feared that their licenses would be revoked, especially after the military government nationalized all TV stations in Argentina.[39]

There were, however, two primary reasons for Globo's success during the military rule. These included: (i) the economic growth and the increase in family income (both of which allowed for the consumption of durable goods and the expansion of audience size) and (ii) the implementation of satellite communication systems (after the state-owned company's Embratel's launching of a Brazilian satellite in 1982). These changes opened a unique window of opportunity for Globo given that Globo had the funds and managerial capabilities required to take advantage of it before the competition. In the short term, the creation of a national television network functioned as a barrier to entry for the TV Globo competitors into a new relevant market – the recently formed national free-to-air television market. When the competition finally managed to establish their networks,

Globo's leadership in the industry had already consolidated and has not derailed ever since.

In the 1990s, Globo made huge investments including entering the market of Pay television and, simultaneously, building its main production studio called PROJAC, inspired by Universal Studio facilities in California.[40] In the broadcasting industry, having its own production studio lead to larger economies of scope that were out of reach for competitors operating in a decentralized manner.

At the same time, Globo made investments to implement underground utility lines in most big cities to allow for the provision of cable television services. It also built the new headquarters of Globo Newspaper. Those investments financially burdened the company because they had been partially funded with loans contracted overseas in a time when the Brazilian currency was significantly overvalued.

As the currency was progressively devalued – the Brazilian Real to Dollar exchange rate increased from R$ 0.92 in 1995 to R$ 3.80 at the end of 2002 – Globo's debt exploded to almost USD 1.7 billion while most of its revenues remained in the Brazilian Real. Expenses were growing faster than expected, and revenues were lower than planned. This is especially because the pay television market performed very poorly during its first decade of operations. Globo was forced to undertake a comprehensive restructuring of its finances. In doing so, it sold several assets (such as NET and its shares in several businesses) and managed to negotiate a solution with creditors that did not include selling shares of its capital. As a result, Globo has been able to remain a family business.[41]

Pay television in Brazil

The business of pay television

Pay television in Brazil differs from that in the US and in other traditional markets. In Brazil, the development of subscription TV had a late start and took longer to consolidate. Nonetheless, it has transformed the patterns of competition in the Brazilian television industry. The main change brought about by the rise of pay-TV was the clear distinction between the markets of content production and of content packaging and distribution. In addition, it has increased competition in the entire market of audiovisual goods and services (which includes broadcasting channels, subscription services, on demand videos, and the incipient internet-based channels and/or independent content providers).

Pay television first became available in the US in 1948. It was established with the aim of providing audiovisual content where broadcast reception was poor. At first, the service only retransmitted broadcasting programming, with subscription channels playing the role of locally based repeater stations[42]. In the 1970s, new technologies and a new business model based on segmented markets emerged and revolutionized the entertainment industry. The use of satellite transmission relaying signals to a cable system allowed for a much larger number of TV channels than the traditional free-to-air terrestrial system could support. Even though investments required to operate a system combining satellites with terrestrial stations were high, financial compensation would easily come from selling packages to several cable TV stations. The TV stations, in turn, were likely to reach a vast number of subscribers.

The business of pay television is fundamentally different from that of broadcasting television. The new technology enabled audience segmentation and offered a large number of TV channels capable of meeting the demands of several distinct groups of consumers and reaching vast, diversified audiences. That is a typical Schumpeterian innovation: technological change creating new business models and entrepreneurs creating new products and generating new revenue streams.

To sum up, since the 1970s, the entertainment industry has experienced technological and structural changes that have given rise to a completely new business. That new business, Pay TV, is radically different from that of the free-to-air broadcasting television. Pay TV operates with content aggregation and packaging into channels and retail service provision. This new business is not a two-sided market. With Pay TV, the revenue model is fundamentally based on subscription fees complemented, occasionally, by advertising.[43]

Pay television in Brazil: from start to the Law 12.485/2011

In Brazil, the pay-TV market developed only in the 1990s. However, the first subscription-based transmissions took place in the 1980s on closed UHF coded frequencies. In 1988, pay television services were subject to regulation by Decree 95.744/88, which established the Special Service of Pay Television (*Serviço Especial de TV por Assinatura* – TVA). This regulation defined the TVA as a telecommunications service established to distribute audio and visual content to subscribers by transmitting coded signals into channels of the radio-electric spectrum. There, the partial use of decoding was allowed at the discretion of the concession-grantor. Like all other telecommunications services, TVA was subject to the general Law of Broadcasting Services of 1963. In December 1989, the Ministry of Communications issued the Ministerial Decree n. 250 to formalize the service of cable television. This decree was entitled Cable Distribution of Television Signals Service (*Serviço de Distribuição de Sinais de TV por Meios Físicos* – DISTV).

Based on that ministerial decree, 96 licenses were issued in 1990 to permit the installation of cable infrastructure in 62 cities throughout Brazil. The pioneer regulation made a distinction between broadcasting television and pay television services. While the latter has been treated as a special service and has been regulated since the beginning, the former has not been (and is still not) subject to the rule of any regulatory body.[44] While the FCC has long regulated television broadcasting in the US, in Brazil, there has always been notable resistance to regulating those activities. This was not the case for the pay-TV services. Upon establishment, they were subject to regulation by the National Telecommunications Agency (*Agência Nacional de Telecomunicações* – ANATEL) and after the

Audiovisual Act of 2011, they were regulated by the National Film Agency (*Agência Nacional do Cinema* – ANCINE).

In June of 1991, the National Communications Secretary issued Ministerial Decree n. 51; this decree transformed DISTV into the Cable Television Special Service. The administrative order opened the regulation of cable television services for debate. This resulted in the passing of the Cable Television Act in 1995.[45] In the early 1990s, some large Brazilian media groups began to invest in the Pay-TV industry. They invested in new technologies and created the first Brazilian Pay TV service providers. In 1990, the group Abril, a large media and magazine publisher, launched TVA and debuted in the market offering a five-channel package. The size of this package was increased throughout the decade. In the same year, Globo established Globosat, the first Brazilian firm to play an active role in both content distribution (aggregation and packaging) and content production and development.

During the first years of operation, the number of pay-TV subscribers was very low – reaching only 400.000 in 1994. Table 3.1 displays this starting point as well as the trajectory of Pay-TV subscriptions. Although subscriber base was initially low, it grew rapidly throughout the decade. For example, the subscriber base grew by 44.4 percent per year from 1994 to 2000! However, in the early 2000s, the subscription-base growth stagnated, and companies became frustrated that their growth expectations went unmet. Between 2000 and 2005, annual subscriber growth barely reached 3 percent. In mid-2004, the number of subscribers in Brazil was much lower than in Argentina and even in Mexico.[46] Since 2010, subscriber-base growth has increased exponentially in Brazil. This uptick has been especially pronounced in the last few years. In August 2015, around 30 percent of Brazilian households held Pay-TV subscriptions.[47]

This erratic growth path, as well as the regulatory and competition debates that occurred during its first decade of operation, explain the prevailing characteristics of the pay television industry in Brazil. Among the distinctive features of its market structure is the high level of concentration in distribution.[48]

In this market, two firms, Net and Sky, have significant market power. In 2014, they controlled 87.8 percent of all subscriptions. No other competitor in the fringe

Table 3.2 Brazil: pay-TV subscriptions – all technologies

Year	Number of subscribers (in millions)	Index number Year 2000 = 100.0	Annual growth rate
1994	400	11.1	–
2000	3,607	100.0	44.3%
2005	4,176	115.8	3.0%
2010	9,769	270.8	17.8%
2013	18,019	499.6	22.6%
2015(*)	19,580		

Source: Authors' elaboration based ANATEL and ABTA data.

(*) Data referring to August 2015.

of the market, including firms originated in the telecommunications industry, holds a market share above 5 percent.[49]

Due to the high concentration in service use, prices charged for retail services in Brazil are significantly higher than those in markets. An interesting comparative study conducted by the Office of Superintendent of Market Analysis of the ANCINE reveals that, in 2012, the price charged per channel in Brazil is the highest among a selected sample of Latin American and European countries.[50]

Immediately following its inception, competition in the pay-tv market was based on product differentiation. Since 1993, the main patterns of competition in the industry were gradually established. At that point, competition was based on product differentiation as evidenced by TVA and Net fighting over exclusivity agreements with major international cable channels. Back in 1994, TVA announced that it had obtained exclusive rights over the sales and distribution of HBO channel and other channels launched before 1997. At the same time, Net announced it had entered into an exclusivity agreement with several American studios such as Fox, Paramount, MGM, and Universal, regarding the distribution of motion picture content in newly created Telecine channels. In 1998, cable assets and several Net local operators (Rio de Janeiro / NetRio, São Paulo / Net São Paulo, Brasília / Net Brasília) were merged into a new company renamed Globocabo. In 2002, Globocabo was, again, renamed, becoming Net Serviços de Comunicação SA.

Competition based on product differentiation did not last long, though. Consumers did not benefit from it, since the offer of a diversified range of content is the essence of subscription television – a market where segmentation is a key feature. Thereby, that competitive strategy, in association with high investments in infrastructure required to further develop the industry, made less capitalized firms more vulnerable and less successful in attracting new subscribers.

At the end of the 1990s, it became clear that it was senseless for small markets (such as the Brazilian market) for major international cable channels to enter into exclusivity agreement with any TV operator in Brazil and, thereby, relinquish market shares.[51] In the early 2000s, Brazil's antitrust agency, the Council for Economic Defense (*Conselho Administrativo de Defesa da Concorrência* – CADE) investigated pay television market corporations' antitrust conducts. The investigations, as well as the review of horizontal mergers in this market, pushed for changes in market structure and towards increased competition not only in content production but also in packaging and retail service provision.

At that time, CADE was primarily concerned with the conditions of competition in domestic content production (which were deemed central to TV operators). Therefore, CADE's major concern was not about the market of Pay TV service provision, per se, but rather about the domestic content production. At that time, Globopar, the parent company of Globo's firms, was reducing its shares in the pay-tv retail service provision and focusing in domestic content production and packaging by means of its subsidiary Globosat.

The topic of domestic content raised another concern: The role of the ANATEL in the enforcement of audiovisual content regulation was ambiguous. This should have been the role of a regulatory authority, ANCINAV, that was never created due to tremendous resistance from the Television Networks and media businesses that feared economic regulation in the media market. In the absence of this regulatory authority, all issues involving television content had to be treated exclusively as a matter of competition – and, therefore, only *ex-post* intervention measures applied. However, many issues concerning the pay-tv market required public policies based on *ex-ante* intervention measures. Applying *ex-ante* intervention measures would only be possible if a regulatory body intervened. This dispute on the regulation of pay tv ended up influencing the debate on the role of the ANCINE.

The ANCINE emerged in 2001 as a part of the restructuring of the cultural sector that had been dismantled during President Fernando Collor's term. At first, it was part of the Ministry of Development, Industry and Commerce (*Ministério de Desenvolvimento, Indústria e Comércio* – MDIC). However, in 2003, ANCINE was transferred to the jurisdiction of the Ministry of Culture. The ANCINE functions as an executive agency with the role of fostering the development of cultural activities. During President Lula's terms, an attempt was made to transform the ANCINE into a regulatory body for the entire audiovisual industry (which included television). This proposed development was to be called ANCINAV.[52] Efforts to construct ANCINAV relied on the assumption that ANATEL, a regulatory body for the telecommunication sector, could not rule over content production for audiovisual and television industries. Resistance to the proposal to construct ANCINAV was fierce. Opposition was especially pronounced among major television broadcasters who alleged that the newly proposed agency would interfere with freedom of speech. This contributed to the abandoning of the proposal to construct ANCINAV. Nevertheless, with the passing of the Audiovisual Act (Law 12.485) on September 12, 2011, the role of the ANCINE was expanded to include several functions originally designed to be under the jurisdiction of ANCINAV. After this expansion in its scope, ANCINE has practically become the regulatory body for the Pay television industry.

In sum, pay television was created in Brazil in the 1990s with a market structure based on product differentiation. After some time, the market structure changed. The introduction of new technologies led TV operators to compete based on price and on quality of access. The main providers of pay TV also began to offer varied TV packages including not only major foreign channels such as Warner, Sony and HBO, but also the domestic ones, such as Globosat's Globonews, GNT, Multishow, SportTV, Telecine. At first, Globosat held a practically monopolistic position in the market of domestic content, as smaller broadcasters such as Band and other public or independent stations posed little threat to it. However, the passing of the Audiovisual Act of 2011 has introduced new regulation requiring a minimum level of domestic content to be purchased from domestic independent producers. As a result, competition in the market of domestic content has increased. More recently, growing amounts of independent content available on the internet has contributed to and enhanced competition in the domestic pay-tv and broadcast television markets.

The market today

Technological convergence has transformed the market structure of audiovisual industries including both free-to-air broadcasting and Pay television. It contributed to the emergence of a single market of pay television services, internet connectivity, and mobile and fixed telephone services. The major difference between the present and past market structures is the increasing competition between broadcast television, pay television and the internet.

Between 2004 and 2013, Brazil experienced a steady economic growth caused by increased commodity prices in international markets combined with domestic public policies aiming at income distribution and credit expansion. The latter helped to expand the domestic market for goods and services. As a result, consumption of electronic goods increased more rapidly than the output growth, leading to the increased consumption of services as well. Just as the increased consumption of TV receivers helped boost broadcast television audiences in the 1960s–1980s, the increased consumption of high-definition television receivers, laptop and desktop computers, tablets and smartphones is increasing the demand for pay television and many internet-based content provision services. Thereby, convergence has created new markets for cultural goods and services. At the same time niche channels have proliferated across the internet, especially on YouTube.[53]

Access to digital technologies and telecommunications networks has grown dramatically in Brazil in the twenty-first century. In the last decade, personal computer ownership among Brazilians increased more than four times (meaning more than half of the population has access to personal computers) while internet access grew 4.5 times (meaning that almost half of the population has access to it). Smartphone ownership has also grown dramatically; approximately 80 percent of the Brazilian population has access to this technology. Therefore, today, the number of mobile subscriptions is larger than the size of Brazilian population, which means that several people have more than one mobile subscription. As smartphones are cheaper and more accessible, they have become the ideal way to browse the internet.[54]

Today both content production and the distribution of broadcast television are headed by five private networks, one public network, and a large number of affiliates' channels.[55] The leading television broadcaster is Globo. Globo commands a network of 122 affiliates, and despite the main network's audience share dropping from 20 percent in 2000 to 13.6 percent in 2013, it still controls more than half of all TV advertising revenues.[56] Owned by an Evangelical Church (the Universal Church of the Kingdom of God), Record Network follows in second place with 56 affiliate stations. The audience share of Record Network increased from 5.5 percent in 2000 to 6.3 percent in 2013. SBT is the third largest network. It has 98 member stations and a dropping audience share – from 10.4 percent in 2000 to 5 percent in 2013. Bandeirantes, in the fourth position, brings together a network of 22 affiliates and has maintained a stable audience share of 2.3 percent since 2000. Finally, there is Rede TV with 21 member stations. The audience share of Rede TV has remained stable (~ 1 percent) since 2000.[57]

As of 2011, 97.4 percent of Brazilian households had a television set.[58] That pervasive penetration makes broadcast television the most important outlet for media advertisement in Brazil; in 2014, it received 69 percent of total advertising revenue. However, broadcast television may have reached its peak or may be close to reaching it in terms of advertising revenues. The shares of advertising revenues acquired by pay-tv and the internet have been increasing. Presently, however, these remain marginal; advertising revenues in the pay-TV and the internet markets only accounted for 13 percent of total revenues in 2014. This said, the future of advertising investments is likely to be in the hands of the new digital media, and there is already evidence of this transformation.

The audience share of broadcasting television channels declined from 38.8 percent in 2006 to 28.3 percent in 2013.[59] The declining use of a once extremely popular media can provide evidence of important changes to come. From 2006 to 2013, pay-tv share of the audience rose by 30 percent per year. In this last year, one third of the Brazilian population used to live in households that subscribe to pay-tv. However, most audience members are viewers of both broadcasting television channels and pay-tv channels; having a pay-tv subscription is a guarantee of higher quality of access and better transmission signals and is often included in a multi-play package with internet connectivity and fixed telephone services. From an advertiser's perspective, it does not matter whether viewers watch commercials from a TV set connected by means of a paid subscription or not.

The internet poses the biggest threat to TV audiences in the media industry. Access to the internet rose by 26 percent per year between 2006 and 2013, and the internet now reaches almost half of the population. The rate of growth of internet users is likely to have been influenced by the ease of access (especially by smartphones) and by internet connectivity being essential to the use of social media.

One might not expect to find similar growth figures in the future. The main reason is that, since 2013, Brazil's economy has entered a turbulent new phase where commodity prices are declining and domestic economic and political problems have been adversely affecting the performance of the economy. The second half of this decade is expected to encompass a time of adjustments with unforeseeable outcomes.

Conclusion

The Brazilian television industry has experienced dramatic changes in its more than six decades of history. Beginning as a high-end service available to a few thousand people scattered throughout a couple of metropolitan areas, free-to-air television broadcasting has grown into the most important mass media outlet in the country and is available to virtually all of the population. This massive transformation was made possible with the introduction of recording and transmission technologies – such as videotape, microwave, and satellite – in the 1960s and 1970s and the subsequent converting of TV receivers into a mass consumption type of good, subject to large-scale production and extended credit. It was unexpected that a national market for television programming would emerge so quickly and that advertisers would become so eager to invest in the media. In the 1990s, a combination of technological and business innovations allowed for the emergence of a new market comprised of more sophisticated audiovisual content targeted at more demanding niche consumers. The Pay-TV market, which provides increased image quality, has rapidly attracted many consumers who were formerly exclusively free-TV viewers. In recent years, the new market of pay television has come to share space with the traditional two-sided market of free-to-air television.

However, technology changes have extended beyond the television industry. Additional information and communication technologies, including the internet, have recently emerged. Mass production has diminished prices and extended credit has become available to consumers purchasing the sets of equipment required to operate the media. The impact of such changes has been much larger than that of the emergence of national broadcasting television networks decades before. While traditional TV and radio sets were built solely for unidirectional transmission, the internet allows for bidirectional transmissions with several complimentary functions. These include content production and distribution by the users themselves.

Many innovative businesses have been created in response to the opportunities generated by the internet. In particular, the once high barrier to entry into the audiovisual industry established in the 1950s, has been lowered. With the aid of the internet, one can engage in relatively low cost content production and distribution to potentially wide audiences and obtain financial compensation from advertisers or sponsors (just like in the traditional television business model). The internet also allows business models with revenue streams based on subscription fees to fund the production of premium content (such as Netflix does). In addition to Netflix, HBO GO and Globosat Play comprise this Brazilian new market of TV streaming services. Despite low market shares, these services have been growing quickly. This new way of accessing audiovisual content, without subscribing to a pay-tv service, might become a large market in the near future.

Therefore, a new, more competitive market structure is in the making. This makes room for innovative business models. The new media are not expected to replace the old ones, just like the television did not make the radio obsolete. However, just as the radio lost relevance in the 1970s, traditional broadcasting television may now be experiencing its final moments of glory.

Notes

1 Vogel, 2011, p.281.
2 Amstrong, 2006.
3 Roman, 2005, ch. 2.
4 Brazil was the first South American Country with a television broadcasting service. In 1950, only Brazil and Mexico had this service. In Europe, which was still recovering from World War II in this period, only UK and France regularly had access to this service. According to an executive of TV Tupy Rio, only five countries in the world had

this service by 1950, and the Brazilian Television channel was able to sell advertisements even though their costs were five times higher than those of the radio. *O Globo*, 21/12/1950, p.15 "Televisão, Uma Realidade."

5 Sobrinho, 2000, p. 193. The first television set had very high prices and became more expensive during the first year of Korean War. See "Os impressionantes Aumentos Especialmente dos Materiais Elétricos," O Globo, 5/5/1951).

6 By December of 1952, the price of a television set (specifically, a 17-inch Zenith model) was CR$ 19.450,00 according to an advertisement in the O Globo newspaper (15/12/1952). This amount is equal to R$15.533,14 (about US$ 4.000,00) in price of November of 2015 (price index, IGP/DI of FGV).

7 The largest Brazilian newspapers produced advertisements informing its readership that RCA was the supplier of the TV equipment for the newly inaugurated TV TUPY in São Paulo (18/9/1950).*O Globo* 18/9/1950.

8 Mattos, 2000, p.87.

9 Mattos, 1990, 2000.

10 Clark & Priolli (2015:position 1451).

11 Clark & Priolli (2015:position 1767).

12 Clark & Priolli (2015, position 1751).

13 Clark & Priolli (2015, position 2125).

14 Cardoso & Roekman, 2005

15 A noteworthy fact is that, in theory, TV Record's programming should have been transmitted in Rio de Janeiro by TV Rio because TV Rio's owner, João Baptista "Pipa" Amaral, was Paulo Machado de Carvalho's brother-in-law and owner of half of the TV Record's quotas. However, family rivalry prevented them from working together. Instead of broadcasting its programs via TV Rio, TV Record sold its videos to TV Globo, its competitor owned by media entrepreneur Roberto Marinho.

16 Clark & Priolli, 2015: position 3411).

17 O Globo, July 8, 1971, p.3

18 The Decree-Law n° 236 of 28/2/1967 is related not only to television broadcasting but also to radio broadcasting.

19 A color camera cost about US$ 150.000,00, meaning that it was six times more expensive than the black and White equipment. Clark & Priolli, 2015: position 4093).

20 Color TV required producers to change equipment and to hope that the public would similarly invest in the new technologies. Clark & Priolli (2015: position 3970)

21 Hygino Corsetti was an engineer and coronel of the army, that was born at the city of Caxias do Sul, in the state of Rio Grande do Sul.

22 See Borgerth, 2003, p.36.

23 See Mattos (1990, 2000); and Memória Globo at http://memoriaglobo.globo.com/acusacoes-falsas/concessoes-de-canais.htm. Accessed on 20.11.2015.

24 Sinclair (1999, Introduction).

25 "Under the contract signed in 1962, Time-Life agreed to supply financial, technical, and management assistance, in the widest sense, covering equipment, financial controls, training, programing, marketing, and commercialization in general. In return, Time-Life would receive 30 per cent of the profits." (Sinclair, 1999:66).

26 Later, in 1990, Time Inc and Warner merger to became the Time Warner Inc, one of the largest entertainment groups in the world.

27 See Sinclair, 1988, p.18.

28 The network purchased this equipment with resources obtained from their agreement with the Time-Life group.

29 The Television equipment cost about 500 and 600 thousand dollars (Wallach, 2011, p.27). The rest of the investments were buildings and funds for the cash flow. See Wallach (2011, p.27).

30 Ver Sobrinho (2000, p.121).

70 *Sá-Earp* et al.

31 All this history is available in the deposition to the Congress CPI, published as DC1S, in 12/01/1967. The deposition of Roberto Marinho was published also in the O Globo in April, 25, 1963, p.10.
32 It seems that Globo was considered guilty by the Congress CPI because Joe Wallach, Time Life employee, was a member of the board that make financial decisions.
33 Ver Wallach (2011, p.229), that published the General Attorney decision. See also further information in http://memoriaglobo.globo.com/acusacoes-falsas/caso-time-life.htm.
34 The hiring of professional executives has reflected in the higher quality of its management and, moreover, through the improvement of their programing by the end of the 1960s.
35 Clark & Priolli (2015, positions 3697 & 3706).
36 Clark & Priolli (2015, position 4110).
37 Sobrinho, 2000, p.114).
38 An example was the 1975 prohibition of the "novela" *Roque Santeiro,* after 36 chapters were recorded. This led to a loss of US$ 500.000,00 in sunk costs. In the next year, the "novela" *Despedida de Casado*, was also censured after 30 chapters had been recorded. http://memoriaglobo.globo.com/acusacoes-falsas/concessoes-de-canais.htm. Accessed on 21.12.2015.
39 Clark & Priolli (2015, position 3880).
40 The name PROJAC is an abbreviation of Projeto Jacarepaguá, that was named the building of the Central Globo de Produções. The investment to build the PROJAC was US$ 110 million (Brittos, 2000, p.68).
41 http://memoriaglobo.globo.com/acusacoes-falsas/bndes-e-renegociacao-da-divida.htm, accessed on December, 26, 2015.
42 See Parsons, 2008 and Cicciora, 1995.
43 For a description of the Productive Chain of Pay TV in Brazil, see the decision of CADE in the merger of Sky Brasil and DirectTV Brasil. It can be found in CADE as AC 53500.029160/2004.
44 Torres, 2008, p.70.
45 Before the 2011 Law, all other technologies were regulated by Executive Orders such as the Decree 2,196 of 2007 and by by-laws of the Ministry of Communication. There were no restrictions for foreign ownerships for those services.
46 See data from Table 3.2 and from Prado & Santos, 2008.
47 Data from ANATEL, available on www.anatel.gov.br/dados/index.php?option=com_content&view=article&id=215, accessinNovember 2015.
48 To see the concentration of the Pay Television service providers market in Brazil, it is useful to compare this Brazilian market to the C2 concentration index of other large Latin American countries. In Argentina, the C2 is 68,7%. In Chile, it is 57,9%. In Colombia, it is 66.4%, and in Mexico, it is 59,0%. Data computed from LAMAC-Latin American MultichannelAdvertisingCouncil/Bussiness Bureau.
49 Data from Anatel and ABTA.
50 See Ancine 2012.
51 According to Possebon (2009, p.127), the Pay Television Service Providers lost interests on contracts with exclusivity rights after 1997.
52 See the proposal law for the creation of ANCINAV, 2004. See Prado (2015) for further information on regulatory agencies in Brazil.
53 A very successful case is the site Porta dos Fundos, that was established in 2012. By 2015, it had reached 10 million of subscriptions, making it the largest internet channel in Brazil, the fifth largest comedy internet channel in the world, and the eighteenth largest internet channel in any content in the world. https://pt.wikipedia.org/wiki/Porta_dos_Fundos. access at November 19, 2015.
54 Data from ANATEL and IBGE (2013).
55 Networks Globo, Record, SBT, Band e RedeTV.

56 The data applies for the total of television sets – that is, both television sets both powered on and off.
57 Data from Becker et al., 2015.
58 This is practically the same share of households with access to electricity (97.8 %) Data from IBGE/PNAD, 2011.
59 Becker et al., 2015.

References

Abreu, Alzira Alves de, Lattman-Weltman, Fernando, Rocha, Dora (2008) *Eles Mudaram a Imprensa: Depoimentos ao CPDOC*, Editora da FGV.
Alves, José Eustáquio Diniz – As Características dos Domicílios Brasileiros entre 1960-2000, IBGE, Textos para Discussão, Escola Nacional de Ciências Estatísticas nº10.
Alves, José Eustáquio Diniz and Cavenaghi, Suzana – Tendências demográficas, dos domicílios e das familias no Brasil em www.ie.ufrj.br/aparte/pdfs/tendencias_ demograficas_e_de_familia_24ago12.pdf acesso em março 2016.
Amstrong, Mark (2006) "Competition in Two-Sided Market," *RAND Journal of Economics*, Vol. 37, No. 3, Autumn, pp. 668–691.
ANATEL (2015) Agência Nacional de Telecomunicações- Estatísticas de Acesso disponível em www.anatel.gov.br/dados/index.php?option=com_content&view= article&id=215, acesso em novembro de 2015.
ANCINE – Superintendência de Acompanhamento de Mercados (2012) *Dados e Estatísticas sobre o Mercado de TV por Assinatura no Brasil e em Países Selecionados-* Rio de Janeiro, Março de 2012.
Balan, Willians Cerozzi (2012) "Um Breve Olhar pela Evolução da TV no Brasil, parte1." *Revista Produção Profissional*, Editora Bollina, São Paulo, abril 2012.
Becker, Valdecir, Gambaro, Daniel and Souza filho, Guido L. (2015) "O impacto das mídias digitais na televisão brasileira: queda da audiência e aumento do faturamento", in *Palabra Clave* – ISSN 0122-8285, Vol. 18, nº 2, Junio de 2014. 341–373.
Bial, Pedro (2005) *Roberto Marinho*. Rio de Janeiro: Jorge Zahar Ed.
Blumenthal, Howard J. and Goodenough, Oliver R. (2006) *This business of television. The standard guide to the television industry*. New York: Billboard Books.
Bolano, César (2004) *Mercado brasileiro de televisão*. Aracaju: Editora UFS; São Paulo: Educ.
Bolano, Cesar R. S and Brittos, Valério C. (2005) *Rede Globo: 40 anos de poder e hegemonia*. São Paulo: Paulus.
Bolano, Cesar R. S and Brittos, Valério C. (2007) *A televisão brasileira na era digital*. São Paulo: Paulus.
Borgerth, Luiz Eduardo (2003) *Quem e como fizemos a TV Globo*. São Paulo: A Girafa.
Brittos, Valério (2005) "Globo, transnacionalização e capitalismo," in Bolano and Britos (2005).
Brittos, Valério (2000) "As Organizações Globo e a reordenação das comunicações," in Revista Brasileira de Comunicação. Vol. XI, nº 1, janeiro-junho.
Brazil – Diário Oficial da União – Diversos Números – disponível em http://portal.in.gov. br/
CADE – Conselho Adminstrativo de Defesa Econômica – Diversos Processos, disponível em www.cade.gov.br
Chaniac, Régine and Jézéquel, Jean-Pierre (2005) *La télévision*. Paris: La Découverte.

Cardoso, Tom and Rockmann, Roberto (2005) *O marechal da vitória. Uma história de rádio, TV e futebol.* São Paulo: A Girafa.

Cicciora, Walther S. (1995) *Cable TV in the United States: An Overview*, Louisville, Co: Cable TV Laboratories Inc.

Clark, Walter and Priolli, Gabriel (2015) *O campeão de audiência.* São Paulo, Summus, 2ª edição.

Dell, Chad E. (2003) The History of "Travelers": Recycling in American Prime Time Network Programming," *Journal of Broadcasting and Electronic Media*, June 2003, pp. 260–275.

Doyle, Gillian (2005) *Understanding media economics.* London: Sage.

Federal Communication Commission, disponível em www.fcc.gov/encyclopedia/ evolution-cable-television, acessado em julho 2014.

Filho, Daniel (2001) *O circo eletrônico. Fazendo TV no Brasil.* Rio de Janeiro: Zahar.

Fox, Elizabeth and Waisbord, Silvio [eds.] (2002) *Latin politics, global media.* Austin: University of Texas Press.

Herz, Daniel (1991) *O superpoder.* Porto Alegre: Ortyz, 14ª edição.

IBGE – Instituto Brasileiro de Geografia e Estatística (2003) – PNAD – Pesquisa Nacional por Amostra por Domicílio.

Jornal Meio e Mensagem (diversos números) – acesso eletrônico em http://www. meioemensagem.com.br/

Júnior, Gonçalo (2001) *Pais da TV.* São Paulo: Conrad.

Kolesky, Fábio Lúcio (2010) *Defesa da Concorrência na TV por Assinatura*, Tese de Mestrado, Faculdade de Comunicação, Universidade de Brasília.

LAMAC- Latin American Multichannel Advertising Council/Bussiness Bureau disponívelem, www.lamac.org.

Lopes, Genésio (2001) *O superpoder, um império da ganância e da lucratividade.* São Paulo: Ibrasa.

Martins, Ana Raquel Paiva & Barros, Denise Pereira – Perspectiva da TV por Assinatura no Brasil: Um estudo sobre o Modelo de Negócio apresentado pela ABTA em 2002 disponível em www.bndes.gov.br/SiteBNDES/export/sites/default/bndes_pt/Galerias/ Arquivos/conhecimento/especial/TV.pdf

Mattos, Sergio (2000) *A História da TV Brasileira: Uma Visão Econômica, Social e Política*, Editora Vozes, 4ª edição.

Mattos, Sérgio (1990) *Um perfil da TV brasileira.* Salvador: Capítulo Bahia da Associação Brasileira de Agências de Propaganda e Empresa Editora A Tarde S/A.

Morais, Fernando (1994) Chatô, o rei do Brasil. São Paulo: Companhia das Letras.

Moya, Álvaro (2010) *Gloria in Excelsior. Ascensão, apogeu e queda do maior sucesso da televisão brasileira.* São Paulo: Imprensa Oficial, 2ª edição.

O Globo (1950) "Televisão, Uma Realidade" publicado em 21/12/1950 , disponível em http://acervo.oglobo.globo.com/

O Globo (1950) – Anúncio RCA, publicado em 18/9/1950, disponível em http://acervo. oglobo.globo.com/

Parsons, Patrick R. (2008) *Blue Skies, A History of Cable TV*, Temple University Press, Philadelphia.

Picard, Robert G. (2002) *The Economics and Financing of Media Companies.* New York, Fordham University Press.

Possebon, Daniel (2009) TV por Assinatura: Vinte Anos de Evolução, Save Produções Editoriais Ltda e ABTA.

Prado, L.C.D and Santos, Marcelo (2008) "Teoria Econômica da Concorrência e Economia da Mídia: Aplicação ao Caso da Fusão Sky-DirectTV," em Mattos, César, *A Revolução do Antitruste no Brasil: A Teoria Econômica Aplicada a Casos Concretos*, Editora Singular.

Prado, L.C.D – "Relações entre Estado e Mercado: Reformas e Agências Reguladoras no Brasil – 1991- 2013" in Sá-Earp, Fabio, Bastian, Eduardo F. and Modenesi, André M. (2014). "A economia brasileira: da diversidade do tema ao exercício da diversidade," in *Como vai o Brasil? A economia brasileira no terceiro milênio.* Rio de Janeiro: Imã Editorial

Rebouças, Edgard (2005) "América Latina: um território pouco explorado e ameaçador para a TV Globo," in Bolano and Britos (2005).

Roman, James (2005) *From Daytime to Prime Time: The History of American Television Programs*, Greenwood Press.

Sá-Earp, Fabio (1981) *Serviços de telecomunicações no Brasil.* COPPE/UFRJ, Tese de mestrado.

Sá-Earp, Fabio and Paulani, Leda (2011) *Mudanças no consumo de bens culturais no Brasil após a estabilização da moeda.* Rio de Janeiro: IE/UFRJ Texto para Discussão 001/2011. Disponível em www.ie.ufrj.br/images/pesquisa/publicacoes/discussao/2011/IE_Earp_Paulani_2011.pdf

Sá-Earp, Fabio, Bastian, Eduardo F. and Modenesi, André M. (2014) "A economia brasileira: da diversidade do tema ao exercício da diversidade," in *Como vai o Brasil? A economia brasileira no terceiro milênio.* Rio de Janeiro: Imã Editorial.

Sinclair, John (1999) *Latin American Television. A global view.* Oxford/New York: Oxford University Press.

Sinclair, John and Turner, George [Eds.] (2004) *Contemporary world television.* London: British Film Institute.

Sobrinho, José Bonifácio de Oliveira (2000) *50 anos de TV no Brasil* São Paulo: Globo.

Sobrinho, José Bonifácio de Oliveira (2011) *O livro do Boni.* Rio de Janeiro: Casa da Palavra.

Torres, Rodrigo Murtinho de Martinez (2005) *O Mercado de TV por Assinatura no Brasil: Crise e Reestruturação Diante da Convergência Tecnológica*, Dissertação de Mestrado, Programa de Mestrado em Comunicação, Universidade Federal Fluminense, Março de 2005.

Vogel, Harold L. (2011) *Entertainment Industry Economics. A guide for financial analysis.* New York, Cambridge University Press.

Wallach, Joe (2011) *Meu capítulo na TV Globo.* Rio de Janeiro: Topbooks.

4 The history of Metal Leve S.A.

From birth to denationalization

Jaques Kerstenetzky

Introduction

Unlike the other business case studies in this volume, Metal Leve (ML) figures as the only unsuccessful one in the fallout from liberalization, a development that was particularly disruptive for Brazilian business activity in the auto parts sector such that even iconic national businesses ended up being denationalized.[1] The account that follows aims to explain Metal Leve's prolific growth and abrupt decline, culminating in the sale of the shares of the tight-knit group – or of their descendants – that controlled it since its foundation to a foreign company.[2]

In this way, Metal Leve's case is emblematic of business in a peripheral country in the era of globalization. During the decades of import substitution industrialization, ML was recognized for its national business excellence, achieving international recognition in the 1980s as a supplier to foreign companies through its exports. However, ML's glory and global prestige were short-lived as it was denationalized several years later in the 1990s. With the onset of denationalization, ownership and control were relinquished to a large German auto parts firm that had already participated in the early phases of ML's history.[3] Though the ML case contains nuances that give it marked characteristics and interest in its own right, it is also broadly representative of the development and transformation of the auto parts manufacturing sector and automobile industry both in Brazil and the world.

The narrative's construction follows an evolutionary conception of business history inspired by Alfred Marshall's writing. An evolutionary approach moves away from ideas of equilibrium in favor of ideas of organic growth trajectory. Marshall's concept of life cycle of firms gives due attention to the accumulation of capabilities and solutions to problems in the different areas of business activity including production and technology, workforce qualification and training, the firm's internal organization, its relationship to the market, as well as financing its operations. The evolutionary conception stresses that the quality of solutions is related to the configuration of elements inside and outside the company that change over time as a result of the firm's and other agents' actions; additionally, the evolutionary stance suggests that growth, itself, brings with it new problems and also that the incapacity to continue introducing effective solutions may be indicative of ossification and decay contributing to decline in the business life cycle (Marshall, 1961, chapter XI §5 and chapter XII §6; Kerstenetzky, 2010: pp. 573–5).

Five phases were identified in the company's life and in its relationship with its business environment. The first phase is the birth of the company in the immediate post-war years. The second is marked by the establishment of the car industry in Brazil followed by the crisis and the slowdown in the Brazilian economy. The third phase is characterized by the return of growth with the cycle of expansion and reversal, starting in 1968 and continuing through the late seventies. The fourth is defined by the issues and contradictions of the troubled eighties. The fifth and final phase is marked by the opening of the economy and globalization, which led to the selling of the company. It is worth noting here that if the firm still exists as a result of acquisition by another company, from the viewpoint of a business history focusing on business capabilities, it is reasonable to consider this as ending the life cycle.

Exemplary as the company was, the ML case raises age-old questions about protectionism and efficiency. *Did the company become complacent under the auspices of protectionism? Were the workings of global competition different from those at home?*

Birth and the first phase (1950–1956): a particular historical context

In the first decades of the twentieth century, fluctuations in international trade linked to the world wars and the Great Depression brought about alternating periods of ease and difficulty in importation. This resulted in the emergence of industrial companies that initially operated precariously but eventually transformed into effective units of industrial production. In the specific case of auto part manufacturers, the fleet of vehicles in circulation[4] required maintenance and replacement of parts worn out as a result of heavy use and precarious road conditions. National piston production could take place at home in periods of heavy importation restrictions by using sand-casting molds and overhauling machines. However, the resulting product from domestic production was high in cost, poor in quality, and small in scale.

The development of production capacity from this fragile base depended on the evolution of foreign trade. The 1929 crisis and, later, World War II contributed to the emergence of auto parts manufacturers in Brazil. In 1941, there were five domestic manufacturers. This number rose to 30 in 1946 and 250 in 1952. The adoption of import liberalization after World War II threatened this precarious domestic production, which managed to proliferate due to fast depletion of exchange reserves accumulated during the war. A new interruption of normality in foreign trade stemmed from the eruption of the Korean War in the early 1950s. Alternation of periods of import easiness and import restrictions allowed the domestic fleet to grow and also for production capacity to take root through the importing of equipment. However, this development was not without moments of real threat to auto parts businesses. These threats stemmed from the unpredictable nature and changes in economic policy guidelines, as are frequently observed in the early days of ML's history.

Metal Leve originated in a company called Motorit, a piston ring manufacturer. Motorit was established in 1941, with Samuel Klabin, A. Buck and Ludwig Gleich as its partners. With import liberalization after the war, the plant was transformed into an overhauling business as it was unable to compete with imported piston rings. Machinery in good condition from the war effort was imported from the US and Switzerland. The firm's difficulties in obtaining pistons led to the idea of producing them inside the company. One of the primary actors responsible for this development was the German emigrant partner of Motorit, Gleich. Prior to his arrival in Brazil, Gleich was an overhauler in Berlin. He attracted the attention of German piston manufacturer Ernst Mahle through their old clientele ties established previously in Germany. Though the future of auto parts production in Germany was still uncertain in this post-war phase, Brazil had distinct advantages for production in its fleet, bauxite reserves, and water power (Penna, 2014). This led Mahle, who was already considering producing pistons abroad, to choose Brazil as a new industrial location in association with the Motorit partners. However, certain steps were required on the Brazilian end before Mahle would make the journey. Those undertaking these necessary steps and the said requisites are described below.

José Mindlin, a lawyer for Motorit, prepared the certificate of incorporation for the new firm and looked to his friend Luiz Camillo de Oliveira Netto, Managing Director of the Banco de Crédito Real in Minas Gerais, to provide the necessary loan. Oliveira Netto could not make the loan himself but recommended Walther Moreira Salles, then Loan Portfolio Manager at Banco do Brasil, to do so. Salles granted the new company a loan of Cr\$400.000,00. It is worth mentioning that this loan was reflected as a 70 percent debt ratio[5] in the new company's first annual balance sheet. Luiz Camillo networked further to ease the necessary bureaucracy and Mahle's way. Once the proper arrangements were made, Mahle immigrated to Brazil and became a partner in the new company. Other partners included Buck, Samuel Klabin, José Mindlin and Luiz Camillo, Gleich, and, finally, Mahle. Mahle contributed his production capabilities and German machinery and operators, thus contributing to the establishment of a company's high technical reputation from the outset.[6]

The company, which included 50 white and blue collar workers, was established on a 2,800m[2] plot in Rua Independência in the Cambucí neighborhood of São Paulo City. There, the office, foundry and machining operated, in a first production line made up of German machines with a production capacity of 220,000 pistons per year.

The history of ML's founding speaks to the exceptional nature of a high-technology industrial company in a peripheral country. Clear opportunities and skills allowed for the emergence of ML, and its development was made possible by following in the footsteps of service providers-turned-industrial companies. As exploration of the company's history suggests, in Metal Leve's case, circumstances and personal ties were decisive. The difficulties and uncertainties of German auto parts firms in the post-war years along with former clientele ties between Gleich and Mahle helped solve the Brazilian industry's technical problem. In a period of strong fluctuations in the trade balance, personal ties and arguments about the benefits of industrialization allowed for an indispensable loan. Moreover, personal and community ties brought together a group of partners and their families for the whole of the company's history; these partners interacted through a consensus-based management style in which robustness, caution, competence, and mutual trust were consistently present. It is also worth noting that these relations, considered to be an asset through most of the company's life, took their toll in its last years.[7] More details on this will be provided later.

Getting back to the story, Ernst Mahle ended up returning to Germany in the 1950s and selling his share in the company. The relationship with the German manufacturer – and subsequently with his German firm, Mahle GmbH – proceeded in a sequence of three assistance contracts. These were renewed until 1975. It is worth saying in advance here that the relationship between ML and Mahle's firm ended due to the condition imposed by Mahle GmbH for the signing of the fourth contract. This proposed contract would give Mahle GmbH a stake in Metal Leve's capital.[8] Instead of signing this contract, ML chose to end the relationship and to allocate the sums that formerly went on royalties to Mahle GmbH to a technology center. In doing so, ML replaced assistance by an effort to enhance their own development. The center was financed with a loan from FINEP, and Mahle GmbH, demonstrating its intentions to remain involved in the Brazilian market, bought the Brazilian piston manufacturer, CIMA, in 1978. We will also return to this later.

Understanding the market prospects of the then-new company requires consideration of the fact that pistons are parts requiring high manufacturing standards and precision to the scale of thousandths of a millimeter. Due to the complexity involved in its production, only a few firms produced pistons at the time. Therefore, Metal Leve, both with German technological backing and through its own development, had only one minor competitor supplying to automobile manufacturers (OEM),[9] CIMA, for much of its existence. It only had a few other rivals in the market for replacement of the fleet's worn parts (the so-called aftermarket). This means that ML was largely dominant in the market. In the mid-50s, for instance, it made up around 75 percent of installed capacity in piston manufacture. Its dominance only began to be seriously challenged with the arrival of foreign companies at the end of the '60s and, even then, market-share losses came about slowly. It is worth pointing out that ML never lost its position as the largest-ever manufacturer and supplier of its products to automobile assembly plants in Brazil.

The company's success, in part, can be attributed to its distinctly conservative management style. This style became entrenched in the company's experience with an episode from its early years (Campos and Pinto, 2007; Kerstenetzky, 1985). In March, 1951, having produced 100,000 pistons, a study carried out due to the suggestion of the Banco do Brasil revealed that a second production line would allow ML to meet the demand of the piston market. Piston imports would then become unnecessary and could be effectively banned through CEXIM[10] controls based on the principle of the existence of a similar national product. Per the study's recommendations, a second line was ordered. However, in April 1951, the government suspended import controls due to fear that conflict from the Korean War might, once again, interrupt overseas supplies necessary for the domestic production of products. This contributed to Ford's suspension of a Metal Leve order of 150,000 pistons. CEXIM accepted import license applications until it became convinced there was sufficient national piston production. Then (in January 1952), piston import licenses were again refused. The temporary suspension of import controls left Metal Leve in dire conditions until all the imported pistons were sold, and the company had to turn to different banks for help. The episode remained in the company's history as a lesson in caution. It served as an example of the consequences of poor financial management. The lesson operated throughout ML's entire history with growth financed by internally-generated resources and a very low level of debt, as we shall see later.

Aside from this extraordinary episode, the market offered remunerative prices and profitability. These were reflected in a reduction in the high initial debt levels, in continual decline after the difficult times of the import liberation episode, and in the attainment of a level of approximately 15 percent of the company's liabilities in the mid-1950s.

To conclude with an assessment of this initial phase of Metal Leve's lifecycle, the replacement market and the protection mechanisms, together with technical quality, the almost complete lack of competition, and the prices charged allowed the company to reduce its debt level (from 70 percent initially to 15 percent in the mid-50s) and simultaneously grow at very high rates. Internally-generated finance allowed simultaneous debt reduction and a fivefold increase in production capacity. This first phase was the most profitable in the company's history. During the subsequent phases, profitability declined with the development of the market represented by the onset of vehicle manufacturing in Brazil, and the entrance of foreign competitors into the market. Nonetheless, we will see that the company could compete with the threat of competition imposed by foreign companies until the onset of the 1990s; at this time, the situation abruptly changed.

Industrialization and Brazilian automobiles (1956–1968)

The industrializing stance the country had adopted during the 1950s became official with the Juscelino Kubitschek's government's Target Plan ("Plano de Metas"). We can identify the beginning of the company's second phase after the establishment of the automobile industry in Brazil in 1956. At this time, the auto parts market started to expand, supplying to both the Brazilian automobile industry and the auto parts replacement market.

With the conception of the Brazilian automobile industry's policy, non-vertical structure was implemented and recommendations were made to manufacturers to subcontract for parts supply. Economic policy guidelines established progressive nationalization targets and conditions favorable to importing equipment and parts that complemented national production.[11] As a result, parts manufacturers, having emerged in a turbulent, precarious environment, not only had their place guaranteed but were also transformed by the presence of demanding buyers, who brought with them an expanding and more predictable market (the OEM). It is significant that the resultant industrial structure represented a peculiar experience of small, flexible parts manufacturers. Given the smaller dimensions of the market and of auto manufacturing, it was impossible to fully enjoy typical economies of scale of the sector at that time. Varied and flexible production remained a national trait throughout the sector's history. International experience, by contrast, showed a greater degree of vertical integration. In the extreme case of the United States, for example, automobile manufacturers produced their own pistons at that time.

Demand trends for vehicles aligned with the Brazilian macroeconomic evolution favored economic predictability. Furthermore, the new phase of industrialization promoted internal dynamics of investment, income generation, and consumption. Transformations included the creation of financing mechanisms for durable goods. A complete cycle of growth and slowdown can, thus, be seen in the Brazilian economy and in its automobile industry, with expansion in 1956–1962 and recession in 1963–1967. Metal Leve's experience mirrored that of the broader automobile industry. These years comprise, what I call, the second phase of Metal Leve's lifecycle.

In 1957, Metal Leve was able to produce 1,200,000 pistons per year, which represented three quarters of national capacity. Of its competitors, only CIMA also sold to manufacturers, but its capacity was only 140,000 pistons per year. Other manufacturers had an individual capacity of no more than 40,000 units and only supplied distributors or retailers (or produced for themselves, as in the case of overhaul services).[12]

Concerning the beginning of the automobile industry, Metal Leve presented a number of expansion projects to the GEIA.[13] The first, which was approved in August 1956, involved the installation of a fourth production line with a capacity for 500,000 pistons. It not only increased capacity by 42 percent but also allowed interruption in the use of the old production lines for repairs. The equipment was imported from Mahle for a sum of DM 999,337.84. This sum was financed over five years at 6 percent interest per year. The second project involved the creation of specific lines for the production of large pistons that had been produced on existing lines and, consequently, caused a great deal of wear and loss of quality due to the high content of silicon in its alloys. The increase in capacity stemming from the new lines amounted to 120,000 pistons annually for tractors and trucks, 1,200 pistons for ship and rail engines and 25,000 pistons for General Motors, in addition to 500,000 pistons corresponding to one more line of light pistons. The equipment to install these lines was also imported from Mahle, for the sum of DM 2,514,894.00, with the same financing conditions as before. The third project, which was approved in September 1958, included the installation of new induction furnaces to complement those already in use. The project was intended to prepare alloys in the factory and to avoid difficulties obtaining them at home and overseas. The project also included enlargement of production capacity of pins and forging presses. The equipment, once again, was imported from Mahle, under the same conditions, for a sum of DM 1,186,790.00. The three expansion projects approximately tripled the existing stock of machines and installations at the end of 1955 (Kerstenetzky, 1985).

The investments above included installing capacity to produce aviation pistons for Pratt and Whitney engines, which Metal Leve developed from unofficial drawings. In 1965, ML signed a technical assistance contract with United Aircraft Co., which granted ML access to technology and its improvements. Soon after, ML was granted approval for its aviation pistons by the Federal Aviation Agency, becoming the first non-American company to obtain this permission. Having acquired this approval, ML expanded its piston sales beyond the Brazilian Air Force. It began exporting to the US, the replacement market, the Lycoming and Continental Motors factories (later Teledyne Continental Motors), and executive airplane manufacturers. Demands made by the FAA in the approval process raised manufacturing standards not only for aviation pistons but for all production lines.

In the same period, Metal Leve also diversified into the production of bearings, another auto part. As early as 1953, Ford suggested that ML start to make bearings and recommended that ML obtain the necessary technology from Clevite,[14] an American supplier. However, difficulties resulting from the period of recessive economic policies between 1954 and 1956 interfered with the implementation of this until the following year. At this time, the equipment was imported from Clevite, with whom a technology transfer agreement was also signed. Approval to import the equipment was given by SUMOC[15] in 1956, and in 1957 the bearings project was approved by GEIA. The financing, granted by the Eximbank, amounted to US$1,250,000, at 5.5 percent interest per year, to be paid off over seven years.

There was a mistake in one aspect of the diversification: the bearings chosen were of the Babbitt kind, made of lead antimony (or white alloy) while the auto industry was shifting to copper lead bearings (red alloy). 2,657,000 bearings were produced in the first year, more than the one-shift production capacity of 2,400,000. Of these, however, 1,857,000 were for the aftermarket, and in the two following years, there were no sales to the automobile manufacturers, which were ordering copper lead bearings (red alloy). In fact, only 17 percent of the bearings used in the assembly lines in 1958 were Babbitt.[16]

Metal Leve, thus, began to make red bearings through a non-continuous process called PAP, the patent for which was acquired (by ML in association with Clevite) from a German company. However, the casting process was very limited in terms of the production scale. On the other hand, the installation of a continuous production line of copper lead bearings would mean an overwhelming investment of US$1.5 million; at that point, the investment was too much for the company, as was the production scale. The solution was to adopt another recent production process, sintering.[17] Advantages of sintering included greater flexibility in terms of scale and lower initial investments; however, in theory, the sintering process produced less resistant copper-lead bearings (compared with die-cast red bearings). The solution took the form of another project approved by GEIA with financing of US$469,000 from Eximbank. The capacity of the sintered line was 1,440,000 bearings and 2,400,000 bushings per year.

Unlike in the US, the Brazilian sintered product became the basic material for Metal Leve bearings and bushings which with the improvement of the production process in the company, gave rise to patenting and resulted in a high quality product. Only in the eighties would Metal Leve install a continuous production line of red bearings after increasing capacity with two more sintering lines.

Two other manufacturers presented projects to GEIA for bearings production. The first was the São Paulo Retífica, owned by the racing car driver, Chico Landi. The São Paulo Retífica serviced customized engines and, thereby, did not represent a threat to ML. The company Sinterosa, by contrast, could threaten ML with its proposed expansion reaching the capacity of 2,400,000 parts per year between bushings and bearings. The project involved association with the American firm Johnson Bronze, one of three large American manufacturers.[18] This American company came on board as co-owner of half of the increased capital, such that Sinterosa would be able to gain access to foreign technology and to become a significant competitor.

Another aspect of Metal Leve's capacitation was the in-house machinery production. In 1960, machines were already produced for replacement and improvement of the production process. In 1966, a machine factory was set up, initially with imported projects, to produce chamfering, automatic broaching machines, and copying lathes. Although clearly signaling technological progress, this development is not unprecedented in this line of business, because machine tools are produced by an assembly of parts.[19] With time, the company worked out its own projects for manufacturing lathes, saws, and semi-automatic milling cutters. Proof of production quality lies in the fact that Metal Leve exported six beveling machines to Clevite at US market prices. At the end of the '60s, manufacturing had reached 200 new machines in addition to the overhaul or modernization of approximately 80 units.

The OEM piston market expanded until 1962. After 1962, the Brazilian economy entered into a recession. The car industry was adversely affected with the economic slowdown. As ML provided almost all piston and bearing supplies to car manufacturers (except for the sporadic or localized, though notably reduced, sales by competitors),[20] the company's sales accompanied the general movement of the automobile industry. ML piston sales followed the heating up and the slowing down of the cycle, rising to 180,000 pistons monthly at its peak and falling to 60,000 units in moments of the most severe crisis. In reality, the fluctuations could be more severe than they were in automobile production, as was the case when a small industry upturn in 1965[21] hiked orders to 230,000 pistons because automobile manufacturers also decided to stock up again. Sales fell again in 1967.[22] The bearings market, on the other hand, as part of a less explored market, expanded until 1964 and then started to fluctuate.

In the aftermarket, on the other hand, piston sales remained stagnant during this whole second phase, which is characterized by an improvement in highways and product quality (as they increased the interval of engine overhauls) as well as the renewal of the fleet. In the case of the bearings aftermarket, there was continuous growth under import substitution until 1963.[23]

Export efforts to other Latin American countries began in 1962. These markets had potential due to the fact that these countries imported rejects from developed countries. However, problems of foreign currency availability in the region meant that exports only became significant in the next decade. In this phase, the successful shift towards the international market took place in the American aircraft pistons market in the way mentioned above. This shift broadened later to include parts from other means of transport, such that the American market became the company's main export market.

As for the financial area, this phase brought lower profit margins for the company than the previous one because the company sold to automobile manufacturers, which held significant bargaining power. The debt level, which had declined to extremely low levels (around 15 percent at the end of the previous phase), grew with the high investments related to GEIA projects to 49 percent in 1962. Later, however, debt levels again declined to levels fluctuating around 35 percent at this phase. These are not high levels, especially if we take into account the major efforts of expansion, quality improvement, and diversification. Since 1962, investments and the debt level decreased (albeit fluctuations), stabilizing at even lower profit margins than before.

With regards to technology, Metal Leve's relationships with foreign firms effectively provided it with independent access to technology (even if technological achievements can also be attributed to ML's own efforts to develop its technological capabilities). The contrasting experiences of ML and Sinterosa make this clear: Metal Leve's competitor in the bearings market needed to cede half of its control to a foreign company in order to gain access to its technology. We must not be fooled by ML's success in its initial relationships with foreign piston and bearings firms: Other experiences of its relationship with foreign firms to obtain technology for diversification in the next phase were not as successful as ML's first experiences, as we will see below. Relationship with foreign companies aiming at technological capacitation is not a simple matter, as it frequently involves partnership with control among the factors that attract the foreign firm's interest.

Resumption and maturity: diversification, technological autonomy and exports (1968–1980)

The company's third phase, once again, followed the movement of the Brazilian economy. The phase started with the economic upturn in 1968 that followed public investments and a spurt in the construction industry. As in other phases, the automobile industry was one of the principle drivers of national growth in ML's third phase.

The automobile industry was reorganized as a consequence of the entry of Ford, General Motors, and Chrysler in the Brazilian passenger vehicle manufacturing market and by company mergers. The industry started to adopt features of international competition, with product differentiation, which was lacking in the implantation phase. Changes in income concentration, transformation of consumption patterns, financing, and the incorporation of families into the market place characterized this phase of the automobile industry. Incentives to export and to attract external capital inflows and easy access to foreign loans contributed to strengthen the industry's expansion until 1974. After 1974, the expansion lost momentum. The automobile industry, which grew by 26 percent (on average) between 1967 and 1974, began growing by a mere 6 percent from 1974 to 1978. Rising international oil prices and their global consequences, external restriction, the rise in inflation and an end to stimulus as represented by new consumption patterns with income concentration contributed to this period of industry malaise.

In the automobile industry, the exports increased due to stimuli of tax exemption, tax credits, and the drawback of import taxes on inputs; consequently, they were expanded in proportion to overall production – 2.5 percent in 1973, 7 percent in 1974 and 8.7 percent in 1978 (Guimarães and Gadelha, 1980). Other trends in the industry were the growth in the production of small vehicles after 1974 (while the recovery in 1968 featured medium and large vehicles) and the substitution of diesel for gasoline in commercial vehicles.

Reflecting the more general movement of the Brazilian economy and automobile industry, Metal Leve's revenues grew at a rate of 20 percent per year in pistons and 24 percent in bearings between 1968 and 1974 and decelerated to 13 percent per year in pistons and 4 percent per year in bearings by 1978. The company's market share remained high, at around 68 percent for pistons and 74 percent for bearings, in value for the period 1973–78.[24] Market-share data compiled by the company for the years 1974–75, in number of parts, indicate a higher share in the market – around 83 percent for pistons and about 96 percent for bearings.[25] What is significant here is that the company's share confirms, according to any criterion, the endurance of the company's almost monopolistic dominance observed in previous phases.

This phase was marked by the entry of foreign auto parts manufacturers into the Brazilian market. In 1968, Volkswagen attracted KS, the other large German piston manufacturer alongside Mahle, offering it half of its piston acquisitions. In the bearings market, Johnson Bronze was bought by Federal Mogul in the US, and Johnson Bronze started to use its new parent company's brand on its products in Brazil from 1971. The loss ML suffered as a result of this purchase was insignificant in this period. An exercise comparing ML's and ML's competitors' sales data for automobile manufacturers and their automobile production shows ML's continued dominance as a piston supplier to automobile manufacturers. Though ML's competitors sold pistons to VW (to be expected because of their invitation to KS), GM after 1972, and Toyota, ML remained dominant.[26] The data clearly show that ML was the only supplier to Ford, Fiat, FNM/Fiat Diesel, Mercedes Benz and Scania at this time.[27]

ML's competitors were even more inferior in providing bearing supplies to car assembly plants: Johnson Bronze/Federal Mogul, which could have been a major competitor, ended up not giving its subsidiary in Brazil the necessary support to establish it as a presence on a par with its headquarters. In Argentina, by contrast, Johnson Bronze/Federal Mogul played a role similar to the one played by Metal Leve in the Brazilian market. John Bronze/Federal Mogul's limited role in the Brazilian market may be a consequence of ML's reaction to the entry of competitors, making long-term agreements with car manufacturers (both for pistons and bearings), in exchange for favorable conditions. The economic slowdown in 1974 may have reinforced entry barriers, as the minimum scale of light piston production at the time was of 500,000 pistons per year.[28] Later, in 1977, one of the largest bearings manufacturers in the world, Glyco, presented a project to the CDI (Conselho de Desenvolvimento Industrial) and set up a small capacity factory in 1978.

Competitors' penetration into the aftermarket was faster than into the assembly market. KS adopted the strategy of making kits including parts other than pistons and of offering a payment timeframe of 180 days (as opposed to ML's 60-day timeframe) to compete with ML's products. ML responded by putting together their kits with their own and with Cofap's products; however, they did not increase the deadlines for payment. As a result of ML's efforts to safeguard its markets, KS's entry brought about more losses to Cima and to other smaller-scale manufacturers.[29]

To defend its aftermarket share, ML developed different strategies to deal with the range of buyers' sizes and market fragmentation.[30] Regional offices replaced regional representatives. Large-scale clients received frequent problem-solving visits. The company used its size to demand exclusivity from distributors. In the small dealer market segment, dispersal and relative insignificance of individual dealers or repair shops were solved by strategies aiming to establish and maintain contact with customers (i.e., dealers, repair shops, mechanics) and to raise awareness among mechanics on the importance of the quality of spare parts (i.e., the importance of choosing ML's products). Contact and quality awareness were nurtured by sending technical booklets and offering local technical courses and factory visits. The first of these courses was provided in 1964, and over time, the duration was extended from 2 to 12 hours.

Export development, which commenced in the previous period, grew in this decade. It increased from contributing to 0.5 percent revenue in 1968 to 21 percent in 1978 in the case of pistons and from 0.01 to 7.4 percent in the case of bearings; growth was continuous from year to year. As mentioned previously, the main export market was the US; the US absorbed between 60 and 80 percent of exports with variation depending on the year, the product, and its value or quantity.

The American market presented special market opportunities for Metal Leve and other auto parts manufacturers' exports due to the American automobile industry's extraordinary degree of vertical integration in auto parts manufacturing. This is due, in part, to each manufacturer's scale and, in the case of pistons and other engine components, minimal concern about fuel consumption, presiding until the oil crisis and the entry of Japanese automobiles into the country. The export opportunities for ML emerged when the competition from Japanese automobiles forced American manufacturers to concern themselves with more modern engine designs; modernizing their products required a decline in the verticalization of the US industry. After 1976, Mahle and KS started to explore the American piston market, with branches being set up. The European markets, on the other hand, had different structures, with smaller fleets, more auto parts manufacturers, and less verticalization.[31] Additionally, due to contractual commitment, Metal Leve did not pursue markets already served by Mahle, until 1978. After the termination of the technical assistance relationship between ML and Mahle in that year, ML began to openly pursue the European market, developing samples and carrying out product quotations for manufacturers.

At this point, it is worth detailing the end of ML's relationship with Mahle. The relationship between ML and Mahle had transformed over time due to the progression in capabilities developed by ML, which were reflected in the different terms in the three technology transfer contracts signed with the German firm. Foreign markets contributed to the emerging dissonance between the two companies in this period: ML was becoming increasingly present in foreign markets, and Mahle, already well advanced in developing its internationalization process, quickly noticed that ML was becoming a serious competitor.

The first contract, signed with Ernst Mahle himself, remained in force until 1968, giving ML access to Mahle's piston-making processes and patents, its developments, and use of the Mahle brand in Brazil. German technicians were responsible for the technical knowledge of process engineering and training the workforce, until they could be complemented or substituted by Brazilian engineers and technicians trained in the factory. The relationship included a training period of Brazilian staff in the German factory. In this way, ML absorbed the production process technology and stayed abreast of its developments. In exchange, ML gave Mahle preference to participate in future business ventures it would realize in the country and remunerated it with 2 percent of pistons revenue.

In 1968, ML signed a new contract, this time with Mahle GmbH, because the German firm had been restructured such that a foundation and management company replaced owners in running the firm (Lippert et al., 2014). According to this agreement, Metal Leve was obligated to share advancements in perfecting production techniques (albeit through remuneration to be agreed on by the companies) while Mahle pledged not to go into partnership, to supply technical assistance to, or to set up business with other firms in Brazil until two years after the end of the contract unless ML had decided not to renew it. Remuneration went down to 0.8 percent of revenue after indirect taxes.

A center for research and development was set up in 1970 to centralize activities that were not directly linked to production, develop ideas put forward by management, and make studies into rationalization of technical problems and cost reduction. After the first few years in which the center carried out studies into the rationalization of processes and operations, experimental projects were implemented and gained importance from 1973.

Metal Leve's exports started to cause problems between ML and Mahle beginning in 1971. ML's contract with Mahle only mentioned the companies' exports between Brazil and Germany and required that these trade relations should be pursued exclusively with the partner company. Mahle feared a move by ML on its international market and, consequently, began to put pressure on ML to award Mahle a share in its capital, the Brazilian market, and even in the management of its pistons division as compensation for the threat it posed. Furthermore, Mahle complained that the licensing fee was small compared to R&D costs. ML sensed Mahle wanted to come to Brazil.

ML indicated their intention to rescind the contract in 1974, and discussions held to settle the differences between the two companies gave rise to a third contract, this time concerning "technological cooperation." The provisions of this contract required both ML and Mahle to take part in joint R&D projects and to jointly cover the costs. Regarding results leading to industrial property rights, the parties to the contract agreed on the right to free use. The earlier commitments related to exports and non-entry of Mahle into the Brazilian market were maintained.

Renewal discussions for a fourth contract proved fruitless, and the last contract between Mahle and ML expired in 1977. In May of 1978, Mahle bought Cima, thus entering the Brazilian market independently of ML. At the time, they also established a presence in the US through foreign direct investment with the capacity to produce 1,200,000 pistons per year.

ML restructured its R&D activity, creating a technical management team which brought together quality control and R&D. R&D started to have a say in decision-making and mobilization of resources, like the other management areas. The main modification was the setting up of a technology center in a building of its own in 1978; this center was complete with chemical, metallurgical, electronic, and photo elastic laboratories as well as 57 staff members, 19 of whom had engineering doctorates, masters or degrees. The center was financed by FINEP.

As for bearings, ML also had access to advanced technology through technical assistance contracts which had progressive technology absorption. The relationship went on to patent exploration contracts with revenue-based payments (which decreased over time). Here, there existed a peculiarity with the transformation that took place with the licensing company Clevite (which, once bought by Gould Inc., a company whose main product was batteries, started to be overtaken by European manufacturers). In the eighties, Gould sold Clevite, freeing it to once again pursue the technological edge in bearings.

Meanwhile, other international bearings manufacturers grew interested in partnerships with ML; perceiving that partnering with other manufacturers would incentivize Gold to establish a presence in Brazil, ML was wary of engaging in these relationships. High profit margins and precarious entry barriers encouraged the company to take added caution. Additionally, the relationship with Gould did not have high costs; it reinforced the relationship with Ford and, above all, ML judged itself capable of following technological developments on its own. In fact, ML accumulated patents in bearings manufacturing and installed the whole range of lines it needed for bearings. In this way, ML allowed itself to become less concerned about the cutting edge technologies of foreign sources of bearings. In the end, however, the main technological efforts were placed on piston research as a result of both the problems and the end of the relationship with Mahle. Consequently, ML ended up lagging behind in bearings technology.

In this phase, ML's move towards diversification began. Around 1972, the company was in a solid financial situation and prospects for the Brazilian economy were good. ML had successfully gone public and had easy access to financial sources. However, there was some internal disagreement on how to best structure ML's future. There were advocates in the company both in favor of diversification (to reduce the risks associated with a sector prone to the entry of foreign companies) and in favor of investment concentration in traditional areas (i.e. no need to seek new knowledge). There were even those who advocated speculation with raw material stocks. The idea of concentrating resources in what "we know how to do" seemed to win the day and prevailed: if we exclude a juice manufacturing business in the North-East of Brazil, Maraú, which benefited from tax incentives and had good export prospects, the diversifications were still concerned, in one way or another, with the firms' traditional areas of knowledge. This bears out Penrose's (1959) theoretical proposition of diversification occurring on the same technical base or in the same market area. Moreover, ML sought to enter into partnership with foreign companies to gain access to technology in the diversification process.

Ex-cell-O Metal Leve Máquinas was set up as a spin-off of ML's machinery manufacturing activities. The chosen foreign partner, Ex-cell-O co., was a cutting-edge American machine tool manufacturer, with 36 factories around the world. ML had the controlling stake in the subsidiary. However, the American firm was inexperienced with technological transfer and, more importantly, showed little interest in the joint venture. As a result, projects took a long time to develop, when, ideally, pre-existing projects would have been adapted to clients' needs; and, without a costing system, sales prices were frequently inadequate. The factory operated with a high idle capacity and low competitiveness and was unable to cover its costs. ML ended up accepting Thyssen Hueller's proposal to take over the subsidiary, with Metal Leve keeping a 30 percent stake. This enabled ML to stay in the sector with technological support, albeit losing its majority stake.

Metal Leve Gould, on the other hand, was founded in 1974 to manufacture sinterized products (that is, products made out of iron and steel powder, replacing cast and forged components) and to supply clients not only from the automotive sector but also from the office machinery, electronics, and refrigerator sectors. This venture can be understood in terms of the good relationship with Gould inc. discussed above.

The turn of the eighties signified the end of this phase in the firm's life. It is marked by the worsening Brazilian economy caused by balance of payments problems related to oil and capital goods imports. These problems manifested after the first oil crisis in 1973; at that time, the government responded by implementing policies of deepening import substitutions between 1974 and 1978 in order to keep the economy growing. Followed by a second oil crisis in 1979 and rising international interest rates, these problems ran rampant and resulted in the so-called "lost decade" of the eighties. During this "lost decade," stagflation in 1981–83 was succeeded by fluctuations in economic activity and a gradual worsening of inflation for the remainder of the decade. The fluctuating pace of production was the result of the increasingly ephemeral results brought about by bold stabilization plans and Brazilian exports favored by the upturn in economic activity of developed countries.[32]

In this context of growing difficulties faced by the Brazilian economy, we can identify Metal Leve's fourth phase. In spite of the previously explained adverse economic conditions, the firm kept on growing, such that it was not immediately affected by the national economic problems.

Golden years? (1980–1989)

ML's fourth phase was even qualified as the "golden years" (Faldini, 2005). The period, however, contains contradictory developments, not only in terms of the firm but also in the contrast between its performance, the difficulties of the Brazilian economy mentioned above, and its reaction to challenges brought about by the great transformations under way in the world economy and automotive industry. We can say in advance that ML achieved great things from the viewpoint of a peripheral country company but that these achievements were not enough to prepare it for the global competition that would mark the following phase.

ML adequately understood the reorganization trends of the world automotive industry and sought to adapt to the transformations. In the new automobile business environment it was no longer enough to master the production process and to produce a good product according to specifications furnished by the automobile producers.[33] In the past, orders for parts came with their specifications, reflecting the fact that automobile projects were completely developed by automobile manufacturers. Changes in the world automotive industry pointed to the need for parts manufacturers' involvement along with the automobile manufacturers in the development of automobile projects. Incorporating parts manufacturers into decision-making roles in automobile projects brought about new technological challenges. Joint development also made parts manufacturers the chosen supplier for the model on a global scale, raising their business challenges insofar as the production scale was concerned. Thus, in addition to diversification and exports begun in the previous phase, which were ongoing in ML's "golden decade," efforts to internationalize were undertaken at the end of the decade and included direct investments overseas.

As mentioned, the Brazilian economy of the eighties experienced a long period of stagnation. The fact that vehicle production did not surpass 1980 levels until 1993 speaks to the particularly severe stagnation within the Brazilian automotive industry. To make matters worse, the lag in Brazil's automotive industry in relation to foreign manufacturing grew. This is, in part, because American and European parent companies, pressured by Japanese competition, were busy trying to adapt to the new competition while their Brazilian subsidiaries remained out of the dispute.

For the Brazilian auto parts sector, exports became the outlet for the use and expansion of its production capacity so much so that it made up for the prevailing

stagnation in the decade. A number of companies in the sector made their presence
felt on the international market, particularly after 1982. Metal Leve was prominent
among these companies newly-emerging on the international market, gaining a lot
of ground in the American market, including quality recognition, as evidenced by
the Caterpillar certificate of guaranteed quality supplier.[34] ML's exports to the
United States represented half of overseas sales. In the European market, their
presence was also felt but to a lesser degree for the reasons outlined above.

Metal Leve exports grew year after year, with few exceptions,[35] and direct
overseas investment began at the end of the decade as a result of a specific order
from an American client who requested for a plant to be installed in the US, as we
will see below. However, hikes in demand caught the company by surprise, and
consequently, ML was unable to deliver on all the national and international
orders. The period from 1985 to 1987 showed, one after the other, an increase in
demand owing to an upturn in the American economy and the Cruzado Plan,[36]
leading the firm to operate in full capacity for three years. In the dramatic year of
1986, installed capacity proved insufficient to meet all the demands such that the
firm was obliged to reduce its exports. This experience was not limited to Metal
Leve; it is indicative of the experience of the whole auto parts sector.[37]

The conjunction of transformations in world industry with the period of
insufficient manufacturing capacity is especially evident in an episode revealed in
the minutes of an executive management meeting in 1986. This meeting was held
to discuss the appropriateness of responding to a call from General Motors
regarding the joint development of the Saturn model (which appears as a pilot of
a new form of structuring and adaptation of GM to the trends under way). The
question under discussion concerned their capability of, should they beat the
competition, becoming an exclusive production supplier of the model given the
commitments already undertaken. One of the executive managers was against
responding to the call, because of ML's high level of capacity utilization. The
discussion develops around the importance of the opportunity and another
executive manager even suggests responding to the call but making it clear that
the company cannot be the only supplier. The proposal is not considered acceptable
because the call is explicit on this point. The discussion moves on to the idea that
staying in this line of business means answering the calls. The incapacity that
emerges in the discussion does not relate to technical competence, but to
production capacity, which is one of the dimensions of the firm's reduced scale
faced with the industry's new challenges.

As a consequence of the capacity shortage, by the middle of the decade Metal
Leve assumed the need to accelerate the growth of production capacity again.
However, in the years following the hike, market stagnation prevailed again in
Brazil, and we find in the press signs of negative expectations concerning
investments and dismay among auto parts manufacturers. Accordingly, we find
reference made to investment projects consisting of equipment rationalization and
modernization in a number of years of Metal Leve's Annual Executive management
reports. In the annual report of 1987, concerning 1986, ML still complained of
instability, lamented late delivery of ordered equipment, and announced that

investments were reduced and that the company was ready to effect additional revisions to its plans. In the context of the prevailing stagnation of most of the decade, rationalization and modernization investments make sense, but the Saturn episode points to vulnerability in an important question of competition in sectors of activity typical of the second industrial revolution – the strategic availability of idle capacity through investment ahead of demand, so as to compete for market shares deftly. In this way, if in the times of the Cruzado Plan, the hike in demand caused by the plan was tackled by resorting to a third production shift, with the advantage of saving on overtime pay, ML was not able to meet all the export demands in 1986. Only in the beginning of 1989, we again find resolute statements of capacity growth in the annual management report and in press interviews with José Mindlin. Mindlin incites other entrepreneurs to invest regardless of the political situation – it was a presidential election year, and Lula[38] was one of the candidates. Mindlin defends the position that there are no alternatives to investing in the country. At least for Metal Leve, the thrust of growth came to the fore again. In agreement with this attitude, the Annual Report of 1989 also mentions ML's acquisitions of companies, which is where we pick up again below.

ML's diversifications at this phase evolved in two ways. Attempts at diversification that were close to the company's main line of business and capabilities were enhanced. Those that were complementary to its main line of business and capabilities, however, did not develop vigorously, and ML ended up abandoning these non-central domains in this phase or in the next. Occasionally, partnerships were dissolved, with ML taking over when capabilities and lines of business were similar and withdrawing from the ventures when they were complementary (non-central).

Metal Leve Controles Eletrônicos was set up in 1984 in an attempt to venture into the area of microelectronics and IT.[39] As part of the same move, ML took up a majority stake in a partnership with the American firm Allen-Bradley. Together, they created Metal Leve Allen-Bradley Sistemas Industriais Ltda and Lógicos Sistemas de Controle Industrial, the former of which acted in the area of electromechanical industrial control products and the latter of which commercially represented these products and those of Metal Leve Controles Eletrônicos. The company divested itself of its three subsidiaries in the next phase in 1992, alleging that the company Rockwell (which had taken over Allen-Bradley) did not want partnerships anymore but only wholly owned subsidiaries. Consequently, ML had to choose between ending the business and branching out alone.

The machinery factory in partnership with Thyssen Hueller (created in ML's previous phase) was sold to the partner, allowing ML to withdraw from the field of special machinery manufacturing and focus on other investment priorities detailed in the management report of 1989.

Other investments in the form of acquiring companies or establishing partnerships took place within the ambit of the auto parts sector. The Metalúrgica Mogi-Guaçu, which resulted from a new partnership with Mahle in 1981, was among those directly linked to the company's key, central area of focus. ML contributed with machining technologies and Mahle with casting.[40] This venture represented diversification in the direction of cast-iron components such as ring carriers, drive camshafts, and cylinders. The partnership between ML and Mahle was lasting and continued until ML was denationalized.

In another development linked to its original core business, in 1989, ML bought out Imperial Clevite's part in its subsidiary of sinterized products set up during the previous phase under the name, Metal Leve Gould. The subsidiary became known as Metal Leve Produtos Sinterizados Ltda. Also in the same year, ML bought the company, Bimetal, a small, American-controlled firm located in Rio de Janeiro and responsible for making bearings and bushings.[41] Even though the plant was not a significant acquisition in terms of state-of-the-art technology, the acquisition marginally strengthened ML's presence in bearings and bushings manufacturing.

These examples of diversification yielded a growth strategy that eliminated, over time, initiatives not strictly connected to the auto parts sector. Although machinery and electronics were strategically developed and linked to the company's activity, they contributed to a change in focus and an outflow of resources and energy such that they were later discontinued.

Particularly significant for the company's history was the beginning of ML's foreign direct investment activity, not only as it represented a watershed in the effort to internationalize but also for the technological content involved in these investments. The latter definitively demonstrated ML's capability of following and keeping up with trends of transformation in the world automotive industry. The foreign direct investment in Orangeburg, North Carolina stemmed from the development of an articulated piston for high-capacity diesel engines developed in the company's technology center in Brazil. ML's product had a competitive edge over those developed by Mahle and KS, with the advantages of having a longer working life, of being smaller, lighter and less polluting. Because of these product characteristics, ML was able to overcome these competitors in the occasion of a call to supply Caterpillar in the US. Other vehicle manufacturers also later adopted this ML piston, including Volvo and Cummings. ML's foreign direct investment was required to fulfill Caterpillar's demand for just-in-time supply. Orangeburg's factory installation began at the end of 1988, with a US$10 million investment project and projected capacity of 230,000 pistons per year. In addition to the pistons factory, ML set up an American extension of the Brazilian technology center in Ann Arbor. This close proximity to American manufacturers enabled ML to discuss their needs and, to pass them on to the production chain.

In Europe, ML's strategy involved setting up commercial subsidiary companies to stimulate ML's exports. Direct investment on the continent was considered at the end of the decade with the creation of the European Union in mind. Portugal was considered a possible location, but the discovery that the EU would not set up trade barriers to the continent meant the move did not proceed beyond the idea.

In this way, ML's "golden years" can be characterized by international consolidation and acceptance of the company's products. In the Brazilian market, ML was able to protect itself against the entry of foreign firms. ML proceeded with relatively high profits initially, with more modest results, however, in later years of the decade.

The main force counteracting Metal Leve's development in this phase, referred to in the beginning of this section, was promoting production capacity growth. ML experienced notable difficulties in this area.[42] The subsidiary Thyssen Hueller was meant to be strategic for the expansion of the parent company's production capacity, but it was unable to meet Metal Leve's needs – there were problems of cost and delivery time in the middle of the decade, marked as it was by a shortage of idle capacity. In any case, ML's diversification which began with Excell-O and continued with Thyssen Hueller never became an effective source of machine supply for Metal Leve. Other Brazilian capital goods firms performed no better as suppliers in the opinion of Metal Leve.[43] Importing the required equipment also failed to solve supply challenges given that imports were adversely affected by the difficulties of the Brazilian economy with external credit due to debt negotiations. Consequently, ML, again, resorted to internal reform and manufacture of machines as a partial solution that, as we saw before, was a characteristic of the sector. However, Metal Leve lagged in this respect when compared with international competitors.

The investment needs of the decade were also thwarted by difficulties in internally generating necessary funds. Metal Leve became aware of a circular problem involving revenue and production capacity: revenue should grow in order to finance capacity growth, and capacity should grow in order to produce more revenue. This problem had to do with the problem of scale that revealed itself to ML in this phase: as competition progressively acquired international dimensions, firm size became critical for competitiveness. The problem of scale was felt in both the production cost of samples for new orders from automobile manufacturers and in the expenses related to R&D activities, because revenues from current activities back both activities. To exemplify, Mahle and Metal Leve were, at the time, developing a similar number of samples, but these represented a much heavier weight for ML than for Mahle because of the much bigger revenues of the German firm. It is worth adding that Metal Leve's subsidiaries could have been part of the solution for the issue of size, revenues, and internal generation of financial resources, but their meager returns implied that they were not able to financially participate in the growth process.

The company's history was transformed quickly from the turn of the decade. The change came primarily from abroad with globalization (in spite of the stagnation beleaguering the Brazilian economy), with trade opening accentuating the long-term weakening of traditional frameworks (which, at the onset of Brazilian automobile manufacturing, reserved the auto parts assembly market purely for Brazilian manufacturers). The company and the sector were swept up in a whirlwind of national changes with very little formulation of development planning. ML and other such companies depended on capabilities acquired until then to navigate unfamiliar waters.

Decline and denationalization (1990–1996)

The fifth and final phase of ML's history starts with the trade opening of 1989–1990 that brought Brazil into line with the globalization process and made ML face foreign competition. However, before the depth of globalization's effects had become clear, the beginning of the phase brought about difficulties of another order for ML and other Brazilian auto parts manufacturers. Following Brazil's economic and automotive problems of the previous decade, the United States recession (caused by the recessive impact of the Gulf War (Zimmerman, 1998)) adversely affected the US automobile and truck market – ML's main export market.[44] In 1990, ML made profits in spite of the hardship imposed by the struggling US markets as it was helped by exports to other markets (such as the European market). In fact, ML managed to raise exports to US$54 million in the same year. Nevertheless, in 1991, ML's accounts experienced losses for the first time since the founding of the company. From 1991 until 1996, ML's performance in terms of profits was negative practically every year, despite the upturn in American and Brazilian automobile manufacturing after 1992 and the increase in the company's sales. ML's only profitable year was 1994 but, even in this year, profits were modest. These results and an assessment of the small probability of reversing the dismal situation coerced the owners of ML to sell their shares in 1996.

Globalization affected auto parts manufacturers particularly severely. Global competition started to incorporate new dimensions in addition to product quality and reliability, by involving systemic questions relating to the world organization of the sector and to the way automobile manufacturers restructured themselves to compete in markets that came to be part of a global logic.[45] Furthermore, with the opening of the Brazilian economy in the 1990s, the auto parts manufacturers' situation was transformed suddenly. Under a set of new governmental incentives to modernize the Brazilian automobile industry and improve its economic performance, foreign automobile manufacturers sought to modernize Brazilian subsidiaries to better correspond with the new dynamics of competition. The decline in protection stemming from the reduction of tariff barriers led to an increase in imports. However facing a decline in tariffs on their products, automobile manufacturers benefited from the reduction in import tariffs on their inputs – auto parts – and from the opportunity to import parts in proportion to their exports. Auto part producers faced a much bigger decline, compared to automobiles, on the tariffs that once protected their products; there were no economic policies designed for the restructuring of the national auto parts manufacturing companies, and there was little time for them to transform to perform well in the new environment.[46] Added to this, later, in 1994, there was the exchange rate valuation caused by the Real Plan. The makeup of the sector experienced a radical change with a reduction in the number of auto parts manufacturing firms[47] due to company closures, mergers and acquisitions, and downsizing of levels of hierarchy in companies. This harsh modification of the automobile business in Brazil was bound to negatively impact Metal Leve's overall performance.

In this phase, ML continued making investments and pursuing the strategy of internationalization with the focus on the North-American market. In 1991, in a joint venture with the second biggest piston manufacturer in the world, KS, ML bought the bearings factory Bohn Bearing in Greensburg, Indiana. It further increased its presence in the American market in 1992 by opening its second American diesel piston factory in Sumter, South Carolina (which held a production capacity for 230,000 pistons per year) and by raising its production capacity in Orangeburg to 600,000 pistons per year. It also increased its export efforts to other markets, gaining new clients, such as Renault and Mitsubishi, in their respective countries of origin. Exports continued with some fluctuation; in general, these stabilized around the US$ 54 million attained in 1988 but rose to US$ 68 million in 1994.

In the two previous phases, we saw how the entry of foreign competitors took place in the Brazilian market but also how the consequences of these entrances was limited to specific markets. In the case of bearings, foreign manufacturing did not prosper and the actual entry of competitors only came to pass in the nineties. In the case of pistons, Mahle and KS occupied markets slowly and gradually formed real competition to ML. Mahle, in particular, focused on especially profitable markets of the replacement segment, like that of a diesel pistons model for Mercedes-Benz vehicles, which had been a hit for ML sales and profitability. With the installation of a modern factory in Brazil, Mahle posed serious competition to the Brazilian firm.

Though losses to competitors were small in the 1980s, in the face of liberalization and globalization, ML's business destabilized. The national bearings markets, which showed the largest profit margins, began to be served by imports at lower international prices. This drastically affected ML's profitability. After two years of losses, ML realized there were structural problems in its operation. During the initial moments of difficulty, some company members defended the position that it was solid in terms of production and claimed that the troubled environment was to blame for the opposite results. Such a position, though mistaken, was comprehensible as it had been conceived over many years of high inflation permeated by stabilization plans that included price freezing and subsequent hikes. The effect on the quality of financial statements and on entrepreneurial calculations was to disturb the whole Brazilian economy – and certainly to keep foreign capital at a distance.[48] In the specific case of ML, the difficulties were aggravated by the fact that the company did not produce any separate verification of results of operations for business units, so that bearings margins were mixed with the lower piston margins. On this note, ML did not know the operational cost for each of its products; additionally, ML's continued role and culture of meeting the whole range of national needs for products also contributed to less favorable results. Consequently, some of the products contributed to the company losses without the possibility of using objective criteria to discontinue them. The possibility of phasing products out was not considered.

In 1993, however, even before the Real Plan stabilized the price system and made it easier to check product profitability, two years of negative results signaled ML's business problems to the company's board; consequently, ML pursued a restructuring process.

In parallel with the restructuring process, ML began to negotiate a partnership with Mahle in pistons, as it was clear to ML that one of the problems confronting the Brazilian firm was related to its lower production scale compared to that of competitors. This problem had different facets. Firstly, ML's small size (in relation to its two biggest foreign competitors, Mahle and KS) disadvantaged the company in the way of costs. This disadvantage did not manifest in the day-to-day production operation but rather in the smaller dilution of the costs of R&D and in producing samples for new orders through revenue. Thus, although Metal Leve had the competitive capability to develop new products, as demonstrated by the episode of the articulated pistons for Caterpillar in the eighties, development costs weighed more heavily on its lower revenue. Secondly, internationalization and following trends in the world automotive industry demanded much greater investment than the company could finance. Not only was it necessary for ML to deepen its presence in markets in which it previously had experience but ML was also required to enter into Asian and Australian markets which it had previously untapped. Negotiations with Mahle advanced the farthest, though the two companies did not reach an agreement. In addition to Mahle, ML also approached other companies such as KS and Dana. In interviews to newspapers given in 1996 (during the sale of ML), José Mindlin explained that the negotiations between ML and foreign companies did not bear fruit because the controlling group did not want to become a minority, and the foreign companies were not willing to consider an alternative arrangement. On this occasion, Mindlin also explained that another option would have been for ML to make an investment that would literally multiply the company's production capacity. However, this solution encountered the well-known (at least to ML's senior management) problem of circularity between increasing revenue and financing investment, making these objectives mutually dependent. Added to this problem of circularity was the fact that difficulties of financing such an effort to raise production capacity were increased during the 1990s because of the vanished profits of the company.

In the context of the restructuring of ML in 1993, the consultancy firm Consemp was hired to evaluate the then implemented correction measures.[49] Consemp's report made clear the enormity of the required restructuring tasks and gave a glimpse of the uncertainties inherent in putting the company back on a competitive footing. Among the recommendations, the needs for relocation, operational reengineering, and change of processes and automation were most prominent. Among the short-term modifications introduced by ML was the reorganization of business units so that production costs by product family were known, involving transformations in IT, with a consequent phasing-out of products.

The restructuring helped ML to return to modest profits in 1994, and other measures were developed with the hope of effectuating longer-term impacts. However, Mahle lowered its prices by 30 percent between 1993 and 1996, and ML was forced to follow suit. It is worth noting that Metal Leve, until its denationalization, remained the largest national piston manufacturer, with a large share of the market and growing sales, remaining from 1994 to 1996 with around 65 percent of the OEM piston market (against 23 percent of the market produced by KS and 11.9 percent of the market produced by Mahle) and 42.1 percent of the aftermarket (against 26.3 percent of Mahle, 16.1 percent, KS, 11.8 percent of a company called Suloy and only 3 percent imports).

In this way, after signs of recovery in 1994 (in which a small profit was realized), losses reappeared in the following two years. What was gained in cost reduction was quickly lost with the continuation of the same detrimental trends. In 1996, the controlling group sold its shares to a group consisting of Mahle, COFAP and Bradesco.

Thus, trade opening (in the context of difficulties for automobile manufacturers and their parent companies and, in particular, of obsolescence in Brazil) brought about a frantic search throughout the sector for modernization with cost cutting. The rush to modernize did not allow ML sufficient time to restructure its business properly. Occasionally, the attempted restructuring proved fruitful, but other efforts remained wanting and further transformations to the production scale were required.

An assessment of Metal Leve's life cycle

Metal Leve's case provides an example of how entrepreneurs accumulate solutions and capabilities in different areas during the company's lifetime and, eventually, arrive at a point where changes in the environment are not accompanied by new solutions, resulting in the cycle closing.[50] This last section gathers elements from areas of capabilities in the ML's history in order to piece together an explanation for the decline.

It is worth starting with management, explaining who the entrepreneur was and who we are referring to when we say anything about decisions made 'by Metal Leve'. The partners who made up Metal Leve established a practice of joint management, with the most important decisions made by the group of managing partners. A collective spirit of agreement accompanied the practice of joint management and instilled unity and mutual confidence in the company's partners. Metal Leve was transformed into a publicly traded company in 1971. Resistance from some of the partners to transforming the legal status of the company and professionalizing company management seems to have been mitigated by the power invested in the board of directors to which the partners were transferred. At the end of the company's history, this board was identified as taking part in all the decisions. Despite its evolution into a publicly held company, ML sought to maintain its status as a family firm with members of the founding families responsible for its operation. On the positive side, this maintained involvement of the founding families meant that the mutual unity and trust as well as the general business model (with lasting values in staff policy and a vision that was not limited to short-term financial results) were preserved. On the negative side, it meant maintaining deep-seated rules of financial management and little flexibility to adjust to changes in the environment.

Moving on from the observation about entrepreneurs, the problem of scale highlighted before will be combined with the firm's capabilities, areas of which, if managed differently, could perhaps have resulted in a different company trajectory than the one deteriorating in ML's final years.

As told in the previous pages, ML's history shows that technology matters received constant and effective attention and management, having been the star and basis for the business success story. In operations, a lag in the production processes in comparison with the competition proved important in the final phase. This lag in production added to the administrative deficiency in cost tracking. Management of the financial area, which was once considered by the company as one of the bastions of its solidity,[51] was compromised at the end of ML's lifecycle. At the end of its lifecycle, ML had to confront the impossible task of financing an investment of US$100 million (which would have provided a solution to the problem of competitiveness by means of the increase in scale). In fact, this financial obstacle reproduces on a larger scale the awareness of investment needs that were greater than the financing capacity, a reality experienced by ML since the mid-1980s.

The pieces presented above – management, technological know-how, operational problems linked to outdated machinery, the problem of scale, and financial insufficiency – can be put together to explain the phase of decline in the firm's lifecycle and how the history of an iconic company of Brazilian industrialization ended.

ML's decision to maintain a notoriously low debt ratio throughout its history can be understood as a self-imposed limit to growth. Such austerity originated in the remote episode of piston imports at the time of the Korean War, which required ML to "go from bank from bank" and evolved into a permanent company attitude of caution and financial self-restraint in relation to government plans and debt ratio. The piston import episode was told and retold to justify ML's attitudes toward austerity. As a result, ML made little use of debt as a way of financing growth.

Self-sufficiency in investment was, for the most part of ML's life, provided by high profit margins obtained through protection. This allowed the company to grow in such a way as to dominate the Brazilian market.[52] However, these margins, which initially fueled exponential growth, decreased over the course of the company's history due to the succession of phases with change in the business environment. At the time of ML's inception, there were premium quality producers' margins at play in the aftermarket, with a 75 percent market share of national manufacturing capacity and protection against imports. Then, at the beginning of the Brazilian automobile industry, average margins fell, with a part of the sales destined to the OEM market. Next, exports grew, and international prices were lower than national ones. Finally, the market was opened to international competition, and all prices were international.

In terms of technology, partnerships made with Mahle and Clevite were fundamental for Metal Leve to get a head start and contributed to ML's ability not only to master the production process but also to develop new products. Having benefited from these good relationships, ML learned more and more to advance by its own means.

ML's other relationships with foreign firms also aimed at obtaining technology and took the form of partnerships. They were strategic to company growth but were not successful like the first two. The attempt to transform capabilities developed internally in equipment manufacture into a machinery company with foreign partnership did not end well. ML had to opt to obtain equipment from other sources. The company's history, again, registered internal equipment manufacture, and later ML sold its participation in the subsidiary. The incursion into the IT sphere in partnership with Allen-Bradley can also be explained as a strategic investment in a source of technologically advanced equipment with numerical control and automation. With the change in the IT public policy that terminated the market reserve for Brazilian firms, the foreign partner lost interest in the partnership, and the relationship ended. Because of the failure of these diversifications, these moves might appear to lack focus, but they can be explained by the need to improve access to equipment in a country in which imports, their financing – which involves international payments and all the resulting issues – and national supply do not offer the same conditions that are presented to international competitors. Unsuccessful as they were, these efforts resulted in an outflow of resources.

Failure in attempts to solve the problem of machinery provision gains special meaning when foreign competitors set up in Brazil with more modern automatized factories. Metal Leve was also able to set up modern, competitive factories in the US with equipment acquired there. In Brazil, ML adapted its production lines with numerical control, but this is not the same as installing lines that are wholly conceived with automation. It is important to note that operational deficiencies and the strategies to obtain equipment are linked to the Brazilian business environment, with its deficiencies and opportunities, and the less than optimal results cannot be entirely attributed to the actions of Metal Leve.

The nuances discussed here allow us to better qualify the importance of protection for the company's survival. It allows us to avoid simplistic and extreme explanations including the attribution of the elimination of the company to globalization and sudden trade opening or, at the other ideological extreme, to the auspices of protection that the company lived under. It ought to be noted that, although protection was shown to be important, achievements in terms of exports and product development indicate that ML was technologically qualified in auto parts manufacturing, and even in the final years of its life, the company demonstrated its capacity in many ways including receiving orders for new projects, winning new clients, and obtaining certifications. ML's ability to beat out international competition to supply sintered connecting rods for a new Volkswagen engine just three months before the company's control and ownership were transferred speaks to its exceptional capacity.

Next, there was the problem of scale, to which we can link the financial area, which was previously described as capable of promoting high levels of growth with a low debt ratio, fed by high but decreasing margins. In the fourth phase of ML's history, when the Brazilian market stagnated in the 1980s, production continued to grow through the exploration of foreign markets. However, in the first half of this decade there was a lapse in expansion efforts as the goals of financial conservatives were realized and with a relaxation in the expansion policy: Piston production capacity rose only marginally and the distribution of dividends was markedly greater than in other periods of its history, exceeding half the profits in three years and, in another year, almost reaching the same level.[53] The lapse resulted in difficulties a little later when installed capacity had to be completely used in the period between 1985 and 1987 and the company could not make the most of all of its business opportunities.

The episode above can even be justified by the recessive state of the national and international economies of the early eighties. Nevertheless, we can speculate that a more aggressive expansion strategy (including going from nationally protected markets to international competition through foreign direct investment earlier than Metal Leve did at the end of the eighties) would have been advantageous. This could have made the company grow faster, so that it would have become more internationalized by the 1990s, with greater revenue and capacity to finance more expansion. It could even have had repercussions from international experience on its national operative practices. Perhaps this strategy could even have benefited from the resources that were alternatively destined for diversifications that I qualified before as complimentary. This line of reasoning is reinforced by Mahle's experience, which bought companies in many countries from the 1960s on, taking over international markets and becoming an engine of growth.[54]

These observations remain speculative: We do not know if companies bought or set up by ML abroad would have been successful in their battle for markets, but we do have the success of Metal Leve's American plants, suggesting that its international expansion was in the right direction. Had it been earlier and deepened, we can risk saying that it would have been a better strategy. If it had been successful, it would have gone towards tackling the problem of circularity between revenue and investment which was discussed by the board in a meeting in 1986 and which became an ever-present problem in the nineties.

Even so, we cannot know if an "earlier internationalization" strategy would have been enough or how much it would have contributed to the improvement of Metal Leve's competitive edge in the globalized nineties. Counterfactual reasoning puts us in a slightly more comfortable position than the position in which businesspeople are placed; however, this does not change the fact that, remembering Keynes, all business activity is speculative.

Notes

1 Cofap and Varga are further comparable cases.
2 This chapter draws on material from my master's thesis on the History of Metal Leve (Kerstenetzky, 1985). The thesis covered the company's history up to 1978. I am indebted to Jacob Frenkel, who advised my master thesis work, and grateful for Metal Leve's support which enabled me to conduct many interviews with company's members provided me with free access to data and archives. For the more recent phases of the business history case study (from 1978 to 1996), I thank Sergio Mindlin, who gave me access to José Mindlin's personal archive and kindly accepted to be interviewed twice. I am also grateful for the comments and suggestions provided by Werner Baer, Eduardo

Pontual, Celia Lessa Kerstenetzky, Jacob Frenkel and the other authors of this publication.
3 The acquisition initially involved other buyers, such as Cofap, but the latter was eventually sold to Mahle. These details are not included in this account.
4 The vehicles were produced abroad and were often assembled in Brazil, as of 1919.
5 Measured by the debt divided by the total liability of the company's balance sheet.
6 Buck was an Austrian Jew-turned-Brazilian citizen and partner in Motorit. Endowed with commercial and financial experience, he played an important role in running the company, particularly in financial matters. Shortly later, Abrahão Jacob Lafer, a relative of the Klabin family, and Aldo Franco, a former Banco do Brasil senior official, became partners.
7 Vassalo (1996).
8 According to an interview given to *Indústria Brasileira* (Campos and Pinto, 2007), José Mindlin replied that the stake was not impossible but that it could not be imposed.
9 Original equipment manufacturer.
10 A Banco do Brasil division that administered import controls.
11 There is no space here to detail the measures, but the literature on Brazilian industrialization is abundant and well-known. See, for example, Baer (2014).
12 See CIMA's investment project approved by GEIA (resolution no. 40). In this project we learn that CIMA would enlarge its capacity by 150 percent. However, CIMA did not manage to get the financing and, in 1960, applied with another project seven times smaller in value.
13 The Executive Group for the Automotive Industry was a government agency set up by the government to advance the sector's implantation.
14 A subsidiary of the American manufacturer Cleveland Graphite Bronze co.
15 Superintendência da Moeda e do Crédito was the body in charge of exchange rate management.
16 See Sinterosa's (a competitor) project, submitted to GEIA and approved in 1959.
17 A process in which copper-lead deposited in a fine powder forms a solid mass with steel strips by using electric ovens filled with exothermic gas.
18 The other two manufacturers were Clevite itself and Federal-Mogul.
19 i.e., a machining line can produce parts for machine-tools like those on the production line. The same technical base is involved.
20 From board meeting minutes and interviews carried out in the 1980s.
21 The upturn followed a reduction in excise tax.
22 This episode is viewed, in twentieth-century literature about manufacturer-supplier relationships, as manufacturers using their bargaining power to shift the burden of fluctuations in demand to auto parts suppliers in the form of storage, opportunity and idle capacity costs, which is done by means of the relationship with manufacturers being based on the proportion of total purchases and not on fixed quantities (Grote, 1971).
23 Which Metal Leve had already done so for pistons at an earlier stage.
24 Estimates based on data from the economic census of 1975, annual industrial surveys, and sales data supplied by Metal Leve (Kerstenetzky, 1985).
25 The company's estimates used data from its main competitors through an exchange of information.
26 Toyota, which at that time was making a small number of commercial vehicles, was the only one not being supplied at all by ML
27 The comparison (Kerstenetzky, 1985) serves more for these general indications than for market share, given the rough character of the estimate of the piston OEM market, based on the number of vehicles manufactured and on the number of cylinders of each of them and not on piston acquisitions from the assembly plants.
28 Considerations based on interviews at ML carried out in the 80s.
29 Based on interviews.

30 The units that make purchasing decisions in this market are not, generally, individual car owners but rather a diversity of professionals and entrepreneurs as the automobile mechanics, retailers, and owners of large fleets.
31 This means less potential market related to de-verticalization.
32 Hermann (2005).
33 Kerstenetzky (1985).
34 A distinction obtained at that time by only 50 out of 4,500 suppliers.
35 Metal Leve Annual Executive management report, various years.
36 A heterodox plan to fight inflation in 1986.
37 From the newspaper, Estado de São Paulo, October 3, 1986.
38 Lula was a leader from the Partido dos Trabalhadores ("Labour Party") who would become president in 2003.
39 More specifically, into the manufacture of programmable logic controllers, with a view to supplying products and services in the industrial control and factory automation market.
40 This confirms José Mindlin's interview comments that the end of the contracts left no hard feelings.
41 The parent company was Federal Mogul.
42 The appraisal that follows in these two paragraphs is based on a set of executive board minutes from 1986.
43 In one of the minutes of the executive management meetings in 1986, an executive mentioned that BNDES had a different opinion in this respect. However, we give more weight to ML's position given that the company was the user of the machines.
44 The American automobile production was already experiencing a slowdown that combined the effects of the penetration of Japanese automakers with a cyclical short-term decline of the sales in the American market, after a four-year period of brisk sales in the second half of the '80's (Wong, 1990).
45 The many aspects involved in this transformation will not be detailed here and can be found in Arbix et al. (1997). Only those most directly relevant to ML's case will be dealt with in this chapter.
46 For a detailed account of denationalization and restructuring of the Brazilian autoparts sector in the years of this last phase of ML, see Posthuma (1997).
47 According to *The Study on the Competitiveness of Brazilian Industry*, the number of auto parts manufacturers fell from 2000 in 1989 to approximately 1200 (p. 268). The year of publication is 1993.
48 Castro (2001).
49 Among the changes there was a reduction of hierarchical levels and big layoffs.
50 Remembering that, in this specific case, if the company continued to exist, management changed and its resources became subjected to another larger hierarchy in a global corporation, justifying the idea of the end of its life cycle.
51 See, for example, the Company's 1981 Executive Management Report.
52 The explanation of Metal Leve's growth must also consider commercial and other areas and capabilities developed over the course of time.
53 In most of the other years as a publicly traded company, distribution of dividends did not surpass 30 percent of profits; actually, it was usually well below this level.
54 I think the comparison is valid even though the difference between the two companies in terms of age and position in the context of the international automotive industry.

References

Arbix, G and Zilbovicius, M. *De JK a FHC. A Reinvenção dos Carros*. São Paulo: Scritta, 1997.

Baer, W. *The Brazilian Economy. Growth & Development*. Boulder and London: Lynne Rienner, 2014.

Campos, I. and Pinto, P.S. "A força de uma vida." Entrevista com José Mindlin. *Indústria Brasileira*, vol.7, n.76, pp.10–16, 2007.

Castro, A. de B. "A reestruturação Industrial Brasileira nos Anos 90. Uma Interpretação." *Revista de Economia Política* vol. 21, n. 3 pp. 3–26, Julho–Setembro 2001.

Coutinho, L. and Ferraz, J.C. (coord.) *Estudo de Competitividade da Indústria Brasileira*. Research report IE/Unicamp, IEI/UFRJ, FDC and FUNCEX, 1993.

Faldini, R. "Experiência empresarial vivida: o caso Metal Leve." IBCG, PDF, 2005. Accessed July 20, 2015.

Grote, H. "Position and Prospects of Suppliers with Special Reference to the Motor Industry." *German Economic Review*, vol.9 n.3, pp. 269–273, 1971.

Guimarães, E.A. and Gadelha, M.F. *O Setor Automobilístico no Brasil*. Rio de Janeiro: Relatório de Pesquisa FINEP, *mimeo*, 1980.

Hermann, J. "Auge e declínio do modelo de crescimento com endividamento: O II PND e a crise da dívida externa (1974–1984). In: F. Giambiagi et al., *Economia Brasileira Contemporânea (1945-2004)*. Rio de Janeiro: Editora Campus, 2005.

Kerstenetzky, J. *A História da Metal Leve S.A.: Empresa nacional líder do setor metal-mecânico*. Rio de Janeiro: IEI/UFRJ, Tese de Mestrado, 1985.

Kerstenetzky, J. "Alfred Marshall on Big Business." *Cambridge Journal of Economics*, vol.34, n.3, pp. 569–586, May 2010.

Lippert, I. et al. *Corporate Governance, Employee Voice, and Work Organization. Sustaining high road, jobs in the automotive supply industry*. Oxford: Oxford U.P., 2014).

Marshall, A. *Principles of Economics*. 9th edition (variorum). London, Macmillan, 1961.

Penna, Maria Luiza *Luiz Camillo: Perfil Intelectual*. Rio de Janeiro: Editora FGV, 2014.

Penrose, E. T. *The Theory of the Growth of the Firm*. Oxford: Basil Blackwell, 1980 (second edition), [1959].

Posthuma, A.C. "Autopeças na encruzilhada: modernização desarticulada e desnacionalização. In: G. Arbix and M. Zilbovicius, *De JK a FHC. A Reinvenção dos Carros*. São Paulo: Scritta, 1997.

Vassalo, C. "Como a Metal Leve perdeu o passo." *Revista Exame*, July 3, 1996.

Wong, D. "The U.S. Auto Industry in the 1990s." *Federal Reserve Bank of Philadelphia Business Review*, July/August 1990.

Zimmerman, M. B. "A View of Recessions, from the Automotive Industry." In: J.C. Fuhrer and S. Schuch (eds.) *Beyond Shocks: What Causes Business Cycles*. FRBB Conference series 42, June 1998.

5 Innovation, state partnership and growth strategies in the software industry

The case of TOTVS

Paulo Bastos Tigre and
Leonardo Fernandes Moutinho Rocha

Introduction

TOTVS is currently the world sixth largest enterprise resource planning (ERP) provider and the largest locally-owned IT company in Latin America. The software industry has being suffering major changes since the diffusion of the cloud computing concept, a technology that enables the development of new business models based on services rather than products. New technology platforms seek to increase demand economies of scale by producing network effects. Although there is room for smaller specialized companies in horizontal and vertical niches, the world ERP market is concentrated on a few large suppliers.

The trajectory of TOTVS reveals a comprehensive growth strategy based on mergers and acquisitions and the consolidation of a proprietary technology platform. By acquiring firms specialized in different market segments, it bought sector-specific capabilities that were further integrated in a system. The development of a technology platform allowed the company to obtain network effects, by increasing the number of users and the value created for each user.

TOTVS has been able to access different funding sources to support its rapid growth, including an initial public offering (IPO) and recurrent financial support from the national development bank (BNDES). By increasing profit margins, TOTVS obtained a significant organic growth and attracted new stock investors. The case is emblematic since TOTVS was founded by technical entrepreneurs counting with little initial capital and is now challenging large multinational companies in specific markets.

Since its foundation in the early 1980s the company pursue a growth strategy based on exploring new technologies to develop vertical and horizontal market niches. Such strategies bore fruit especially in the segment of small- and medium-sized enterprises (SMEs) that need software solutions adapted to their size, management culture and local legal rules. TOTVS now leads the lower end of the ERP market in Latin America, but faces strong barriers to enter into larger international markets.

Before analyzing the TOTVS' case, we will review the impacts of recent innovations on the software industry in the first section and analyze the characteristics of the Brazilian ERP market in the second section, where the company earns the majority of its revenues. The third section looks at TOTVS rapid growth trajectory based mainly on mergers and acquisitions (M&A) while the fourth section makes a more detailed analysis of the company's competitive strategies. Finally, the fifth section looks at future challenges.

The impacts of innovation on software industry

The advent of cloud computing is transforming the software market from the provision of software products to the supply of information services (Software as a Service – SaaS), thus accentuating its characteristics of non-rival good. The SaaS can be shared and distributed without significant additional costs. Hardware and software no longer need to be owned by users, a feature that reduces costs, increases flexibility and speed technological updating. Users become locked in in proprietary technological standards on which they have almost no control. With the spread of mobile devices, the cloud is able to integrate all systems on a single network. Access to cloud-based services can permeate the various device interfaces, facilitating end-user operations.

The ERP system is composed of several business management modules. It can be defined as "modular commercial software packages or services, aiming to support business processes" (Pavin and Klein, 2013, p. 3). According to Rashid, Hossain and Patrick (2002) there are ten main ERP modules: accounting, finance, manufacturing, production, transportation, sales and distribution, human resources, supply chain, customer relationship management (CRM) and E-business. Cloud-based ERP systems provide modularity, integration, flexibility, mobility and enable the incorporation of new business processes by users.

Confronted by growing competitive pressures, user firms seek to reduce costs throughout their value chains, to shorten supply chains, to reduce inventories, to increase the variety of products, to improve quality, to provide reliable delivery services, to enhance after-sales services, and to improve overall coordination with suppliers and consumers. An integrated management system allows the restructuring of business processes and facilitates the incorporation of best practices observed in different segments of economic activity. Large ERP vendors seek to take over specialized software firms in order to acquire technological capabilities in specific business processes. New technology partners add expertise in a wide range of economic activities in manufacturing, services and agriculture. By incorporating these areas of expertise, ERP systems embody best practices in business processes and make it available to other users. Table 5.1 summarizes the advantages of ERP use in organizations and provides a definition of these benefits based on the review of recent literature on the subject.

It can be noted that the implementation of an ERP system is not limited strictly to software acquisition, since several previous steps are necessary. Elmeziane (2012) points out that along with the acquisition of software, the user firms need

Table 5.1 Main advantages of ERP use in organizations

Advantages of ERP use	Definition	References
Productivity gains	• ERP allows the redesign, optimization and automation of activities, thus improving organizational processes. • Users have access to more information and can perform their tasks better and faster, with higher productivity.	Turbam et al. (2001); Saccol et al. (2004)
Increased organizational effectiveness	• ERP improves the decision making processes by providing access to real time information. • Decentralization improves decision making and contributes to increased efficiency.	Saccol et al. (2004); Veleu (2007); Ross (1999)
Increased organizational efficiency	• ERP provides more information about products and services, improving the organizational processes. • Greater flexibility and better information quality increase organizational efficiency.	Saccol et al. (2004); Gattiker & Goodhue (2005); Hsu & Chen (2004); Spathis & Constantinides (2004) Zwicker & Souza (2003)
Improved communication	• Improved communication between different units of an organization. • Co-ordinate manufacturing and sales thus reducing inventories and delivery time.	Hsu & Chen (2004)
Better relationship with suppliers	• ERP reduces lead time by improving interaction and information exchange with suppliers.	Turban, Mclean, Wetherbe (2001); Saccol et al. (2004); Veleu (2007)
Better relationship with customers	• ERP provides more information about customer demands and thus helps to improve the relationship with them.	Ross (1999); Veleu (2007)
Cost reductions	• Reduction of administrative costs (ex: accountancy) • Lower costs with faults and errors in the products and processes information.	Spathis & Constantinides (2004); Poston & Grabski (2001); Veleu (2007)
Higher market value	• Financial markets tend to reward ERP adopters with higher company market value.	Hitt, Wu & Zhou (2002)
Maintenance costs	• Maintaining and updating ERP generates permanent costs.	Zwicker & Souza (2003)
Increased surveillance and control	• Company is integrated by a single system; it means that employees are under control and surveillance.	Wood Jr. et al. (2003)
Increased standardization/ bureaucratization	• Companies using the same ERP systems become standardized and this may eventually affect competitive advantages	Wood Jr. et al. (2003)
Dependence on ERP vendor	• The adopter company becomes more dependent on the ERP vendor thus increasing transaction costs.	Zwicker & Souza (2003)

Source: Pavin and Klein (2013)

to undertake a business processes reengineering. Considering the modularity and flexibility of ERP systems, it is possible to adapt customers' needs, by incorporating legacy systems and critical organizational routines. In this way the supply of ERP is not limited to software implementation, but involves a whole range of additional services required for system customization and/or transforming the clients' business process to match benchmark models.

Software providers search for network effects by incorporating new customers and partners in a single technology platform. To build a successful network platform, a software firm must add value and innovations to users. Large ERP suppliers usually manage technology platforms, train users and provide technical assistance (mainly at distance). Partners operating under franchise agreements are in charge of opening up new regional markets and providing physical support.

The ERP market is segmented by sector and size of firms. While large corporations need more robust and holistic solutions, smaller companies prefer more simple and inexpensive services. Competition is therefore based on price, easiness of use, reliability, adaptation to different regulatory environments, compatibility with other ERP systems, mobility and accessibility. For Rashid, Hossain and Patrick (2002), companies must constantly update their systems and add new components in order to transmit an image of technology strength to their customers. As ERP is a long-term relationship, goodwill and good support services are key advantages.

The software industry is, according to Pavitt's taxonomy, a technology transmitter sector. In Brazil, this role can be evidenced by a survey ranking innovative activities perceived to be of high importance by industry (PINTEC). Table 5.2 shows that the acquisition of software, which was not even mentioned in the 2000 and 2003 editions of the survey, was considered the sixth most important source of innovation in 2005, moving to fifth position in 2008 and third place in 2011 and 2014. Such changes indicate that software is becoming a major

Table 5.2 Ranking of innovative activities considered to be of high importance by Brazilian firms

Innovative activity	2000	2003	2005	2008	2011	2014
Acquisition of machinery and equipment	1	1	1	1	1	1
Training	2	2	2	2	2	2
Industrial design and other technical preparations	3	3	3	3	5	4
Internal R&D activities	4	4	5	6	6	6
Introduction of technological innovations in the market	5	5	4	4	4	5
Acquisition of other external knowledge	6	6	7	7	7	7
Acquisition of external R&D	7	7	8	8	8	8
Acquisition of software	–	–	6	5	3	3

Source: PINTEC 2000, 2003, 2005, 2008, 2011 and 2014.

source of innovation in the manufacturing industry. The increasing complexity of technological systems and the trend of outsourcing ICT enable firms to focus on their core activities while leaving information technology (IT) to specialized suppliers. Firms using in-house developed systems have the tendency to become outdated, since they usually lack the required capabilities to continuously keep pace with the state-of-the-art of technology.

Brazilian ERP market

Brazil represents about 3 percent of world and 46 percent of Latin America software market, according to the software association ABES. In 2014 the local market grew 6.7 percent, reaching US$ 60 billion but a setback in the Brazilian economy restrained growth rates in the following two years. The ERP market is essentially international, since users face almost no tariff or regulatory barriers to access technology. The high concentration observed in the world market can be attributed to the network economies and costs associated with the development and provision of information-intensive goods. In Brazil TOTVS, SAP, Oracle and Infor are major players with an overall market share of 36 percent, 30 percent, 16 percent and 5 percent respectively. However, leadership varies according to the market segments: high end, mid-range and low end (see Figure 5.1). The high end is largely dominated by SAP and Oracle witch hold, together, 72 percent of the user segment using more than 700 keyboards. In Brazil there are about 9,000 firms counting with more than 500 employees. Since many of them are foreign owned, they usually use the same ERP systems adopted by the corporation or business network as a whole and seldom source locally. TOTVS has a 20 percent share of the upper end market by attending mainly locally-owned firms or government organizations. Competition in this market segment is fierce since global players are reputed to offer robust solutions and to support large and complex data flows.

On the lower end of the market (under 170 keyboards), TOTVS holds a confortable 51 percent market share. It adopts a strategy combining low-cost enter packages and focus on user needs to attract small business. In recent years, small Brazilian entrepreneurs are becoming more concerned with fiscal rules, due to a stricter law enforcement control system. New fiscal legislation is simplifying tax procedures, although these rules are still considered to be too complex and time-consuming for most firms. For Araújo and Souza (2014), new tax rules have encouraged SMEs to adopt ERP. The low end market presents a good growth potential, since less than 10 percent of small companies already adopt ERP solutions.

TOTVS strategy to capture small clients is based mainly on partnerships with local software houses. In Brazil, there are more than 5,000 software firms which could potentially act as local distributors, since they are usually open to network with larger technology and business communities. TOTVS seeks to consolidate its network by encouraging mergers and acquisitions among its associates in order to boost economies of scales and to better organize regional scope of operations.

In the last years, the number of regional franchises dropped from 230 to 56 channels, revealing an intense process of fusions and acquisitions supported by TOTVS. Larger distributors are more able to increase bargaining power, reduce costs, provide better maintenance services and access to financial resources.

Despite marketing efforts, SAP and Oracle hold, together, only 19 percent of the lower end of Brazilian ERP market. The main reason for this relative weakness is that few products are specifically designed for local small firms. Global players usually focus on developed countries markets where the business environment requires advanced systems. For small Latin American firms, however, these solutions may be too expensive and ill adapted to local needs. Microsoft, in particular, is quite active in this market globally, but lacks a good local structure to directly support SMEs.

TOTVS also leads the mid-segment of the ERP market (from 170 to 700 keyboards) with a 40 percent market share. Typically, users are medium-sized firms, employing from 100 to 499 people, which demand reliable information systems, but usually lack technological capabilities and financial resources to implement best practices in IT use. They would rather transfer IT infrastructure to a consistent outside SaaS provider, and link their employees to the cloud according to different functions in business processing. To access this market, TOTVS has acquired technology capabilities in a wide range of business processes.

However, a clear segmentation between the low and the high end of the market is now blurring. On the one hand, global players are increasing their focus on SMEs. In 2006 German-owned SAP established a R&D center at the southern University UNISINOS and integrated it to a network of 14 laboratories around the world. SAP Labs Latin America's R&D activities include mobility solutions,

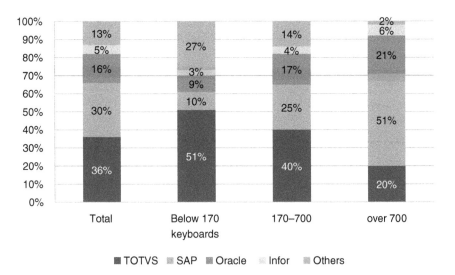

Figure 5.1 Brazilian ERP market, 2014–2015

Source: Pesquisa Anual de Uso de TI (2015)

bigdata analytics, and the design of specific products for smaller firms. One of the first products developed locally was a "Tax Declaration Framework," a full tax management system specifically designed to meet fiscal needs of firms operating in Brazil. On the other hand, TOTVS seeks to enlarge its high end market penetration by greater specialization in horizontal segments, such as agro-industry, manufacturing, trade, finance, health, education, logistics and distribution. By focusing on sectoral specialization, rather than business size only, TOTVS wish to grow with their clients, eventually following their expansion outside Brazil. Figure 5.1 shows the participation of the leading companies in the Brazilian market in function of the size of the users according to the number of connected devices.

Despite market concentration, it can be noted that smaller Brazilian ERP providers have managed to thrive in some specialized niches by obtaining a higher growth rate than TOTVS. In 2014, while TOTVS revenues grew 10 percent, Linx grew 25 percent in the retail segment and Senior Systems grew 36 percent in general ERP. These firms have become major takeover targets due their capacity to enlarge the market with the development of new applications.

Growth trajectory

TOTVS has its origin in Microsiga, a company founded in 1983 with the goal of developing integrated management systems for SMEs. The advent of micro-computers, more economical and flexible than mainframes and minicomputers that dominated the market of information technologies at this time, has opened a window of opportunity to explore the low end segment of the business automation market that was practically unexplored in Brazil. Due to high costs of systems based on larger computers, only large users were able to automate. By developing low cost solutions based on microcomputers, Microsiga were able to promote downsizing and capture a fast-growing market niche.

In the first 15 years of operations, Microsiga grew organically, achieving a turnover of R$ 35 million in 1998 (Table 5.3). By that time, the company launched its own technology platform, a feature that has proved essential to integrate different software used by customers and also to differentiate its services in the market. The platform offered an integrated portfolio of solutions that preserve customers' investments in legacy systems and managerial processes. To enlarge the spectrum of customers, Microsiga has created different licensing models, with features and level of complexity defined according to the size of the client and its business sector. At this time the firm promoted an aggressive expansion of franchises in order to enlarge its customer service to the whole country.

In 2000 Microsiga set the goal of becoming the larger ERP provider in Brazil by reinforcing a strategy combining organic growth with mergers and acquisitions in different segments of the software market. Microsiga has explored different external financial sources, including venture capital, IPO (initial public offer) and a long-term partnership with the national development bank (BNDES) (see Table 5.3).

In 1999 Microsiga obtained resources from the US private equity fund Advent International and started its acquisition route. In the following year, it launched a

Table 5.3 Revenues, profit margins and relevant facts

Year	Revenue (R$ million)	Yearly growth %	EBITDA (%)	Relevant facts
1983	–	–	–	Foundation of Microsiga
1996	17	–	–	Quality certificate ISO 9001
1997	24	41	–	Opened a subsidiary in Argentina
1998	35	45	–	
1999	63	80	9.8	Private equity by Advent
2000	98	56	10	Launched its own technology platform
2001	106	8	8.4	Established the goal of becoming ERP market leader in Brazil
2002	110	4	6.5	Strategic plan presented to BNDES
2003	126	15	12.4	Purchase of Sipros (México)
2004	173	37	12.4	Purchase of Logocenter
2005	247	43	13.9	BNDES funding (R$ 40 million) obtained. New company name (TOTVS)
2006	392	59	18.4	IPO. Purchase of RM Sistemas
2007	490	25	21.9	Purchase of Midbyte and BCS Informática.
2008	760	55	20.6	New BNDES funding obtained (R$ 404 million). Merger with Datasul
2009	1,080	42	25.2	Unification of TOTVS and Datasul franchise network.
2010	1,233	14	25.6	Purchase of SCR
2011	1,343	9	24.1	Purchase of GENS and Totalbanco
2012	1,557	16	26.7	
2013	1,600	3	25.1	New BNDES funding - R$ 650 million. Purchase of PC Sistemas, PRX, RMS and Seventeen.
2014	1,669*	–	26.5**	Purchase of Ciashop
2015	2,200***			Purchase of Bematech

Source: www.totvs.com.br

EBITDA: profit margin before financial expenses and taxes
* 12 months until the 1st trimester; ** 1st trimester 2014; *** Estimative after Bematech purchase (Valor, 15/8/2015)

proprietary technology platform in order to integrate new acquisitions in a single technology base. Another decisive step was taken in 2002, when it proposed to BNDES an ambitious plan to create a national champion in the Brazilian software industry, capable of directly compete with world leaders. The aim was to multiply its revenues by ten, reaching R$ 1 billion in 2010, thus matching a goal established by the new industrial policy[1] launched by the recently elected Workers Party. For policy makers, the promotion of mergers and acquisitions (M&A) was a necessary condition to generate economies of scale and scope to participate in the global software industry. In January 2005, BNDES acquired a 7.6 percent market share in Microsiga (now TOTVS), by investing R$ 40 million. The money was used to buy Logocenter, then the fourth largest ERP in the Brazilian market. The acquisition was an excellent opportunity to enter the high end of the ERP market since Logocenter had a well-built client base among medium and large manufacturing companies. In March 2006, TOTVS successfully launched an IPO and BNDES took this opportunity to sell out its equity participation. From this time on, TOTVS experienced a two-digit annual growth and almost doubled its gross profit margin from 12 to 22 percent. It also started a new round of acquisitions aiming at diversifying its market range into retailing and legal software services. In 2008 TOTVS merged with DATASUL, the second-largest Brazilian software company and market leader in the manufacturing sector. To enable this operation, BNDES invested R$ 404.5 million, half of which in loans and the other half in equity shares. The enhanced company reached 50 percent of the Brazilian market and entered in the top ten world ERP ranking. In 2013, TOTVS obtained another loan from BNDES summing up R$ 650 million and two years later made an offer to buy Bematech, the largest independent retailing automation provider in Brazil. TOTVS now offer a wide range of products and services including Customer Relationship Management (CRM), Business Intelligence (BI) and Supply Chain Management (SCM). In 2015, total turnover was estimated at R$ 2.2 billion. It has now about 26,000 clients and employs 7,000 people directly and another 6,000 indirectly through exclusive franchises.

Competitive strategies analysis

The fast growing path pursued by TOTVS in the last 15 years was supported by a combination of seven persistent corporative, technical, financial and marketing strategies.

Revenue stability

In the software industry, recurrent revenues are obtained by means of long-term licensing and maintenance contracts. Currently, 50 percent of TOTVS's revenue derives from systems maintenance contracts, while 23 percent comes from software licensing. Only 27 percent are non-recurring revenues, usually related to systems implementation services. However, the supplying of these services can eventually generate systematic revenues later.

Having most of its revenue guaranteed by service contracts is an important financial asset because it signifies greater relationship stability. Intangible investments carried out by users on proprietary solutions tend to generate lock-in. Customers tend to adapt their business processes to benchmark solutions developed by SaaS providers and become dependent on them to obtain information technology. Customers often rely on suppliers' proprietary software on which they have only a slight control. In order to maintain control over their legacy systems, some qualified IT users would rather develop their own solutions applicable to open multiple platforms.

Software companies that provide the traditional maintenance services to systems installed on their client premises also have stable revenues but this business model is being challenged by the SaaS form. Analysts from Gartner Consulting attributed the fall of 2 percent on Oracle's global revenues in 2013 to the on premise model, arguing that it nourishes complacency and the tendency to procrastinate innovations. This business practice tends to shrink because it faces competition from cloud computing, considered to be a more flexible, efficient and technologically dynamic model. Broadband infrastructure is now widely available, giving support to the cloud computing model and new software solutions can be implemented faster and cheaper

Seeking to explore new technological opportunities, TOTVS has being pushing its clients to the SaaS model. Since programs run remotely over the internet, there is no longer software installed on the client's premises. The sharing of hardware and software substantially reduce staff costs, maintenance and energy consumption, thus benefiting both clients and suppliers. Software SaaS providers also take advantage of technological improvements on the demand side.

Single platform technology

The main source of innovations and productivity growth in the world manufacturing industry is the purchase of machinery and equipment. Conversely, in the software industry, hardware no longer constitutes a critical asset, because it has become cheaper and more efficient over time. For software companies, main technological assets include technological standards, intellectual property, R&D capabilities and management skills. These assets are intangible and are often embodied in software programs.

TOTVS invests from 12–14 percent of its turnover in R&D activities, which are decentralized and usually located in former headquarters of software firms acquired along the time. R&D location reflects the range of skills acquired via M&A: The state of Rio Grande do Sul focus on system development for the health industry; Santa Catarina explore its tradition in manufacturing automation processes; São Paulo brings together the development of solutions for retail and services; Minas Gerais is specialized in education and building construction systems; and the Goiás state develop systems for logistics and transport.

A small but important R&D facility is located in California's Silicon Valley. It plays the role of providing TOTVS with an international identity, putting it "on the map," facilitating involvement in global networks and increasing opportunities for innovation. Also, the California Lab search for scientific and technology services provided by research centers such as technology components development and software testing.

In 2013, TOTVS launched a new technological platform (FLUIG) oriented to integrate business processes, data and identity management. According to its website, "FLUIG is an agnostic management platform based on a single interface management for collaborative communication. Developed 100% as SaaS (software as a service), it stores all content in the cloud. The user accesses the information safely, anytime, anywhere and on any device. The new platform promotes the flow of information within the enterprise and permeates the entire management, through a single platform. There is a paradigm shift: the processes assume the leadership of corporate management. The standardization of procedures ensures more security and predictability, because it reduces errors and increases productivity."

Network economies

According to the "Metcalfe's law,"[2] the more users link to a network the greater the possibility of communication between its members and the usefulness of the network to its members. Technological coordination of a platform shared by a wide network of customers, franchisees, distributors and development centers generates opportunities for obtaining network economies. The extensive virtual network created by TOTVS allows generation of external economies through increasing demand economies of scale. Being a non-rival good, software, once developed, can be shared by different providers and users without relevant cost increase. The larger the network, the greater the possibilities for exchange of innovations and access to critical technology skills.

If it had relied on organic growth only, TOTVS wouldn't be capable of capturing new clients in such a diverse range of economic activities. Mergers and acquisitions enabled increasing participation in horizontal and vertical segments of the ERP market. The acquisitions of firms specialized in technological solutions typical of sub-segments of industry, services and agriculture, saved a long and uncertain process of learning about new business. There was, in fact, a dual synergy. TOTVS increased the economies of scope derived from the wider dissemination of its technological platform while developers and users absorbed by M&A benefited from participating in a larger knowledge network, having access to new tools and innovations.

Training and human resources management

Acquisitions are not always successful, in view of differences in technical and managerial cultures. TOTVS employs thousands of people, either directly or indirectly, with heterogeneous technical backgrounds. Knowing how to gather the best of different cultures requires not only flexibility and skill, but also the ability to reproduce successful experiences revealed in the process of selection, negotiation and implementation of M&A – a process described as knowledge management. To deal with these matters, TOTVS has developed a methodology for integrating different organizations in which technological and commercial synergies are evaluated, procedures for reintegrating people and measures to minimize the impacts of cultural changes are defined.

Sharing and reusing knowledge constitute a major challenge for any organization. A good knowledge management is essential to expand competences in different areas and a single technological platform facilitates internal training. Many TOTVS consulting and maintenance services employees end up being contracted by the client himself. Despite representing a brain drain in the short term, the job switch ultimately encourages brand loyalty and disseminates the technological culture within its customer base. Training employees, distributors and customers is being increasingly provided by e-learning. TOTVS provides a library of courseware, helpdesk services and encourage discussion groups in the community of users.

Brand creation

Since the establishment of the new company name, brand-building is one of the pillars of TOTVS business strategy. Advertising campaigns in mass media channels transformed TOTVS into the twenty-second most valuable Brazilian brand, according to Millard Brown. In IT, a reputed brand is an indication of capacity to provide reliable services. To a user company's IT manager, it is safer to source from well reputed brand than from a less known one. Problems in IT services delivery always happen, but unknown suppliers are usually blamed more than leader firms.

The strengthening of the brand name not only benefited the commercial side, but also helped TOTVS to attract new investors, raising its ability to gather more funding. By looking for a secure image of transparency and good management, the firm adopts corporate governance practices that seek to exceed the standards required by law. Spraying of capital led to a separation between management and shareholders through an independent Board of Directors. Only the President of the company participates in the Council, as well as representatives of major shareholders and with independent members capable of adding expertise and helping to draw the company's strategy.

Alignment with public policies

The alignment between public policies and business strategies is an essential element for economic development. Albert Hirschman (1958) argues that some sectors of activities create a "multidimensional conspiracy" for development, inducing business synergies, creating positive externalities for the rest of the economy and shaping interests of political groups in a developmental coalition. He believes that the "entrepreneurship" is the missing ingredient of the conceptions of development, because the State needs private companies capable of making the necessary investments to enter the most dynamic segments of the economy. In this process, Hirschman believed that the capital is not the main element lacking to late developing countries, but rather, the willingness of entrepreneurs to invest in promising productive activities.

The prominent development economist Alexander Gerschenkron highlighted another aspect of the importance of public–private partnership in industrial processing. For him, the development process requires that investments grow faster than consumption. In this context, entrepreneurs are faced with new technologies and large competitive challenges without having sufficient resources to invest. Given the reluctance of the private sector to finance riskier activities in the long term, the State must exercise this role through development banks.

TOTVS's case illustrates a successful case of public–private cooperation with the aim of developing a sector capable of creating positive synergies in the national economy. On the one hand, the company was able to realize opportunities to grow rapidly in a very dynamic and competitive segment of the software market. On the other, the BNDES has identified a strong partner to fulfill its goal of supporting the development of national software companies capable of competing internationally and transferring advanced technologies for its users.

The accomplishment of the requirements made by BNDES for investments in equity shares served as "seal of quality" to attract other institutional investors, such as pension funds. In order to show greater transparency and credibility to prospective investors, TOTVS fitted itself in the rules of "New Market" that, according to the nomenclature of the Bovespa Stock Exchange, ranks companies that reach the most advanced level of corporate governance. Companies agree to, on a voluntary basis, adopt practices that exceed the requirements of the legislation in relation to corporate governance and shareholder's rights. Among other requirements, companies can only issue equity shares with full voting rights.

Internationalization

Entering into ERP foreign markets is a slow and difficult process, since it requires an internationally reputed brand, previous relationships with large multinationals and capacity to adapt general solutions to local needs. TOTVS successfully entered into major Latin American countries, but these markets are relatively small in world terms. While the US spend about 1 percent of GNP in IT services, Latin America spend only 0.23 percent. Considering the different GNP levels, the US market is more than 15 time larger in absolute terms.

TOTVS external sales represent today less than 4 percent of its total turnover. Latin America constitutes its main external market summing up 600 customers. The company has own subsidiaries in Argentina and Mexico, the latter responsible for the software translation and adaptation to the Hispanic-speaking markets. In other countries operations are made through franchises or direct worldwide contracts with multinationals. As in Brazil, TOTVS leads the low end of the market in major Latin American markets but seldom reach subsidiaries of large multinationals.

A major source of exports outside Latin America is Brazilian multinationals which operate in Portuguese speaking countries like Portugal, Angola and Mozambique. The R&D center in California also plays an important role in making the brand more global. To be in Silicon Valley increases commercial visibility and helps to reduce foreign mistrust in relation to a company coming from a country with little notoriety in software technologies. According to a study conducted by McKinsey, the lack of visibility has been an important barrier to Brazilian software exports. TOTVS holds about 2 percent of the ERP world market, occupying the sixth position in the overall ranking.

Future challenges

Since its foundation, about 30 years ago, TOTVS has being growing fast by adopting successful business models. TOTVS' phase 5 strategic planning foresees the transformation of the company into a global reference, but keeps Brazil as the main strategic focus. Growth would draw from further specialization on clients' size and business sectors and the exploration of new opportunities for acquisitions. Enhanced clients fidelity will be searched through brand strengthening, further development of process-oriented technology platforms, and focus on recurrent revenues. Profit margins would be kept by R&D productivity gains, better management of software life cycles and software components reuse. Larger penetration in international markets is also a target.

TOTVS position in Brazil and some Latin American markets seems to be secure, since its revenues are mainly recurrent and customers are somewhat locked-in to cloud services based on a proprietary technology platform. However, solutions that may have been fruitful at some point in the life cycle or historical moment could stop working if they are not improved, reformulated or replaced as the technological and competitive environment evolves (Kerstenetzky, 2015).

One immediate challenge is the deterioration of Brazilian political and economic situation. Since 2015, the national GNP has been falling considerably and many TOTVS customers were affected by this. However, the impacts of economic slowdown on the software market are still unclear, since business process automation is a tool for increasing efficiency and to reduce costs. Thus, some users may rather increase the use of ERP in response to the crisis.

A second challenge concerns the access to financial resources to further explore a growth strategy based on mergers and acquisitions. The BNDES has been a key partner, not only by providing substantial and timely supply of resources, but also by adding a "brand" capable to leverage other investors. Due to the fiscal crisis, BNDES is under pressure to reduce its role in the Brazilian economy and may eventually be more hesitant to invest heavily in a single firm. However, TOTVS is today a typical open company since about 68 percent of its shares are sprayed on the capital market (free float) of which 82 percent are held by foreign investors. Consequently, TOTVS may become less dependent on BNDES in the future and rely more on its shareholders to obtain new investment money.

The third challenge faced by TOTVS is obtaining a larger penetration in international markets. TOTVS holds today about 2 percent of the global ERP market acting essentially in a subcontinent that represents only 3 percent of the world total. Roughly speaking, TOTVS already holds two-thirds of the targeted market of SMEs, leaving a slight margin to further expand its market share. In order to increase its global market share, the company may need to increase its participation in the high end of the ERP market which is now dominated by few large multinational companies. Also, TOTVS need to raise its presence in the highly competitive North American market which represents about 50 percent of the world's total. By keeping Brazil as the main strategic focus, the company may defend its impressive and hardly conquered customer base but would hardly become a global player.

Notes

1 The Brazilian Industrial Technological and Foreign Trade Policy (PICTE) elected the software industry as one of its strategic options.
2 Network externalities served as basis for Bob Ethernet create a rule to calculate its value. If there are n people in a network, the network's value to each one of them is proportional to the number of other users, so that the total value of the network (for all users) is proportional to $n * (n-1) = n{-}n^2$. That means that if the value of a network, to a single user, is R\$ 1 for every other network user then a network with 10 participants have an approximate value of R\$ 100. In contrast, a network with 100 participants have a value estimated at R\$ 10,000. Therefore, an increase of 10 times the size of a network leads to a 100 times increase in its value. (Source: Shapiro and Varian, 1999).

References

ABES. (2015). *Mercado brasileiro de software: panorama e tendências* (Vol. 1).
Araújo, B. C., and Sousa, R. A. F. de. (2014). *Liderança de mercado no setor de tics brasileiro: estudos de caso da TOTVS e da Positivo Informática S/A* (No. 1917). *Texto para discussão*. Brasília.
Elmeziane, K. (2012). Enterprise Resources Planning Systems Implementation Success In China. *Business and Management Review*, *1*(12), 1–9.
Hirschman, A. (1958). *The Strategy of Economic Development*. Yale University Press.
IBGE. Pesquisa de inovação tecnológica (PINTEC).
Kerstenetzky, Jaques (2015) "Uma sugestão de abordagem teórica para estudos de casos de história empresarial com base na teoria da firma de Alfred Marshall." Anais do XI Congresso Brasileiro de História Econômica e 12a. Conferência Internacional de História de Empresas. Vitória, ES: ABPHE.
Meirelles, F. de S. (2015). Tecnologia da Informação - 26ª Pesquisa Anual do Uso de TI. Retrieved from http://eaesp.fgvsp.br/ensinoeconhecimento/centros/cia/pesquisa
Pavin, R. D. P., and Klein, A. Z. (2013). Mobile ERP systems adoption: case studies in Brazil. In *CONF-IRM 2013 Proceedings*.
Rashid, M., Hossain, L., and Patrick, J. (2002). The evolution of ERP Systems: A historical perspective. In *Enterprise Resource Planning Global Opportunities and Challenges* (pp. 1–16). Hershey, PA: Idea Group Publishing. http://doi.org/10.4018/978-1-931777-06-3

Roselino Jr., J. E., and Carlos, D. J. A. (2014). Redes Globais de Produção e Inovação em Software e Serviços de TI: Uma sugestão de tipologia. In *Cadernos Temáticos do Observatório: Pesquisa, Desenvolvimento e Inovação em Software e Serviços de TI* (pp. 11–30). Campinas, SP: Softex. http://doi.org/10.1017/CBO9781107415324.004

SEBRAE software de gestão – ERP 2008

Shapiro C. and Varian, H., 1999. Economia da Informação. Editora Campus.

SOFTEX - Associação para Promoção da Excelência do Software Brasileiro. Software e Serviços de TI: A Indústria Brasileira em Perspectiva, Vol. 2, 2012

TOTVS. Apresentação Institucional. Agosto/Setembro 2013.

6 Brazil's EMBRAER

Institutional entrepreneurship

Werner Baer and Joseph L. Love

The emergence of EMBRAER was largely the product of "institutional entrepreneurship." In some ways this is different from Schumpeter's entrepreneur, whom he viewed as an innovator who succeeds in introducing a new good, or a new method of production, or opening a new market, or arranging for a new source of raw materials. This is achieved with the aid of a banker (or a whole banking system) who was persuaded by the entrepreneur of the feasibility of the project.[1]

The rise of Brazil's aircraft manufacturer, EMBRAER, was not the result of the efforts of one entrepreneur, but rather the result of institutional developments which brought forth entrepreneurial efforts. Yet one person stands out in the development of EMBRAER, so this case shows the significance of the combined importance of institutions and individual leadership. Our interpretation builds on two valuable sources of information: Rodengen's detailed history of EMBRAER[2] and Ramamurti's early analysis of the firm, but our study also includes a variety of other sources, including treatments of recent developments.[3]

Brazil's early interest in aviation

Brazil's interest in aviation dates back to the beginning of the twentieth century. Brazilians consider Santos Dumont, rather than the Wright Brothers, the true inventor of the airplane. In 1906 Santos Dumont was the first individual to fly a self-propelled plane.[4] And in 1910 a monoplane was built in Brazil for the first time; this was followed in 1918 by the production of a military trainer biplane and in 1922 by a twin-engine airplane. By 1936 Brazilian companies had begun the serial production of trainers for flying clubs.[5] Both the army and a number of private groups showed an early interest in acquiring aviation technology through joint ventures with foreign firms. In the 1920s Brazil's armed forces invited French aviators to explore the possibilities of setting up joint ventures in designing planes, while a number of private Brazilian groups attempted to design and build aircraft in the 1930s. The Lages company designed, and eventually produced, a three-engine plane that made its maiden flight in 1943. However, production was ultimately discontinued because of a lack of orders.[6]

Most private sector initiatives relied on government support.[7] For instance, the building of the Galeão airplane factory in Rio de Janeiro in the 1930s was the result of a joint venture of the Brazilian navy and a German aviation firm. By this agreement, the navy would construct the hangars, while Germany's Focke-Wulf built some of the trainer planes in the facility. Forty planes were constructed. The program ended, however, with the outbreak of World War II. The Galeão facility was subsequently taken over by a joint venture with the Dutch firm Fokker to produce 100 units of S-11 trainer planes and 50 nose-wheel undercarriages. This collaboration came to an end in 1963.

Meanwhile, in 1931 a private firm, Ypiranga Aeronautics, designed a plane (EAY-201 Ypiranga, also known as Paulistinha). It was a two-seat high-wing monoplane, which went through several design modifications before being officially approved. It flew for the first time in 1935 and more than 1,000 units were sold over the next few years. However, the company was never a commercial success. In 1942 the São Paulo industrialist, Francisco Pignatori, founded the Companhia Paulista Aeronautica (CAP), which bought the rights to the EAY-201 Ypiranga. After some adjustments in the design the aircraft was approved by the Brazilian government and a large number of Paulistinhas were subsequently produced.

Thus, during the first half of the twentieth century one finds attempts by various Brazilian private and public groups to design and produce planes, drawing on foreign technical knowledge. By the second half of the twentieth century this effort had produced a fairly large scattering of technical talent in aircraft manufacturing. Ramamurti reported that between 1910 and 1970 about 700 prototypes were built in Brazil, mostly by Brazilians educated abroad. However, only a small number were commercially exploited.[8]

Institutional developments

Brazil's government entered the scene in 1941 with the creation of the Ministry of Aeronautics. It controlled both civil aviation and the country's air force. Following the end of World War II the ministry created the Centro Tecnico Aerospacial (CTA) to deal with projects in the aircraft sector, and within that new center the Instituto Tecnológico da Aeronautica (ITA) was created with the collaboration of the Massachusetts Institute of Technology. One of its main missions was to train aeronautical engineers, the first class graduating in 1951. ITA rapidly became one of the country's leading engineering schools; it also provided the human capital base for the future EMBRAER. By 1988 ITA had already trained 800 aeronautical engineers, and 2,200 in other specialties (Fritschtak, 1992).

Private sector initiatives in the post-World War II period

A few private firms turned out commercial aircraft from the 1940s to the 1960s. The CAP produced a few hundred single piston-engine planes that were bought mainly by Brazilian flight clubs. Another firm, Neiva, was established in 1953 and produced its first plane (a single piston-engine trainer for the air force) in 1961. Over the next decade and a half Neiva turned out 100 such planes for military use.

Finally, AEROTEC was founded in 1962 and produced 100 single engine trainers. These firms never produced twin-engine aircraft on a commercial scale and were always dependent on orders from the Brazilian air force. However, they would later become important subcontractors of EMBRAER.

The emergence of EMBRAER

In the 1950s the government tried to advance the aeronautical sector by attracting specialists from Europe. It invited experienced engineers from Germany to help design new combat planes and helicopters. As part of this attempt it set up the Instituto de Pesquisas e Desenvolvimento (IPD) within the CPA. Although the German collaboration was dissolved after a few years, this connection helped to strengthen Brazil's technical base in the field of aeronautics.

In 1965 a new project started in the IPD under the direction of Captain Ozires Silva, a 1963 graduate of ITA. He was sent to the California Institute of Technology, where he received a master's degree in aeronautical engineering in 1966.[9] The new undertaking was to develop a twin-engine turboprop transport plane for the Brazilian air force; it would replace an older fleet of Beech-18 planes. The project benefited from the expertise of Max Holste, a French aeronautical designer who helped Ozires Silva's group develop an 8–10 seater, non-pressurized twin-engine turboprop. This transport plane, the IPD-6504, was christened the Bandeirante.[10] To build the prototype, thousands of pieces had to be built with hand-held hammers, finely crafted to assure the interchangeability of parts. Many of these parts, as well as technicians, came from abroad. This was the beginning of a new assembly-line production of planes in Brazil.[11]

Research had found an underserved segment of the market outside the large urban centers; "feeder lines" would fill the gap. Ozires and his colleagues affirmed that there was a market for a small turboprop passenger aircraft robust enough to land on Brazil's many unpaved runways. The IPD-6504 was a perfect model as it "focused on simplicity. It featured two Pratt & Whitney Canada PT6A turboprop engines, low metallic wings, and retractable tricycle landing gear, with a maximum takeoff weight of 4,500 kilograms."[12]

Work on the plane began in 1966. Rodengen describes the ordeal which Ozires and his group underwent to bring this project to fruition. They did not have their own budget, and funds for the IPD-6504 project came from various other concurrent government projects. Rodengen notes that "From the start, the practical, bureaucratic, and funding problems seemed insurmountable. The CTA's only computer, 3 kilometers away at ITA headquarters, was constantly overbooked by students and engineers throughout the day. Yet the IPD-6504 team persevered, piling into a Volkswagen van and driving to the nearby ITA campus to pull all-nighters. According to Ozires, the lessons learned during those early experiences, despite the long odds, proved invaluable for the development of EMBRAER."[13]

The first prototype was flown in October, 1968, and, as noted above, it was baptized the Bandeirante. At this time the government decided to create EMBRAER, which would mass-produce the plane.[14] According to Ramamurti, the initial motivation for creating the firm was that "the unexpected success of the aircraft design group could be capitalized upon to launch a Brazilian aircraft industry of some sophistication."[15]

The technical success of the Bandeirante in its maiden flight did not result in the immediate availability of funding. Ozires had a difficult time in obtaining the necessary US$ 150 million to begin serial production. By May 1969 he had not succeeded in obtaining resources from the business community. But a special opportunity arose when the plane of the current military-imposed president of Brazil, General Arthur da Costa e Silva, was forced to land on the CTA airstrip and wait for an hour before taking off again. Ozires used the one-hour layover to talk to Costa e Silva about the Bandeirante project. In an interview with Rodengen, Ozires related that:

> I described to him what I thought EMBRAER would look like in the future, making different aircraft, selling them to the world. I told him we went to the private sector first, and why I thought foreign capital would be a bad idea. Then I told him "Mr. President… there is a provision in the Brazilian legislation that makes it possible for the government to create a corporation in partnership with the private sector. We can start with the State, then we can privatize. What do you think?"[16]

Ozires convinced the President, who upon his return to Brasília told his Aeronautics Minister, Márcio de Souza e Mello, that Ozires had the right idea. The Minister followed up by writing to the President, requesting that the government make aircraft manufacturing a national priority, thereby allowing the Aeronautics Ministry, together with the Industry and Trade Ministry, to work with foreign entities on technology transfer agreements.

With the creation of EMBRAER on August 19, 1969, by decree 770, with 51 percent government and 49 percent private ownership, Brazil's government resolved to make the firm a "national champion" of the aircraft industry. Ozires was to be the chief executive. Most engineers and technicians who had worked on the Bandeirante prototype were transferred from the CTA to EMBRAER, while personnel from various metalworking industries were also recruited. The government purchased land to construct EMBRAER's offices and factory close to CTA's offices in São José dos Campos, São Paulo. This arrangement allowed the new firm to continue to use the specialized labs, testing facilities, and the airport of the CTA.

The government continued to strengthen the new firm in various ways. It implemented a special tax provision which made it possible for individuals and corporations to convert 1 percent of their income taxes into EMBRAER shares; and the air force ordered 80 Bandeirantes, paying between 30 and 40 percent of the manufacturing costs upfront, and the rest upon delivery. Sales of the Bandeirante were financed by the government development bank, BNDES, because commercial banks wouldn't make large loans at reasonable interest rates in an era of rapid inflation.[17]

The Aeronautics Ministry transferred an ongoing IPD project to EMBRAER to develop an agricultural aircraft adapted to local conditions; equally importantly, the air force decided to purchase 112 new attack aircraft, the Xavante (named for an Indian tribe) through EMBRAER instead of through Italy's Aermacchi. The latter then entered into a licensing agreement with EMBRAER, allowing it to acquire expertise on the establishment of serial production of aircraft. Such skills were then applied to the production of the Bandeirante plane. The agreement with Aermacchi also provided for 20 Brazilians to receive training in Italy, and for Italian specialists to make lengthy stays at EMBRAER's plant.[18]

The Bandeirante was a 19-passenger aircraft designed for short-haul feeder lines, as well as for military transport, air drops, search-and-rescue operations, ambulance service, aerial phogrammetry,[19] and remote sensing. Most successful was the civilian version. By the end of 1991 of the 491 units that were delivered between 1973 and 1991, two-thirds were operating in more than 45 regional airlines in 36 countries, with the US gradually becoming the most important market.

The collaboration with Aermacchi also resulted in the production of the EMB 326 Xavante trainer plane, which had its maiden flight in September 1971, and eventually resulted in the sale of 167 planes to the Brazilian Air Force and a small number to Paraguay and Togo. A third project, a crop duster named Ipanema, was undertaken to replace imported Piper planes. The government financed 10 percent of the first prototype. Over the following decades more than 1,000 Ipanemas were produced. By 1970 work had begun on developing a third Bandeirante prototype for Brazil's new national space agency. It would be designed for remote sensoring applications. This new prototype was to be the plane's first civilian aircraft model.[20]

EMBRAER's engineers emphasized complying with strict FAA certification standards, which resulted in CTA's approval for commercial passenger flights in Brazil, and was the key to obtaining certification not only in the United States but around the globe. FAA certification came in 1978. Meanwhile, serial production on the 12-seat EMB 110 began in 1972 and the plane entered commercial airline service in 1973. EMBRAER sold 15 passenger Bandeirantes to Transbrasil Airlines and 5 to VASP Airlines. This plane opened new markets, servicing smaller cities.

The directors of the company soon realized that lasting success depended on continuous product innovation and diversification. Emphasis was placed at first on developing and perfecting pressurized cabin technology, and was soon followed by the decision to develop a whole family of aircraft. The company developed a number of pressurized turboprops: the EMB 120 Araguaia, the EMB 121 Xingu, and the EMB 123 Tapajos. The Araguaia and the Tapajós were larger planes, seating 20 passengers. However, the oil price explosion of the 1970s made these planes uneconomical. This was not the case of the Bandeirante nor the six-passenger Xingu, which was developed for taxi services and training purposes.

In designing the Xingu EMBRAER engineers "blended a pressurized fuselage and new Pratt & Whitney PT6A-28 engines with Bandeirante-style wings and streamlined engine enclosures. Engineers described the Xingu design process as similar to cutting out parts from other EMBRAER aircraft and putting them together like a [jigsaw] puzzle."[21] Only 105 Xingus were sold, the largest number to the French air force.

Despite the commercial failure of the Xingu, EMBRAER decided to continue producing light aircraft, whose world market was expanding in the 1970s. It signed a licensing agreement with the Piper company in 1975, under which it would manufacture six different models. Eventually EMBRAER sold 3,000 Piper models. The agreement was crucially important because it enabled EMBRAER engineers to learn the latest techniques in the production of light aircraft.

At the same time EMBRAER made a licensing deal with the Northrop Corporation to produce components for the F-5 fighter. This not only produced a source of revenue flows, but also allowed EMBRAER also new manufacturing technologies, such as metal bonding, machining aluminum-magnesium, and manufacturing aluminum honeycomb.

First exports

EMBRAER began exporting airplanes in 1975. It sold five EMB 110 Bandeirantes to the Uruguayan Air Force and marketed the EMB 200 Ipanema crop duster to Uruguay's Agricultural Ministry.[22] It expanded its business with France in 1977 as an agreement was reached to sell Air Littoral the EMB 110P2, which was a 21-passenger, elongated version of the Bandeirante. This was the first overseas sale of a commercial aircraft to a country with a major aircraft industry.

To expand its export business, however, EMBRAER needed the certification of the US Federal Aviation Administration, whose seal of approval, as noted above, was the key to major sales. In December 1977 France had granted the Bandeirante flight certification, and the following year the British Civil Aviation Authority and the Australian Department of Transportation also certified the Bandeirante. The difficulty with the US was that the FAA would not consider the Brazilian aircraft unless a US firm was interested in purchasing the plane. This event occurred only in 1978, when Mountain West Airlines ordered three Bandeirantes. This arrangement brought the US Department of State and the FAA into a bilateral aviation agreement with Brazil's CTA, thereby permitting the first certification of a Brazilian manufactured aircraft in US airspace.

Between 1979 and 1982 there was a pronounced growth of small passenger aircraft (15 to 19 passengers) in the international market, and EMBRAER's share amounted to 31 percent. Between 1975 and 1985 the US became EMBRAER's most important foreign customer. Of 480 Bandeirantes delivered, 130 operated in the US. Rodengen observed that these planes "were renowned for their rugged durability and low maintenance requirements, as well as their flexibility to alternate between cargo and passenger applications."[23] Also helping sales was the fact that EMBRAER was able to offer buyers a 45-day delivery deadline and lower interest rates – 9 percent compared to 15–18 percent for US aircraft.

EMBRAER entered the US market at an opportune moment. On October 24, 1978, President Jimmy Carter signed the Airline Deregulation Act, which made it possible for new regional carriers to serve smaller, previously unserved cities. In October 1979 EMBRAER opened its first center in the US in Florida. It functioned as a sales, service, training and repair center. By 1983 EMBRAER's success selling its Xingu plane in France led it to open a center at Le Bourget airport.

Two events in the 1970s contributed to the further growth of EMBRAER. Cessna discontinued its T-37 pilot trainer and the US announced a boycott of Brazil on the sales of defense materials and equipment based on charges of human rights violation by the military regime. Brazil's air force then urged EMBRAER to develop replacements for the components involved. The result was the development of the EMB 312 trainer, which was named Tucano. This new plane, according to Rodengen, "featured a full cover Plexiglas canopy, retractable landing gear, modern avionics, and specialized hardpoints designed to carry external fuel or munitions. The standard Tucano was equipped with the Pratt & Whitney PT6A-25C, which powered the three-bladed propeller aircraft to a maximum speed of 448 kilometers per hour."[24] In 1982 the Brazilian air force ordered 118 Tucanos, with options to buy 50 more. In the same year the Honduran air force ordered 10 of these planes.

Shortly thereafter EMBRAER made an agreement with the Egyptian government to provide 120 Tucanos, with an option of 60 more. Of these, the first 10 would be produced and assembled in Brazil, while the rest would be assembled in Egypt. An arrangement with the UK firm Short Brothers soon followed to jointly manufacture Tucanos for Britain's Royal Air Force. The RAF ordered 130 of these planes, with an option to buy 15 more. These planes were produced at the Short Brothers' facilities in Belfast, Northern Ireland.

At the time of the Tucano's development, EMBRAER began negotiations with Italy's Aermacchi, with which, as mentioned above, it had already collaborated in building the Italian designed AT Xavante. By 1980 EMBRAER had already delivered 167 of these planes to the Brazilian air force. In 1981 Brazil's Aeronautics Ministry signed an agreement with Aeronautica Militare Italiana to develop the AMX jet fighter program, which would give the Brazilian air force highly advanced technology. This action brought computer integration and fly-by-wire[25] technology to Brazilian aircraft manufacturing, which would gradually be used in the manufacture of even bigger planes. EMBRAER had 30 percent of the responsibilities by value for the construction of the plane. These including the wings, engine air intakes, weapons pylons, fuel tanks that could be jettisoned, main landing gear, and parts of the electrical and navigation attack systems, plus an electronics subsystem.

From the Brasília to the ERJ 145

Following the success of the Bandeirante and the advances in technology that were included in the Xingu, EMBRAER embarked on a new venture. It designed and produced three prototypes of the Brasília-EMB 120, which was a pressurized twin turboprop for 30 passengers, designed to appeal to regional airlines. This prototype made its first flight on July 29, 1983. This came at a time when most US regional airlines were in the market to replace older regional aircraft. The Brasília turned out to be the fastest and most economical plane in the 30-seat passenger category. It was designed to comply with FAA certification requirements. According to Rodengen, "EMBRAER engineers designed the Brasília with a focus on the specialized needs of the airline industry. As airports faced pressure to lower noise levels, the Brasília featured reduced internal and external noise compared with that of its competitors... In addition, the Brasília offered comfort and luggage space previously unavailable to regional airlines."[26]

The Brasília was certified by the FAA in July 1985, and the first planes were delivered to Atlanta Southeast Airlines in October of that year. Serial production of the plane continued until 2001 and it was ultimately purchased by 29 companies in 14 countries.

In 1984 EMBRAER established a new division called EMBRAER Equipment Division (EDE), which would serve as a components and engineering division. It specialized in landing gear manufacturing (from concept to design), components maintenance and repairs. EDE remained part of EMBRAER until 1999, when a joint venture was formed with the Swiss company Liebherr; the enterprise came to be known as EMBRAER-Liebherr Equipamentos do Brasil, S.A., and produced and exported aerospace equipment. In July 2008 EMBRAER bought out the entire enterprise, and the company became known as ELEB Equipamentos Ltda.

The emergence of the regional jet

In the mid-1980s EMBRAER and Argentina's Aerospace Materials Factory (FAMA) agreed to collaborate in the development of a regional jet, which would be a successor to the Bandeirante. The former would pay for two-thirds and the latter one-third of the development costs. The new plane was to be a 19-seater known as the CBA 123 Vector. Its design was based on a lengthened version of the Xingu plane and it was first unveiled at the 1987 Paris Air Show. According to Rodengen, the aircraft "had a revolutionary design with propellers mounted aft of the engine, thus pushing the aircraft rather than pulling. Designers foresaw the installation of more aerodynamic[ly] efficient wings."[27]

EMBRAER expected to sell between 1,500 and 2,000 planes of this type. However, the costs of the project were high and the promised Argentinean and Brazilian funding did not materialize as expected. EMBRAER accumulated losses of about US$ 280 million before the plane made its inaugural flight in 1990. And by the time the plane was ready for delivery, the oil price hike had hit the market.

Although this project was a failure, the technology and experience acquired in developing the CBA 123 would be crucial in the future development of the EMB 145 regional jet.

The 1980s and 1990s were difficult years for EMBRAER. The company had over-relied on defense and other government contracts. As foreign defense markets declined, it became obvious that the firm had paid greatest attention to technical achievements, without due concern for the market. As the economic performance of EMBRAER became increasingly precarious, a US firm (Comair), which had been an important purchaser of the EMB 120, inquired about the possibility of EMBRAER's constructing a large plane, seating as many as 50 passengers. EMBRAER would respond with the ERJ 145, which was a jet-powered version of the Brasília, extended to accommodate 50 passengers. However, the costs of modifications and adjustments required to make the plane viable and commercially attractive were extremely high. Given the development costs and the rising debt of the company, it became clear that the firm would be more viable if it became a privately owned company. This transformation occurred when Coronel Ozires da Silva returned to lead EMBRAER in 1991 after leaving the presidency of Petrobras.

The late 1980s and early 1990s were difficult times for EMBRAER, because it had accumulated a huge debt and was experiencing substantial losses. The company sustained itself by loans from the Banco do Brasil and from a few private creditors. It was also able to surmount this difficult period by subcontracting. In 1987 it obtained a subcontract from McDonnell Douglas to build outboard flaps. In 1990 it obtained a subcontract from Boeing to manufacture mechanical flap supports for the Boeing 747 and 767 aircraft. This, in turn, led to other contracts to supply components for Boeing's 777 planes. These subcontracts not only helped the firm to overcome some of its financial problems, but also to keep up-to-date technologically.

With the financial burden of its debt in the late 1980s and early 1990s, EMBRAER postponed its new aircraft programs. It did not want to curtail its customer service, that is, the provision of maintenance parts and services. This solidified its world reputation as a reliable company.

The ERJ project was put on hold until October 1991. When it was reactivated EMBRAER was able to obtain letters of intent from 14 airlines (Australian, US, European, and Latin American). Because of EMBRAER's solid international reputation and the broad recognition of the viability of the project, suppliers of structures and components were willing to provide the necessary engineering resources.

As the construction of the ERJ 145 proceeded, a number of modifications were made. Rodengen reports that,

> the engines were moved back to the rear of the fuselage and then inched forward for aerodynamic effect. The landing gear was redesigned and the passenger doorway was modified. However, the aircraft retained many features developed for EMBRAER's previous aircraft.... Commonality of design and parts with other EMBRAER aircraft saved the company valuable time and money, and costs were shaved by utilization of many solutions originally developed for the CBA 123.[28]

ERJ 145's success

The plane proved to be a huge success. By 2001 monthly production reached 18 aircraft. The major competitor was the Canadian firm Bombardier which had developed a similar plane, the CRJ200. According to the *Official Airline Guide*, the ERJ 145 had a lower fixed cost for short distance flights for 110 or fewer passengers. Moreover, the EMBRAER plane was less expensive than its Canadian rival – US$ 17.6 million, compared to US$ 21 million.[29]

Military planes

In the 1990s EMBRAER also attempted to develop previous military training models by incorporating the latest technology, teaming up with the Northrop Corporation. Although the joint venture lost out to another consortium, EMBRAER gained a substantial amount of technological experience which was later incorporated in the redesign of planes for the armed forces.

Privatization

The greatest crisis in EMBRAER's history, according to its long-time director, Ozires Silva, came in 1990, when a recession was accompanied by the rapid advance of globalization in all forms of production. Ozires, as previously stated, was called back to direct the company.[30] Yet in a few years EMBRAER's economic situation had improved considerably, and when its inclusion in the government's privatization program was announced, its share values in the São Paulo stock exchange (BOVESPA) shot up 2,000 percent. And as privatization neared, the Brazilian government agreed to absorb US$ 700 million of its debt. It also "set a low reserve price on company shares, and allowed for partial payments in bonds that traded at 50 percent of face value."[31]

Privatization finally took place in December, 1994, under President Itamar Franco, but arranged by the outgoing Finance Minister, Fernando Henrique Cardoso. The Brazilian senate had approved auction details in September 1994, and on December 7, a 55 percent controlling stake of EMBRAER was sold at auction to a group of investors, which included Bozano-Simonsen, Previ, Sistel, and a boutique New York investment bank, Wasserstein Perella.[32] The Brazilian government maintained 20 percent ownership; another 10 percent was given to EMBRAER employees, while the remainder was sold to the public.[33]

The early period as a privatized company was difficult. In the first months after privatization more than 2,000 employees were laid off. With revenues of US$ 230 million and losses of US$ 330 million, EMBRAER was essentially bankrupt. Its debt amounted to US$ 400 million and its backlog of orders was only US$ 170 million. Everything rested on the future of the ERJ 145.

The new management obtained a loan of US$ 106.5 million from Brazil's government development bank (BNDES) to help complete the ERJ 145 test flight program, and the major new owners injected an additional US$ 150 million. It also engaged in a number of cost-cutting measures, which included salary reductions and job cuts. At the same time the new management adopted a "niche strategy" which included such features as ability to take off from shorter runways, more easily fulfilled maintenance requirements and the ability to operate under harsh conditions that prevailed in many minor airports. The company also streamlined its operations, decreasing its lead time for new projects from 12 to 5 months. It made extra efforts to accommodate customers' wishes, such as redesigning interiors.

The newly designed ERJ 145 was unveiled at the Paris Air Show in 1997. It had already received FAA certification in November 1996. This plane would eventually turn EMBRAER into a global player. Sales of the plane grew continuously. Continental Express ordered 25 ERJ145 in the fall of 1996 and reserved options for 175 more. Shortly thereafter American Eagle ordered 42 of these planes. Already by September 1997 EMBRAER announced profits of US$ 10.4 million. By the end of that year 85 percent of the company's sales were international.

Many airlines chose EMBRAER's ERJ 145 for their regional jet fleets. As expected, the most intense competition came from Canada's Bombardier. EMBRAER outsold the latter. By 1998 it had 182 firm offers, with options for 245 more. At the same time, EMBRAER gradually abandoned the turboprop market. The success of ERJ 145 led to international litigation, because Bombardier alleged that EMBRAER received subsidies from the Brazilian government contrary to WTO rules. However, EMBRAER retaliated by accusing Bombardier of using inappropriate marketing methods to commercialize its plane.[34] In 1999 and 2000 the WTO issued several rulings, finding that both companies had received illegal subsidies from their governments.[35]

Growth and diversification

Derivatives of the ERJ 145 followed. For instance, when Brazil created the Amazon Surveillance Program (SIVAM), it needed specialized aircraft. EMBRAER adapted some of its ERJ 145 for that purpose.[36] Over the following years a family of products were developed: the ERJ 135, ERJ 140, ERJ 145, ranging from 37 to 56 seats per plane. 95 percent of the parts of these planes are interchangeable. The ERJ platform was also used to develop new designs for executive-class jets, such as the Legacy aircraft.

In the twenty-first century EMBRAER developed an entirely new family of planes (EMBRAER 170, 175, 190 and 195) designed for the newly-emerging market for 80 to 122-seat planes. They were certified to operate in the Americas, Europe and Asia.

By the beginning of 2015 EMBRAER had 60 firm orders for the EMBRAER 175 plane. It was outcompeting Bombardier's equivalent plane, the CRJ 900. The DRJ900 and EMBRAER 175 entered service in 2003 and 2004 respectively, and until 2012 "Bombardier held a sizable edge in sales, with the CRJ900 winning 314 orders compared to just 181 for the E-175. But for the past two-plus years,

Table 6.1 EMBRAER: commercial aircraft deliveries

1996–	4	2001–	161	2006–	130	2011–	204
1997–	32	2002–	131	2007–	169	2012–	205
1998–	60	2003–	101	2008–	204	2013–	209
1999–	96	2004–	148	2009–	244	2014–	
2000–	160	2005–	141	2010–	246		

Source: Wikipedia.

EMBRAER has dominated the sales competition, winning 240 E-175 orders compared to only 70 CRJ900 orders. The E-175 had vaulted past the CRJ900 in lifetime orders, now leading 421 to 384."[37]

According to Karp, the explanation of EMBRAER's greater competitiveness owed to the fact that it "modified the E-175's wing to lower the fuel burn by 6.4%, and airlines looking for looking for 75–90 seat regional jets increasingly gravitated to the EMBRAER aircraft over the CRJ900."[38] In addition EMBRAER added bigger wingtips to the EMBRAER 175 and extended the wing size by almost 9 ft., totaling 92 ft. It also strengthened the wing skin. Karp reported that EMBRAER had originally told its customers that such aerodynamic modifications would reduce the EMBRAER 175's fuel consumption by 5.5 percent, but "the Brazilian manufacturer bested that figure by nearly a percentage point, to its own surprise."[39] The first modified EMBRAER 175 were rolled out in March 2014 and are now operating in the US market.

Lessons from EMBRAER's success

What accounts for EMBRAER's success? The firm was not conceived within a typical entrepreneurial milieu, where it was possible for individuals with new ideas to bring their projects to fruition. We have seen that Brazilian interest in aviation dates back to the beginning of the aircraft industry, as various individuals and firms tried to construct different types of planes. None became commercially viable.

It was ultimately the state sector that made possible a commercially successful firm in airplane production in Brazil. Entrepreneurial individuals within the newest branch of the country's armed forces, the air force, helped create ITA, the necessary training facility. With its special emphasis on aeronautical engineering, ITA produced a large cadre of specialists. Many of them would remain in EMBRAER, the emerging firm.[40] Outstanding among ITA graduates was Ozires Silva, who had led the company initially and came back to supervise its privatization.

In reviewing EMBRAER's growth, Avrichir stresses the fact that in order to develop a global market, "knowledge was a key production factor in the contemporary economy." For Avrichir, EMBRAER's success in the world market is best explained by its sustained investment in advanced and specialized technology.[41] Throughout its existence EMBRAER has continuously emphasized the acquisition of new knowledge, based not only on its own experimentation, but also on making strategic alliances with foreign firms from which it could acquire new skills and technology.[42] Avrichir states that: "The aeronautical industry is the only case of continued investment in advanced and specialized knowledge in Brazil... This investment allowed EMBRAER to acquire influence, and [its success] became a national priority."[43] A broader contributing factor was Brazil's industrialization, which had begun in the 1930s and went into high gear in the 1950s. This situation made it possible for Brazil's industrial firms to become suppliers of components. In particular, new technology companies tended to congregate in the Paraíba Valley near the EMBRAER complex in São José dos Campos. Of course, many components were imported. This is, however, the nature of aircraft production. Even such giant firms as Boeing and Airbus import a large proportion of their components from around the world.

Another distinguishing attribute of EMBRAER's management was its capacity to spot and exploit niches within the world aviation market. Even though EMBRAER was a state enterprise until the 1990s, its growth and development was in large part also due to the administrative and political skills of its managers, who succeeded over many years in maintaining government support for their projects.

As a rule, state-sponsored enterprises in Latin America are precarious undertakings. They face the risk, on the one hand, of featherbedding by political appointees who lack the incentive to maximize profits, and, on the other, of being curtailed or abolished by governments with priorities different from outgoing administrations. Centeno and Ferraro present a case study of the Brazilian computer industry, established by the government of General Emílio Medici, the successor of the General-President who authorized the creation of EMBRAER, Artur da Costa e Silva.[44] We may summarize their findings as follows:

The Comissão de Coordenação das Atividades de Processamento Eletrônico (CAPRE) was set up by Minister of Planning João Paulo dos Reis Velloso, who held a Master's degree in economics from Yale and presided over the "Brazilian Miracle" in his ten-year tenure as planning minister (1969–1979). CAPRE, created in 1972, gave fiscal incentives to nascent Brazilian computer firms, and was remarkably successful for almost a decade. By 1982 local firms had produced two-thirds of the installed minicomputers (with original architecture) and accounted for 18,000 jobs. The Brazilian firms had gross sales of $667 million, which accounted for about 46 percent of total gross sales. A Brazilian minicomputer outsold those of foreign-licensed companies.

But when General João Figueirdo took power in 1979, he dissolved CAPRE and established an agency of informatics. CAPRE was purged, and its professionally-trained employees were simply replaced by political appointees. CAPRE's dissolution destroyed public trust in the local computer industry and the networks of suppliers, training programs, etc. The new agency also made inconsistent political decisions, first favoring local firms and then giving IBM the right to produce medium-sized computers with proprietary techniques and software. Figueirdo reversed that policy, but the fumbling administrators (political appointees) delayed decisions on critical rulings. Local companies became less innovative, and the public lost confidence. Subsequently, the Collor government introduced neoliberal policies in 1990. The computer regulating department was dissolved, and its informatics policies were abandoned. The big winners under deregulation were Japanese computer companies, according to Centeno and Ferraro.

EMBRAER, like the computer firms, was a government-nurtured "hothouse" enterprise. But EMBRAER enjoyed continuous political cover by the air force. Even after privatization in 1990, EMBRAER operated under an arrangement whereby the government held a minority of shares yet had a veto power. Furthermore, EMBRAER was widely regarded by successive governments as the prime example of Brazilian industry's ability to enter a highly competitive world market, in which continuous innovation[45] was necessary for success.[46]

EMBRAER's post-privatization recovery owes a lot to the actions of the new management. It added to the firm's core technical competence a capacity to react quickly to market signals. According to Goldstein,

> Various forms of organizational changes… led to innovations and improved performance. The hierarchy was flattened by cutting the number of managerial levels from ten to four, and performance-related remuneration was also introduced for all employees. Most importantly, a number of activities – among them strategic planning, overall quality management, intelligence about the market, …and the analysis of system performance feedback – were formalized and endogenized in the company's routines.[47]

Like other high-tech industries, the aircraft sector changes rapidly with new opportunities and new players. In mid-October, 2015, EMBRAER announced its intention to begin the production of unmanned aircraft – drones – in collaboration with the Israeli firm Elbit Systems. EMBRAER will have 51 percent ownership, and the initial focus will be on supplying drones to the Brazilian air force to protect Brazil's borders.[48]

While EMBRAER seeks to obtain a niche in the rapidly growing drone industry, and Bombardier attempts to enter the market for trans-Atlantic jets – perhaps relieving some of the pressure on EMBRAER – a powerful rival in the production of regional jets looms on the horizon, the Mitsubishi Aircraft Corporation. The government of Japan is paying about a third of the development costs, and the state will be among Mitsubishi's first customers. Mitsubishi presented a scale model of its jet at the Paris Air Show in 2007, but the initial production scheduled for 2012 was repeatedly pushed backward, with 2018 being the latest estimate. Mitsubishi executives initially expected their regional jet to use carbon-fiber-reinforced polymer composite materials for its airframe – yielding a lower fuel bill than aluminum planes – but in September 2009 the company announced that it would use aluminum at least in its wings. The Mitsubishi aircraft will nonetheless have a wider and higher cabin than those of EMBRAER and Bombardier. According to the *New York Times*, "Mitsubishi saw an opening when Bombardier focused on building a bigger jet… and EMBRAER initially failed to offer a new version of its regional jet with new, more fuel-efficient engines."[49]

EMBRAER must therefore constantly innovate to expand or retain its market share, and indeed, even to survive. But it has a strong record of development and transformation. The corporation in 2010 has a research and development budget of $70 million, helping Brazil achieve first place in Latin America in R&D as a share of gross domestic product in 2012, the last available year in World Bank data.[50]

Notes

1 Schumpeter, The Theory of Economic Development (1934).
2 Rodengen (2009).
3 Ramamurti (1987).
4 The Wright brothers had used a catapult to get their plane aloft.
5 Ramamurti (1987), pp. 182–3l; see also Rodengen (2009), p. 20 for a discussion of Brazil's early aviation pioneers.
6 Rodengen (2009), p. 22.
7 This was also the case in the US, where government support was necessary in the development of the computer industry.
8 Ramamurti mentions a French government study which found that Brazilians were the largest group of foreigners who studied aeronautical engineering at French Universities. Ramamurti (1987), p.183.
9 Silva, p. 127.
10 The bandeirante was a pioneering backwoodsman, famous in Brazilian mythology for opening the frontier from São Paulo.
11 Ibid., pp. 134, 147, 149, 155, 165.
12 Rodengen (2009), p. 36.
13 Ibid.
14 Max Holste moved on to Uruguay, but left the design in the hands of the Brazilian engineering team that had participated in the project. Ramamurti (1987), p. 184.
15 Ramamurti (1987), p. 184.
16 Rodengen (2009), p. 40.
17 Silva, p. 259.
18 Ramamurti quotes EMBRAER's technical director, Fontegalante Pessoti, describing the benefits which resulted from the agreement:

> "It was a very interesting cooperation, because it brought a lot of technology and expertise that we did not have at that time in Brazil – for example, in such areas as tracing technology, assembly of planes, organization for the procurement of materials, quality control, technical documentation, organization of assembly lines, etc.
>
> We did not manufacture any parts for the Xavantes here since for that small number of planes it would not have been economical. But we did redesign some parts of the Bandeirante with the cooperation of Aermacchi engineers. For instance, at that time we didn't know how to design integral tanks. So we sat with Aermacchi and learned how to do it for the Bandeirante. This was an important change with respect to the original prototype."
>
> Ramamurti (1987), p. 185.

19 The science of measurement based on aerial photographs.
20 According to Rodengen (2009), this new model's "shape was greatly improved with more aerodynamic lines…completely redesigned..wings,…integrated fuel tanks …and a smoother, more dynamic windshield. Even the engines were upgraded", p.50.

21 Rodengen, p.56.
22 Rodengen (2009), p. 63.
23 Rodengen (2009), p. 74.
24 Rodengen (2009), p. 78.
25 According to Wikipedia, "Fly-by-wire (FBW) is a system that replaces the conventional manual flight controls of an aircraft with an electronic interface."
26 Rodengen (2009), p. 88.
27 Rodengen, p. 100.
28 Rodengen, p. 120.
29 Ibid., p. 122.
30 Silva, p. 333.
31 Rodengen, p. 126.
32 Wasserstein Perella pulled out of the purchase agreement and its shares were purchased by the Bozano Simonsen group.
33 Vitor Hallack of the Bozano Simonsen group later stated that: "We learned in the context of due diligence that the ERJ 145 project was under severe cash restraints....We called a group of investors together. It was a huge risk, but, but big challenges and big opportunities usually come together. We saw in EMBRAER a hidden asset with outstanding human capital. That was our main motivation, but the ERJ 145 project was just a bet. If the odds were in our favor, we would succeed." Rodengen, p. 134.
34 Avrichir (2015), p. 286.
35 "Bombardier Aerospace and EMBRAER S.A. government subsidy controversy," Wikipedia.
36 Rodengen, p. 156.
37 Karp (2015), p. 2.
38 Karp (2015), p. 2.
39 Karp, (2015), p. 2.
40 A survey of the Association of Engineers (AEITA) in 2002 found that of the 393 engineers who graduated from ITA between 1997 and 2001, 29.5% were working in the aviation industry. (The others were trained in fields other than aeronautical engineering.) Of the 186 engineers working at Embraer in 2002, 26% were ITA alumni; of the 27 managers, 66% were alumni, and 4 of the 6 directors were alumni.
41 Avrichir (2015), p. 283.
42 Goldstein (2002) shows that the initial rise of EMBRAER was the result of capacities acquired through cooperation and licensing agreements, which enabled it to develop core competencies.
43 Avrichir (2015), p. 285.
44 Miguel Centeno and Agustín Ferraro, "With the Best of Intentions: Types of Development Failure in Latin America" (MS, August, 2015). The following three paragraphs are based on their research and findings.
45 Continuous innovation in highly competitive international markets was also the prescription for successful growth in the "neostructuralist" doctrine of the Economic Commission for Latin America and the Caribbean (ECLAC), formally adopted in 1990. See ECLAC [Fernando Fajnzylber, principal author], Changing Production Patterns with Social Equity (Santiago, Chile: United Nations : ECLAC, 1990).
46 Of course, the government could still intervene in EMBRAER as a minority shareholder. At a theoretical level, the conditions for such intervention ("residual interference") are discussed in Musacchio and Lazzarini, Reinventing State Capitalism, pp. 231–232.
47 Goldstein (2002), p. 107.
48 "Brazil's EMBRAER to Begin Building Drones," Latin American Herald Tribune [Caracas], Oct. 13, 2015.
49 "Mitsubishi Regional Jet," Wikipedia; "Japan Nears Test Flight for Long-Delayed Regional Passenger Jet," and "Japan, Seeking to Regain Manufacturing Might, Bets on Aerospace," *New York Times*, Sept. 1, 2015; Aug. 22, 2016.

50 Martin Grueber and Tim Studt, "BRIC-Brazil" www.rdmag.com/article/2012/12/bric-brazil; World Bank, http://data.worldbank.org/indicator/GB.XPD.RSDV.GD.ZS

References

Avrichir, Ilan (2015). "International Competitiveness of Brazilian Companies: The Much that can be learned from EMBRAER," *Business and Management Review*, (January).

"Brazil's EMBRAER to Begin Building Drones," *Latin American Herald Tribune*, Oct. 13, 2015.

Centeno, Miguel, and Agustin Ferraro, "With the Best of Intentions: Types of Development Failure in Latin America" (MS, August, 2015).

Fritschtak, Claudio R. (1992). "Learning, Technical Progress and Competitiveness in the Commuter Aircraft Industry: An Analysis of EMBRAER." (The World Bank, Industry Development Division), June 15.

Goldstein, Andrea (2002). "EMBRAER: From national champion to global player," Cepal Review 77, August.

Grueber, Martin, and Tim Studt, "BRIC-Brazil", www.rdmag.com/article/2012/12/bric-brazil

"Japan Nears Test Flight for Long-Delayed Regional Passenger Jet," *New York Times*, Sept. 1, 2015, p. B6.

Karp, Aaron (2015). "CRJ900 vs. E-175: microcosm of Bombardier's troubles," AirKarp, Feb. 17, 2015.

Musacchio, Aldo, and Sergio G. Lazzarini (2014). *Reinventing State Capitalism: Leviathan in Business, Brazil and Beyond* (Cambridge, MA: Harvard U. Press).

Ramamurti, Ravi (1987). State-Owned Enterprises in High Technology Industries: Studies in India and Brazil. (New York and Westport, CT: Praeger).

Rodengen, Jeffrey L. (2009). The History of EMBRAER. (N. P.: Write Stuff [sic] Enterprises, Inc.)

Schumpeter, Joseph A. (1934) *The Theory of Economic Development: An Inquiry into Profits, Capital, Credit, and the Business Cycle*, tr. by Redvers Opie (Cambridge, MA: Harvard University Press).

Silva, Ozires. A decolagem de um grande sonho: A história da criação de EMBRAER (Rio & SP: Elsevier, 2009).

World Bank, http://data.worldbank.org/indicator/GB.XPD.RSDV.GD.ZS

7 Entrepreneurship and competition in Brazil's music markets

A taxonomy of two eras

Marc Hertzman and Ronaldo Lemos

Two topics central to this volume – entrepreneurship and competition – raise interesting questions when considered within the music industry. What exactly is musical entrepreneurship and how does it compare to other industries? What is the appropriate unit of analysis for studying competition – artists? Record labels? Something else? (How) have these things changed over time? A subtext running through each question is the understanding that music is a business (and also, of course, much more than that). The very inclusion of our chapter in this volume is significant; far too often, scholars treat music as being divorced from professional or financial forces and institutions. Thinking seriously about music's relationship to banking, the auto and airline industries, and other topics considered in this volume promises to sharpen our understanding of music and other topics more familiar to economists, historians, and others.

Towards that end, we begin with baseline definitions of competition and entrepreneurship. For the former, Baer suggested the following: "A competitive market is one where there are numerous producers that compete with one another in hopes to provide goods and services we, as consumers, want and need. In other words, not one single producer can dictate the market. Also, like producers, not one consumer can dictate the market either."[1] For now, we will define entrepreneurship as a broad array of practices and initiatives, undertaken by individual actors seeking entrance into (or stronger positions within) a given market, often but not always stemming from or otherwise related to technological or other forms of innovation. But, as we will see, the nature of entrepreneurship takes on distinct meanings depending on context.

Working from these bare-bone definitions, we propose a taxonomy of the record industry during two eras. Often treated as a monolith, Brazil's record industry is, in fact, a set of distinct, though often overlapping, spheres. The vast majority of studies about the economics of contemporary Brazilian music deal specifically with a small handful of companies and other "formal" institutions that exercise a great deal of control over music creation and consumption, often glossed as the *indústria fonográfica* (record industry).[2] In this chapter, we propose to break that larger category down into the following subcategories:

a   the (traditional) legacy record industry;

b   the independent record industry;
c   decentralized music scenes;
d   peripheral music scenes.

Our chapter is split into four main sections, one for each category. We develop our taxonomy in dialogue with the past, tracing the outlines of the contemporary market while considering its relationship to the one that preceded it by a century. Between 1877, when Thomas Edison invented the phonograph, and the late 1920s, when new advances ushered in the era of electrical recording, music and the various forms of entrepreneurship and competition that drove it changed in unprecedented ways. Never before had it been possible to "freeze" sound and then release it, theoretically at least, at any time and in any place. These changes, in turn, reshaped the landscape of property and musical commodities, both of which could now more easily be made concrete and lucrative, and unleashed new kinds of entrepreneurship and competition.

Fast-forward a century, and we find a similarly momentous, tumultuous landscape, this one shaped by the internet, file-sharing, and newly accessible recording technology. Between 1999, when the record industry hit a new apex, exemplified by the launch of the album *Millennium* by the Backstreet Boys, which sold more than 1 million copies in its first week of release and established a new record of 11 million CD shipments in one year, and the late 2010s, a lot changed. The record industry continues to face a steep decline in CD sales and the shattering of its traditional business model with new players such as Apple's iTunes stepping into the picture. This, combined with the emergence of file sharing and the decrease of production costs, now accessible to a vast number of home-based studios and producers worldwide, makes today's market as turbulent and full of possibility as the one propelled into existence a century ago.

In considering the past in conversation with the present we try to avoid easy parallels and oversimplified connections. The four categories that we use to describe today's markets are meant to serve as guides rather than straight jackets for discussing the late nineteenth and early twentieth centuries. As we will see, concepts whose definitions are easily taken for granted today had different meanings a century ago. Similarly, various spheres of the music market exist in different forms and share different relationships with each other today. All of this is to say that our taxonomy is offered in the spirit of stimulating further conversation and debate rather than suggesting a fixed or uncontestable framework.

The (traditional) legacy record industry and the first majors

The first subsection of the music market that we investigate is the legacy record industry, which might also be referred to as the traditional record industry. Like legacy industries in other sectors, this one is comprised of a small group of "heavyweight" corporations, in this case the vaunted "majors"—Universal Music Group, Sony Music Entertainment, and Warner Music Group. These multinational companies are the product of an intense process of mergers and acquisitions that accelerated after the advent of the internet and the development of digital technology in the late twentieth century. The record industry was one of the first to face the challenge of rapid disruption caused by the internet and digitization. Napster, a file sharing service created in 1999, caught the industry thoroughly unprepared, and major players had to quickly choose between fight and flight. The Bertelsmann Group, a massive German media conglomerate with stakes in the US majors, announced in May 2002 that it would acquire Napster in an effort to assimilate it as an asset to the record industry. A few months later the deal collapsed because of the copyright lawsuits filed by the other record industry groups. The industry soon consolidated its position to fight file sharing and started to take fierce legal action against internet services and individual users. At the same time, the most powerful companies moved to consolidate their economic positions. In 1998 the so-called "Big Six" – Universal Music Group, Warner Music Group, BMG Music, EMI, Polygram, and Sony Music – dominated the record industry. In 2013, they had been reduced to the "Big Three": Universal, Sony and Warner.

Significantly, the upheaval was the product of innovation that emerged from actors not previously part of the music industry. New services and products like Napster, the iPod and other MP3 players, and iTunes combined with an increasing number of file sharing platforms (Gnutella, Emule, Kazaa etc.) to quickly fill the innovation gap left by a record industry that had stagnated technologically just as consumer demand rose for new services more in line with the internet and digitization.

In many ways, these changes have altered the nature and meaning of competition within the legacy record industry. Universal, Sony, and Warner compete for market shares, but the very nature and idea of the music market has been transformed, and splintered into a number of new business models, only a few of which were being delivered by the legacy record industry. New players – legal and illegal – stepped into the picture to deliver digital content to avid music lovers underserved by the traditional industry. If competition at one point was a relatively straightforward question of a small number of large producers vying to provide goods to consumers, the rise of Napster and other new technologies and products turned the world upside down by creating new goods and services and new kinds of demand for them. Further, over time, innovation within the legacy record industry has been replaced by rent seeking, that is, leveraging intellectual property to control new music products, services or devices. That is not to say that there is no innovation within the legacy record industry. However, in economic terms, it is not central.

This is seen further in the nature of entrepreneurship. Though the internet and other sources of "disruption" have turned music upside down in the last two-plus decades, capital, ownership of musical repertoires, and contractual control of stables of popular musicians all play much greater roles than technological innovation within the legacy record industry. Those who own or control the largest, most profitable portion of these resources are best positioned to dominate and to seek rent from their properties by means of various forms of music licensing.

Today's legacy record industry is hardly the first music sector dominated by a small handful of multi-national conglomerates that leverage capital to control market shares. Indeed, a similar description would be apt for Brazil's original record industry, which formed first as a niche import market serving a small group of affluent elites during the late nineteenth century and then grew steadily (and at times exponentially) after the first Brazilian sound recording in 1902. Today's legacy industry descends from a long line of corporations, technologies, and innovations that originated during this earlier period and that we refer to here as "The First Majors."

At this group's core stood the original "Big Three" – Edison, Victor, and Columbia. Then, as now, competition was intense but highly concentrated among a small number of corporations. However, the means by which the original Big Three arose suggests an important difference between today's legacy industry and the first record companies. Whereas the original Big Three evolved from small enterprises established by inventors, today's majors are, as we have seen, the product (at least in the most immediate sense) of mergers and acquisitions. Mergers and acquisitions also played an important role for the original Big Three, who over time consumed their competition. But while today's firms are propelled by the ability to capture and dominate market shares, technological innovation, above all else, first drove Edison and the others to prominence and success.

During the late nineteenth and early twentieth centuries, technological innovation was entrepreneurship and by extension the main axis of competition. After Edison invented the phonograph in 1877, others scrambled to create their own better machines with improved formats for recording and playing sound. Frustrated that Edison beat him to the punch, Alexander Graham Bell wrote in 1878, "It is a most astonishing thing to me that I could possibly have let this invention slip through my fingers."[3] In the years ahead, Bell, Edison, the German-American inventor Emile Berliner, and other entrepreneurs competed to develop new technology and bring it to market.

Over time, their laboratories and workshops evolved into integrated, multi-national corporations involved not only in recorded sound but also the nascent film industry and other areas. The new technology was so revolutionary that it promised to reach into and change every imaginable aspect of life. "There were," writes Andre Millard, "as many business enterprises as there were uses for recorded sound technology: talking dolls, speaking cash registers, and automatic coin-in-the-slot phonographs which could be used in amusement arcades."[4] Edison and the others endeavored to replicate the models of nineteenth-century magnates like John D. Rockefeller and J.P. Morgan and pursued the same goal as those men: "a monopoly or oligarchy in which a few large companies fixed prices and standardized output."[5] Advertising was crucial. The Big Three spent millions of dollars hawking and trumpeting the superiority of their wares.

Success in the first record industry and today's market depends on the ability to secure and control intellectual property. A century ago, musicians were, in some senses, less important than patents, which firms horded. Edison even resisted putting the performer's name on a recording, including himself instead in order to emphasize the machine and the novelty of his inventions. When many of the original patents for phonographs and gramophones expired in 1917, the First Majors saw their competition multiply dramatically. In 1914, the US had 18 companies in the recorded sound industry. Four years later, there were 166.[6]

The emphasis on patents and intellectual property did not make musicians altogether unimportant; even in the early industry, famous performers gained and wielded great currency, and the large firms were best positioned to sign the biggest stars. Though owning the rights to the newest and most marketable technology was paramount, controlling the rights to songs written or performed by the most popular stars was, too.

Today, aspects of that same structure are still in place, but with one significant difference. When the legacy industry reached a peak in the 1990s, people would stand in line to purchase a new record. Since 1999, lines form more often to purchase new devices, not the music they play. In this sense, today's music industry, writ large, revolves around technology, much as it did a century ago. Crucially, though, more and more of the newest, most desired devices are created, controlled, and sold not, as they once were, by the companies that produce and sell music, and instead by new or outside players. Apple's seemingly endless lineup of must-have hardware is a perfect example of the enduring importance of technological innovation and the legacy industry's ever-slipping grasp on it. Then and now, intellectual property and technological innovation are coins of the realm, but today's majors are as increasingly dependent on musical repertoires as they are seemingly unable to create and control the kind of hardware that the original Big Three were once known for and that today fall more and more under the purview of Apple and other industry "outsiders."

During the early twentieth century, the Big Three expanded its reach across the globe. Edison, Berliner, and others sold their patents to foreign investors and contracted local agents to sell their products. In Brazil and elsewhere, local actors mediated the Big Three's presence. In Rio de Janeiro, the efforts of Fred Figner, a pioneering European immigrant who amassed fabulous wealth, were transformative.[7] Figner recounted in an unpublished memoir that he decided to alight to South America after a fellow traveler in the US told him "Go to Brazil and you'll get rich."[8] Whether true or not, the anecdote captures basic truths about the early international music industry: power and resources were centered in the global north, whose wealthy executives generally viewed the rest of the world as unexplored territory, ripe to be developed into profitable markets. The resulting power relations and economic arrangements were, in fact, much more complex, but there is no doubt that Figner and others – including natural-born Brazilians – who sought to "get rich" in Brazil had to negotiate an unleveled playing field that privileged agents in the US and Europe.

In 1902, ten years after he arrived in Rio, and after a string of frustrated attempts to attract an expert who could help him record Brazilian artists, Figner finally convinced music magnate Frederick Prescott to send a German technician to help make the first recordings on Brazilian soil.[9] Prescott had his hands in all corners of the global music market. He exported Edison's phonographs from New York, which Figner bought in Brazil along with wares traded by other vendors. Prescott also represented Napoleon Petit, the inventor of the two-sided record, an innovation brimming with marketing potential. As Prescott put it to Figner, the new technology would allow him to "give to the public the equivalent of two records for the former price of one."[10] Figner pounced, securing a Brazilian patent for Petit's invention and agreeing to make regular purchases from Prescott. The agreement, and Figner's eventual success in convincing Prescott to provide the means to record music in Brazil, illustrates one important dynamic of Brazil's early music industry. Competition was not simply a matter of foreign interests carving up and dominating new markets. Another component was the wrangling that Figner did to secure relationships with those foreign interests and in doing so beating to the punch other local competitors – for example, record store proprietors Arthur Augusto Villa Martins and Arthur Castilho Natividade de Castro in Rio; Figner's own brother, Gustavo, who founded the Phoenix label in São Paulo; Savério Leonetti in Rio Grande do Sul.

Figner bought from and distributed for the Big Three and its European competitors Zonophone, Odeon, and Fonotipia. His entrepreneurial success depended not only on import contracts but also patents and trademarks, which he both monopolized and evaded. While he proudly advertised his exclusive right to sell Petit's two-sided disc, on other occasions he brazenly ignored others' rights, skillfully navigating the many holes and inefficiencies in the new and evolving legal frontier of intellectual property rights. Figner was also a skilled marketer, who, like Edison, often privileged the power and draw of the machine over musicians and composers. Figner named his Rio de Janeiro store Casa Edison, and the cover of its 1902 catalog featured photographs of Edison and Figner, self-described in bold letters as "Importer of Phonographs, Gramophones, and American Novelties."[11] The cover also displayed US and Brazilian flags, a duality that Figner reproduced on his two-sided discs, which included a national musician on one side and a foreign artist on the other.

Figner's successes and challenges suggest both the similarities and differences between Brazil's first record market and today's legacy industry. In both contexts, success – and the high bar of entry for entering the small circle of competitive players – depended on leveraging capital and controlling song libraries. In the earlier period, technological innovation played a more fundamental role than it does in today's legacy industry, where entrepreneurship is less significant than it was a century ago. The relationship between entrepreneurship and competition also seems to be qualitatively different today than it was a century ago. In vying to conceive, control, and disseminate the latest technological breakthrough, individuals like Edison and Figner made entrepreneurship, technological innovation, and competition one and the same. Today, at least within the legacy industry, innovation has much less to do with entrepreneurship or competition than capital accumulation and the ownership of musical repertoires. This, however, does not mean that we are living in an era void of innovation. To the contrary, and as we have already hinted and will see in more detail below, quite different dynamics govern other market sectors.

Today's independent industry and its semi-independent precursor

The companies that comprise Brazil's contemporary Independent Record Industry for the most part mirror the organizational model of – but should not be confused with – today's three majors. They are called independents because they do not affiliate directly with Universal, Sony, or Warner. Functioning on different scales (small, medium, and even large), independent record companies utilize similar artist contracts and similar production, recording, editing, distribution, and artist development practices as those used by the majors. Though today's independents constitute themselves in all kinds of ways and engage in diverse practices, sometimes acting in partnerships, sometimes hiring third parties, and also by innovating, there are more similarities than differences between independent and legacy companies.

Legacy and independent companies belong to different trade associations. The majors organize themselves in the Brazilian Association of Record Producers, (Associação Brasileira dos Produtores de Disco, ABPD), while most of the independents belong to the Brazilian Association of Independent Music (Associação Brasileira da Música Independente, ABMI), which includes small record companies, labels, and publishers not directly affiliated with the majors. A good example of how independent and legacy companies nonetheless share much in common is seen in the case of the popular label Biscoito Fino.[12] When the majors began to struggle under the pressure of new technologies and forms of listening to and producing music, they started shrinking their list of contracted artists. As a result, big names of MPB (Brazilian Popular Music, Música Popular Brasileira) started fleeing to the independent labels. Biscoito Fino was a primary beneficiary and released new albums by artists such as Maria Bethânia, Daniela Mercury, and Chico Buarque, all luminaries of the Brazilian music.

Historical equivalents for Brazil's independent record industry are slightly more difficult to identify than for today's legacy industry, whose very origins trace to the turn of the twentieth century. Today's independents are defined as such largely because they exist apart from the power players of the legacy industry. At the turn of the twentieth century, such dichotomies did not exist, at least not in the same form. Winners, losers, and power in general changed along with technology, which evolved at a remarkable pace. With inventors and entrepreneurs scrambling to create the newest, best technology and capture markets around the world, the nascent record industry was marked by a degree of fluidity and change not seen today. The original Big Three's place at the top of the food chain was neither predestined nor unopposed. Europe's dominant record companies, especially Zonophone and Odeon, posed credible threats to the US's Big Three, though both were eventually swallowed up by their competitors, with Victor acquiring Zonophone and Columbia buying Odeon. Perhaps, then, an argument could be made to classify Zonophone and Odeon as independents that met the same fate as many similar enterprises today. We resist this temptation because before being acquired the European giants functioned more as equals to the Big Three than plucky outsiders. Because the Big Three was itself an evolving entity, whose primacy was not unchallenged, today's familiar establishment-independent dichotomy was not nearly so clear a century earlier. We opt instead to discuss today's Independent Record Industry in conversation with a group of entities and actors that congealed around (and included) Figner and that, as we explain below, functioned as a powerful, semi-independent sector of the market.

In Brazil, Figner's successful cornering of technology, patents, and trademarks made him the dominant force. Once he began to record Brazilian musicians in 1902, he became, in effect, Brazil's independent record label. In the early teens, Figner established a factory in Rio that produced the first records made entirely in Brazil. But the factory burned down after a few years, and even when it stood the process itself still depended on imported materials and was funded by Odeon.[13] Calling Figner an "independent," then, distorts a more complex reality. His dependence on foreign actors like Prescott and on stages of production located overseas severely limited his autonomy, even despite his expert ability to navigate those relationships. Further, Figner's dominance makes it all but impossible to draw a parallel between even the largest, most powerful independent labels of today and his sprawling domain, which had the look, feel, and domestic reach of the same international firms to which he was often beholden. However paradoxically, Figner's simultaneous dominance and dependence distinguish him from today's independents, and so we choose instead to characterize his empire as powerful and semi-independent.

The dynamics governing Figner's world are illustrated via two turn-of-the-century contracts. In one, signed in 1907, Columbia granted to Figner and his brother the "singular and exclusive" right to sell Columbia phonographs and accessories in all of Brazil, except for the states of Rio Grande do Norte, Ceará, Piauí, Maranhão, Pará, and Amazonas. There, the Figners were still welcome to sell other talking machines, and Columbia was forbidden from selling Brazilian records. A second contract, from 1911, granted A. Campos & Cia., a Figner competitor, the right to sell Columbia graphophones, graphonolas, and discs and accessories in Brazil, with the notable exception of São Paulo, Paraná, Santa Catarina, and a minutely defined area in southern Minas Gerais, which already "belonged" to Gustavo Figner.[14] Like generals dividing up the spoils of war, Figner and Columbia carved up a map of Brazil, staking claim to specific regions. Neither completely dependent on nor free from the powers of the global north, Figner and his competitors were unique products of their time.

The overlap and close relationships between the original Big Three and a powerful semi-independent like Figner made the kind and degree of entrepreneurship in both spheres very similar. In broad terms, the same is true for competition, though a brief discussion will deepen our understanding here. While competition among inventors and the record industry's elite was intense, that competition did not necessarily result in an abundance of choice for consumers, whose options were limited by the arrangements made by Figner and others. Nor, at least as far as we know, did competition dramatically drive down prices. In Brazil's early record industry, owning a talking machine was an exclusive privilege. That being said, the Big Three were certainly not the only game in town, nor was Figner. In addition to European competitors, Brazilian entrepreneurs and labels also vied for space with Figner. This, he once boasted, was of little concern. "I never, not for a single moment, worried about my competitors."[15] Like the "Go the Brazil and you'll get rich" story, this statement may be read as both revelatory and exaggerated. There is no doubt that Figner ruled Brazil's early music industry, and the fact that a number of Figner's competitors were closely tied to him may have given him reason to not fear them. In addition to Figner's brother, Gustavo, oversaw his own empire in São Paulo, Julio Bohm, the founder of the important firm Bohm & Cia., was Figner's brother-in-law. But other labels and firms – including Casa Ao Bogary, E. Bevilacqua & Cia., and Casa Buschman & Guimarães – sold music and machines on which to play it, and therefore represented threats with varying degrees of potency.

At the turn of the twentieth century, the line between the Big Three and others was both pronounced and blurry. The big firms' ability to control new technology cemented their place at the center of the market, but that center was not always as stable or defined as it is today. The category "independent," so recognizable today, makes less sense in that earlier period. Nonetheless, if it does not make sense to talk of an independent record industry in *belle époque* Brazil that does not mean that there were not other vibrant and lucrative musical scenes that existed beyond, and often functioned autonomously from, the nascent world of recorded sound.

Decentralized music scenes

Brazil's contemporary legacy and independent record industries exist alongside a rich collection of decentralized and peripheral music scenes. Today's decentralized scenes arose thanks to the decrease in price and the increase in access to the technical means of production, recording, distribution, and even marketing of music during the late twentieth century – video cameras, personal computers, tablets, high-quality microphones, musical production software and various other necessary inputs that made musical production accessible both in terms of access and price. Such changes allowed new groups and actors the ability to produce and distribute music. The scene they created includes everyday people all over the planet producing musical tracks on their laptops, tablets, or even cell phones. These same actors (and others working in close proximity) also carry out a great part of the distribution and marketing of the music they produce.

The decentralized scene includes a vast number of bands, individual artist, singers and composers that are not affiliated with the majors or with the independent record industry. In many cases they produce music on their own, or with the support of small, independent studios. Most of their works are self-released online. In many cases, artists run things as amateurs, without much consideration to the business side of it, or as micro and small enterprises, with a slightly higher degree of formalization. Much of the work being produced could be characterized as "bedroom music" – the fruit of creative, ambitious young people making music at home and exchanging it online. It is an amateur movement in the sense that many (perhaps most) participants create music less to make money, and more because they love what they do. The level of entrepreneurship is, in principle, low, and there is a lot of cooperation involved in producing and circulating works among vast, informal online networks.

This is not to say that money is entirely absent. The decentralized scene includes electronic music producers who release their tracks directly on online music services such as Beatport, Spotify, and Soundcloud. Some artists do so with the hope or expectation of being contracted by either an independent or major label. The folk singer Mallu Magalhães became a hit artist on MySpace in 2007 with songs she composed and recorded on her own. Sony later hired her, but that happened after she had established herself as an "internet artist." Others have no such goal in mind and prefer instead to conduct their music activities with no strings attached. All are beneficiaries of the technological transformations in the music business initiated from the mid-90s onwards that allow more musicians to produce music on their own terms than perhaps ever before. This includes artists who have dropped the major and independent record companies altogether and taken their careers into their own hands.

Artists in the decentralized music scene take advantage of social networks, instant messengers, websites such as YouTube, torrent-sharing sites, and a new wave of self-management tools enabled by the internet. This is a scene characterized by a great degree of informality, seen, for example, in the frequent appropriation, reappropriation, and remix – sometimes without a proper copyright license – of records whose rights belong to companies in the legacy or independent industries.

Often operating on small scales and in out-of-the-way markets, artists in the decentralized scene are rarely subject to legal or juridical pressure. There is a tolerance for these practices perhaps because it would be practically unviable to effectively rein them in. This is what Lemos calls the power of the "social commons," or, a social milieu in which intellectual property protections are irrelevant, unknown, unviable, or simply unenforced.[16] Significantly, much of the entrepreneurship in the decentralized scene depends on the idea of a "social commons," and if in the future a more effective and efficient system of enforcement of intellectual property is put in place and able to prevent all forms of unauthorized "a priori" use, music scenes like this one will suffer. Music in the decentralized scene grows in the cracks and inconsistencies of existing intellectual property regimes, capitalizing on the opportunities presented by remixing, sampling and the appropriation of third party content to enable their own creations. In other words, many members of this scene see every song ever created as raw material and fair game for inspiration or appropriation. Entrepreneurship here depends on a belief in communal creation and an understanding of property as something that is shared. This is a highly collaborative scene, in which money is not always the primary motivation or engine, and in which members of the scene exchange services, support, production, transportation, marketing and so on among each other, and generally on an informal basis.

Once again, finding a parallel from the turn of the twentieth century is challenging, but not impossible. On one hand, the rise of today's self-produced amateur music may be considered absolutely unique. Never before have so many had so much access to the tools of production and dissemination. On the other hand, journeying back in time to the early twentieth century, one would find a number of Brazilian music scenes not incorporated into (or only loosely affiliated with) any kind of record industry. In Rio de Janeiro, for example, the city's musicians often launched new creations at the Festa da Penha in November, introducing new compositions that they hoped would become popular hits during the Carnival season a few months later. In some cases, this would provide entry into the world of Fred Figner and the larger recorded-sound industry. Competition was fierce, and an entrepreneurial spirit (sometimes but by no mean always connected to technological innovation) was key.

Outside Rio, all kinds of music scenes flourished. In some cases, rising talents made their way to Rio and entered the market centralized there. In other cases, they remained closer to home, building careers in regional and local scenes. And of course there were the countless jam sessions taking place across Brazil in all kinds of contexts. Pixinguinha, Donga, and João da Baiana, three giants of early-twentieth-century Brazilian music, each recall the seemingly endless parade of musicians who gathered in neighborhood homes to play music.[17] In many cases, these were just friends getting together to play, a rough turn-of-the-century equivalent to today's "bedroom" artists. Other times, the line between amateur and professional bled freely and could create no small dose of enmity. Such was the case for "Pelo telefone" (On the Telephone), the foundational 1917 song, often inaccurately described as Brazil's "first samba," that traveled a treacherous path from an ostensibly friendly jam session to a national hit whose provenance is still fiercely debated a century later.[18]

If jam sessions like the ones that created "Pelo telefone" bear a basic resemblance to the "bedroom music" of today's decentralized scenes, a number of differences distinguish them. First, the artists who make up today's decentralized scene often work in isolation, interacting with others online but not as often in person. This is a far cry from the intrinsically social musical gatherings – in many cases, parties – of the past. Second, if recorded sound made it easier for early-twentieth-century listeners in Mato Grosso, for example, to purchase music made in Rio, performers and music flowed less frequently in the other direction. While the revolution that produced recorded sound helped carry music from geopolitical centers to out-of-the-way places, it did much less to democratize access to recording technology, a hallmark of today's decentralized scenes.[19]

Third, there is also a telling difference between the relationships that today's decentralized scenes and those of a century ago share with more centralized institutions. Today, decentralized music has displaced and continues to threaten the legacy industry and independent labels, both of which depend on similar, long-standing norms of access, property, and distribution. Just the opposite was true when recorded sound burst on the scene. In the late nineteenth and early twentieth centuries, Figner, Edison, and other powerful, wealthy inventors, and entrepreneurs "disrupted" music markets and the processes of dissemination and sales, all of which previously relied on some dose or combination of live performance, word of mouth, and written notation. One hundred years later, the legacy and independent industries that those men helped spawn are being overturned and disrupted by processes that decenter and unsettle the same commodity at the center of the original revolution: a song or set of songs tethered to a single physical object (cylinder, record, tape, CD, etc.).

Today's decentralized scenes generally create opportunities for otherwise unknown artists, who gain notoriety and in some cases money. By contrast, while the invention of recorded sound created new prospects and new scales of potential earnings, the number of artists who could profit from those new opportunities was relatively small. The most talented and best connected might become wealthy, but the market's democratic effects were severely limited and carefully mediated by Figner and other gatekeepers. For a musician who enjoyed moderate success and notoriety at the Festa da Penha or in bars around town, the advent of recorded sound and the rivers of cash flowing from it represented a fantastic but all too elusive opportunity. Some artists became centerpieces of Figner's empire. But the vast majority of artists who signed contracts with him recorded just a few songs for which they earned little money.[20] We do not have good economic data (or much economic data of any kind) for the Festa da Penha or other important turn-of-the-century music scenes located outside of Figner's central orbit – popular circuses, or the teatro de revista, for example. But there is no doubt that such scenes flourished before and after the advent of recorded sound, often serving as a training or proving ground that fed into the record industry, sending some of the most popular artists on to recording careers, and in other cases providing visibility and perhaps livelihood for artists who eschewed or were excluded from the record industry but enjoyed success in any number of live settings. The lack of data makes characterizing entrepreneurship and competition in these earlier contexts difficult. It seems reasonable to surmise that musicians in those settings, much like those in today's decentralized scenes, did not necessarily consider a recording contract a primary or even desired goal. And yet there is no doubt that successfully pushing a composition through the Festa da Penha-Carnaval-record contract pipeline was a cherished accomplishment. Our best guess is that today's decentralized scenes are defined by more cooperation and less intense competition than their rough equivalents from a century ago, but further research is needed to make a more definitive conclusion.

Peripheral music scenes

The fourth major component of Brazil's contemporary music market is its vibrant collection of peripheral music scenes. By peripheral we do not mean "marginal" in any sense other than that these scenes are outside the legacy and independent industries. As Lemos has written elsewhere: "the idea of 'periphery'… does not have much to do with a geographical concept. Nor does it have any relation to the separation between rich and poor, developed and developing, or even North and South. These music scenes … emerge in any place where there is a computer, creativity and people wanting to dance."[21]

Most of Brazil's peripheral scenes rose along with the decentralized scenes and thanks to the decreased price of and greater accessibility to the means of musical production and dissemination that allowed individuals to produce, record, launch, develop, and represent artists, their music and products connected to it.

The difference between peripheral and decentralized scenes is a matter of organizational unit and level of entrepreneurship. The peripheral music scene constructs more tightly-knit production arrangements than those found in decentralized scenes and that are, in fact, more along the lines of what we see in the independent and legacy record industry, though put towards different ends and with unique components.

The peripheral scene is more entrepreneurial and more lucrative than the decentralized scene. The two spheres are connected (and, indeed, in previous publications we have treated them as one), but recent developments and this collaborative reflection suggest to us a need to distinguish between them. Though the peripheral scene resembles the decentralized scene in key ways – artists creating music on their own and with no necessary connection to independent or legacy companies – the peripheral scene has come to structure itself in economic terms. There are a number of entrepreneurs who organize parties, buy trucks to transport equipment, sign contracts with musicians, composers and performers, hire dancers for live performances, produce music videos and so on. At the same time, they are not record labels or record companies, and instead self-made entrepreneurs who know as well as any legacy executive that music is good business. Like those who run legacy and independent companies, peripheral artist-entrepreneurs often hire musicians as employees, for example, and pay them a monthly salary. Unlike the more traditional sectors, peripheral artist-entrepreneurs have fully embraced the internet and technology as their key allies and means for distribution. In fact, this peripheral scene only exists because of the internet and digital technology.[22] Another primary characteristic is a significant degree of informality, though few if any of these peripheral scenes are completely informal.

The hallmark elements of the independent and legacy record industry – formal contracts governing author's rights, distribution, and editing – are not found here. Whether due to neglect or because these elements are considered inefficient or excessively bureaucratic, peripheral scenes generally reject them. Instead, flexibility, innovation, and individual entrepreneurship are key currencies. Approaches to intellectual property and author's rights are especially fluid in this arena. In some cases, intellectual property is observed and respected, and in others it is not. Many situations are governed by "tacit" agreements that themselves create modalities of "social commons" in which actors in each scene know that their creations are being appropriated (or are appropriating other creations) but take no action. This is frequently tolerated as part of the *modus operandi* of a given scene and is often, in fact, responsible for its economic and creative vigor. In other words, while the skirting of intellectual property law is often always taboo in the legacy and independent sectors, and in the decentralized scenes it is generally understood as part of an artistic process but not primarily a means to financial success, here it can be a primary entrepreneurial strategy.

From the perspective of entrepreneurship and competition, this is arguably the most exciting scene of all. Brazil's peripheral music scene has created a vibrant and innovative market. This is not your standard "niche market" and instead a multi-million dollar industry that rivals, and perhaps even greatly surpasses, the legacy record industry in Brazil. Since there are no numbers or formal metrics with which to measure its size or market cap, it is hard to gauge the sector's reach. But YouTube views provide grounds for an educated guess, and here peripheral artists often thoroughly outdistance those affiliated with traditional major labels. In Brazil, "peripheral" artists are now some of the most consistent hit makers. In the past few years, the list of breakout peripheral artists is extensive. Just in São Paulo, artists such as MC Daleste, MC Guimê, and more recently, MC Bin Laden have become celebrities and gained massive national audiences.

The peripheral scene also creates large ecosystems of complementary economic activities: video production companies, audio recording studios, transportation networks, booking agents, tour managers, makeup artists, costume designer, internet strategists, and so on. Though all of these things may sound like components of the legacy industry, this is a whole new animal. It is almost as if from the ashes of the old record industry another emerged, one that plays by different rules, embraces rather than fights the internet, digitization and disruption, and that is genuinely "made in Brazil."

A classic example is *Tecnobrega*, a musical scene in the northern state of Pará.[23] As Lemos has shown, Tecnobrega not only operates almost entirely independently of record labels – nearly nine of ten artists have never had any contact with record companies of any kind – but also eschews the elevation of intellectual property above all else. Indeed, much of Tecnobrega's success stems from its reliance on distributing music for free or at little cost, a practice now followed in a number of other sectors and one that hardly limited the music's financial impact, which at the turn of the twenty-first century, Lemos estimates, was as high as US$5 million per month in Belém, the capital of Pará.

Tecnobrega is only one of many peripheral music scenes found all over Brazil: *forró eletrônico* in the northeast; *lambadão cuiabano* in Mato Grosso (in the Center-West); *tchê* music in southern Brazil; *pisadinha*; *carioca funk* from Rio, but popular nation-wide; *reggae maranhense*, from Maranhão (Northeast); *arrocha* (Bahia in the Northeast); and various forms of *sertanejo* music, a rough equivalent to country music. All of these genres have strong connections to peripheral music scenes. In many cases, peripheral artists not only operate separate from any legacy or independent label, but also with no affiliation to the copyright collection organizations that dominate the way that royalties are collected and distributed in Brazil. For a large number of peripheral artists, it is more profitable to make money by touring and receiving revenue share payments from YouTube views than from the collection societies, which for decades shared a tight (though not always amicable) relationship with traditional and independent labels. Another characteristic of the peripheral scene is that its artists generally have little or no presence in the traditional media (newspapers, television, and radio). That absence does not prevent artists from garnering tens of millions of views on YouTube and other internet outlets. To the contrary, it is usually success on the internet that catapults peripheral artists onto the radar of newspapers, television and radio.

When these artists first appear on television, it is the networks that need them, and not the other way around.

Some peripheral artists not only have dialogue with radio, television, and other components of the traditional media but also sign formal distribution agreements with the "majors."

The emphasis on entrepreneurship and financial success by means other than the legacy or independent record industries lend today's peripheral scenes a resemblance to lucrative settings such as Festa da Penha and other popular festivals from the late nineteenth and early twentieth centuries. Though of course without access to the internet or digital technology, Brazil's nineteenth- and early-twentieth century musicians leveraged resourcefulness and creativity in wildly creative and successful ways to carve out semi-professional creative spaces for themselves.

Today's peripheral scenes are distinguished from earlier contexts by the new degree of access to technologies that allow amateurs to create, produce, and capitalize and plug into often-massive transnational networks. These things, more than anything else, distinguish today's peripheral artists from their nineteenth- and early-twentieth-century forebears, who, despite remarkable ingenuity did not have access to the means of recording, production, and dissemination in ways that approximate today's stars of "the periphery."

Interestingly, the way that today's peripheral musicians alternately embrace and skirt intellectual property law resonates not only with practices from decentralized and peripheral scenes from a century ago, but indeed nearly every corner of that early industry. As noted above, Figner flaunted the law as often as he used it to protect his fortune, and the landscape of early intellectual property law resembled a kind of Wild West. Brazil's first significant intellectual property law, passed in 1898, provided only basic provisions and was revised and tinkered with for years to come. Article Six stipulated that in the absence of a contract, the author "is always presumed to be in complete possession of his rights."[24] This was a nice sentiment, but it did little to adjudicate disputes or any number of sticky questions that arise when authorship is contested. This is indicative of the larger milieu that was famously summarized by the great musician Sinhô, credited with first saying, "Samba is like a little bird: it belongs to whoever grabs it."

Today's peripheral scenes are governed by a regime that, at least in theory, both serves individual artists more effectively and, as in the case of the artist MC Daleste, for example, allows them to determine the rules of the game more effectively than many could a century ago. MC Daleste, whose name comes from the Portuguese contraction for "from the East," a reference to São Paulo's massive East Zone, was slain on stage in 2013. Before his death, his work was viewed over 100 million times on YouTube. Remarkably, his massive online presence (complemented by hundreds of thousands of Twitter and Facebook followers) hardly registered in what we might once have called "mainstream" media outlets, a category that loses a great deal of meaning in a case like MC Daleste's, whose "peripheral" presence far outstripped the typical reach of all but the most popular "mainstream" stars. As Lemos writes, MC Daleste is a perfect example of today's "small entrepreneurs who have mastered the art of online promotion" and therefore enter and negotiate stardom with few of the strings or limitations as those operating in the legacy and independent industries.[25]

Conclusions

As the forgoing discussion indicates, none of the categories proposed here are pure or autonomous. Rather, there is a great deal of interrelationship among them, and one scene often adopts the strategies and practices of the next. In sum, the practices of each scene ends up being "remixed" with the practices of the other, thus creating a state of almost permanent transformation of economic, professional, and creative arrangements.

That being said, we propose the following schema (Table 7.1) as a visual short hand for our taxonomy.

In addition to generating future discussion, this taxonomy should point us towards at least three large conclusions about entrepreneurship, competition, and Brazil's music markets. First, when considered together, today's technological innovations and those of the nineteenth and early twentieth centuries suggests an interesting inversion. Where new technology originally willed the record industry into existence, it is now tearing it down. A century ago, innovation, entrepreneurship, and competition were tightly woven strands of the record industry. Though capital and intellectual property have always been important, today they are even more significant in the legacy industry, as it continues to fight for survival as innovation courses around it.

Second, the role of intellectual property is very different for each of these categories. For the legacy record industry, intellectual property rights are a central element. A significant portion of the revenues of the legacy record industry comes from licensing deals to new distribution actors (such as iTunes, or streaming services like Spotify, Apple Music, Pandora, YouTube, and others), and royalty collection from public performance (including radio and TV). In this context, the legacy music industry's historic control over its catalogue by means of intellectual property is an important asset and a key portion of revenue sources. The same is true for the independent record industry.

Intellectual property plays a very different role for the decentralized music scenes and the peripheral music scenes. Neither have any sort of pre-existing "catalogue" on which to rely for revenue or notoriety. Their catalogue is built almost entirely "on the fly" and is infinitely smaller than the ones controlled by the legacy and independent music industries. At the same time, the decentralized and peripheral industries embrace new forms of revenue generation, which include performing in live events, collecting advertising sharing from platforms such as YouTube, touring extensively, engaging in marketing initiatives, and so on. In the decentralized music scene and the peripheral music scene, music artifacts are often treated as some form of "commons," freely shared and distributed online, and treated as raw material for sampling, remixing and other transformative practices.[26] Of course licensing deals, royalty collection and other forms of

Table 7.1 Taxonomy of organization, entrepreneurship, and competition in Brazilian music markets

	Level of formalization	Respect for author's rights	Primary unit	Origin of economic structure	Economic activity estimated by institutional type	Level and kind of entrepreneurship	Level and nature of competition
Today's legacy (traditional) record industry	High	High	Large multi-national conglomerate	Industrial (physical objects)	High	Generally low and limited to a few large corporations with access to massive amounts of capital	High, concentrated
The first majors (19th and early 20th Centuries)	High	Generally high, but with exceptions	Large multi-national conglomerate	Industrial (physical objects)	High	High and tied closely to technological innovation and the control of patents and trademarks	High, concentrated
Today's independent record industry	High	High	National company, formally constituted	Industrial (physical objects)	Low, medium, and high	Similar to the legacy industry, though at times slightly higher	Similar to the legacy industry, though at times slightly higher
Fred Figner's powerful semi-independent industry (19th and early 20th Centuries)	High	Wildly variable: in some cases high, in others blatant disregard	Large multi-national conglomerate and national company, formally constituted	Industrial (physical objects)	High	Similar to the First Majors	High, concentrated
Today's decentralized music scenes	Low	Low (with exceptions)	Individual artist	Internet (digital technology)	Low (with exceptions)	Individual initiative and networking are important, but end goal is rarely financial	Relatively low. Cooperation is as important as competition

	Level of formalization	Respect for author's rights	Primary unit	Origin of economic structure	Economic activity estimated by institutional type	Level and kind of entrepreneurship	Level and nature of competition
Earlier decentralized scenes (19th and early 20th centuries)	Low	Low (with exceptions)	Individual artist	Festivals, private gatherings, sheet music.	Uncertain, but estimated low and medium	Uncertain, but perhaps slightly higher than today's decentralized scenes, though less tied to technology	Uncertain, but perhaps slightly higher than today's decentralized scenes
Today's peripheral music scenes	Low	Low (with exceptions)	Individual artists and hybrid or national companies (non-specialized)	Internet (digital technology)	Low, Medium, and High	High, based on innovation	High. Akin to the levels of competition in the contemporary legacy and independent industries
Peripheral scenes (19th and early 20th centuries)	Low	Low (with exceptions)	Individual artist	Festivals, small commercial establishments, teatro de revista, circuses, sheet music	Estimated high	Estimated high, with multiple financial ends other than record contracts	High. Akin to the levels of competition in the contemporary legacy and independent industries

intellectual property based revenue forms are used in those industries as well. However, they are not their main economic or creative drive. Free cooperation, sharing, remixing, sampling are activities inherent to these music scenes.

Third, there remains much work to be done to fully understand the contours of Brazil's contemporary and historic music markets. Are the four categories proposed here appropriate for the rest of the twentieth century? What about before the advent of recorded sound? And looking to the future, what will the recent restructuring of Brazil's musical intellectual property regime mean for each scene and the role and meaning of entrepreneurship and competition in each? Finally, what will historians of the twenty-second century write when they look back at our current moment, and what categories and units will they use to understand their own era and its relationship to ours?

Notes

1 Personal communication, March 27, 2016: http://study.com/academy/lesson/competitive-market-definition-characteristics-examples.html.
2 This focus is evident, for example, in the influential volume, Morelli, Rita C. L., *Indústria Fonográfica, Um Estudo Antropológico*, Editora Unicamp, 2ª edição (2009), 1ª edição (1991).
3 Millard, Andre. *America on Record: A History of Recorded Sound*, Second Edition (New York: Cambridge University Press, 2005), 26.
4 Ibid., 40.
5 Ibid.
6 Ibid., 72.
7 Further research is needed about other early Brazilian record magnates and the origins of record the industry in São Paulo, Salvador, and elsewhere.
8 Franceschi, Humberto Moraes. *A Casa Edison e seu tempo* (Rio de Janeiro: Sarapuí, 2002), 17.
9 See, Ibid.
10 Hertzman, Marc A. *Making Samba: A New History of Race and Music in Brazil* (Durham: Duke University Press, 2013), 71.
11 Franceschi, *A Casa Edison*, 42.
12 More information about each is found at their respective websites: www.abmi.com.br; www.abpd.org.br; www.biscoitofino.com.br.
13 *Casa Edison e seu tempo*, 195-203, 214.
14 Franceschi, Humberto Moraes. *Registro sonoro por meios mecânicos no Brasil* (Rio de Janeiro: Studio HMF, 1984), 67.
15 *Registro Sonoro*, 31.
16 Lemos, Ronaldo. From Legal Commons to Social Commons. http://www.area-studies.ox.ac.uk/sites/sias/files/documents/R.%2520Lemos80.pdf
17 Antônio Barroso Fernandes, ed. *As vozes desassombradas do museu: extraido dos depoimentos para a posteridade realizados no Museu da Image e do Som* (Rio de Janeiro: Museu da Imagem e do Som, 1970).
18 Hertzman discusses this in *Making Samba*.
19 Of course, recorded sound also facilitated music "gathering" projects such as those led by Mário de Andrade, for example, or the Lomax brothers, in the U.S. Though this kind of project aimed to move music from margin to center, its focus on "preservation" and collection distinguish it from the decentralized scenes under consideration here, both of which disseminate music widely and informally.
20 See, Hertzman, *Making Samba*, 73–77.

21 "To Kill an MC: Brazil's new music and its discontents" in *Postcolonial Piracy: Media Distribution and Cultural Production in the Global South*, Lars Eckstein and Anja Schwarz, eds. (London: Bloomsbury, 2014), 197. Available at: https://publishup.uni-potsdam.de/opus4-ubp/files/7218/ppr89.pdf.

22 For a full account of this scene, see, Lemos, "To Kill an MC."

23 Lemos, Ronaldo, and Castro Oona. *Tecnobrega: O Pará reinventando o negócio da música* (Rio de Janeiro: Aeroplano, 2009).

24 http://legis.senado.leg.br/legislacao/ListaPublicacoes.action?id=60815&tipo Documento= LEI&tipoTexto=PUB. Accessed August 15, 2016.

25 Lemos, "To Kill an MC," 201.

26 For a more comprehensive description of IP rights in the context of the decentralized and peripheral music scenes, please see Mizukami, Pedro Nicoletti, and Ronaldo Lemos, "From Free Software to Free Culture: The Emergence of Open Business, in Access to Knowledge in Brazil," in *Access to Knowledge in Brazil: New Research on Intellectual Property, Innovation and Development*, Lea Shaver, ed. (New Haven: Yale Law School, 2008), 25–66, available at http://isp.yale.edu/sites/default/files/publications/A2KBrazil_bkmk.pdf. The terminology in that article is different, since the terms "peripheral" and "decentralized" music scenes are not employed in it, but the subject matter analyzed is the very same one referred to by these terms.

References

Fernandes, Antônio Barroso, ed. *As vozes desassombradas do museu: extraido dos depoimentos para a posteridade realizados no Museu da Image e do Som* (Rio de Janeiro: Museu da Imagem e do Som, 1970).

Franceschi, Humberto Moraes. *A Casa Edison e seu tempo* (Rio de Janeiro: Sarapuí, 2002).

——. *Registro sonoro por meios mecânicos no Brasil* (Rio de Janeiro: Studio HMF, 1984).

Hertzman, Marc A. *Making Samba: A New History of Race and Music in Brazil* (Durham: Duke University Press, 2013).

Lemos, Ronaldo. "From Legal Commons to Social Commons." www.area-studies.ox.ac.uk/sites/sias/files/documents/R.%2520Lemos80.pdf

——. "To Kill an MC: Brazil's new music and its discontents" in *Postcolonial Piracy: Media Distribution and Cultural Production in the Global South*, Lars Eckstein and Anja Schwarz, eds. (London: Bloomsbury, 2014), 197. Available at: https://publishup.uni-potsdam.de/opus4-ubp/files/7218/ppr89.pdf.

Lemos, Ronaldo, and Castro Oona. *Tecnobrega: O Pará reinventando o negócio da música* (Rio de Janeiro: Aeroplano, 2009).

Millard, Andre. *America on Record: A History of Recorded Sound*, Second Edition (New York: Cambridge University Press, 2005), 26.

Mizukami, Pedro Nicoletti, and Ronaldo Lemos, "From Free Software to Free Culture: The Emergence of Open Business, in Access to Knowledge in Brazil," in *Access to Knowledge in Brazil: New Research on Intellectual Property, Innovation and Development*, Lea Shaver, ed. (New Haven: Yale Law School, 2008), 25–66, available at http://isp.yale.edu/sites/default/files/publications/A2KBrazil_bkmk.pdf.

Morelli, Rita C. L., *Indústria Fonográfica, Um Estudo Antropológico*, Editora Unicamp, 2ª edição (2009), 1ª edição (1991).

Websites

http://legis.senado.leg.br
http://study.com
www.abmi.com.br
www.abpd.org.br
www.biscoitofino.com.br

8 Nationalism and the development of the Brazilian steel industry

Jerry Dávila

> The country, or productive sector, that does not plan its economy, in terms of legitimate national interest, is at the mercy of the planning of other parties… Without [industrial development] the adequate use of the resources of our nation's territory would be impossible, and the integration of our People into the rhythm of modern progress would not be achieved with the necessary speed. Industry is a formidable tool that must be managed to the benefit of national economic growth.
>
> Edmundo de Macedo Soares, on becoming president of
> Brazil's National Confederation of Industry, 1964[1]

In the twentieth-century world, few industrial sectors seemed more important than steel to the process of national economic development. The development of a national steel industry was not just a core element of the process of industrialization, it was a symbol of national progress, sovereignty, and national security. Steel's significance was rivaled only by that of oil. From an economic standpoint, a steel industry in Brazil would transform the nation's abundant natural resources, and would provide material for other industrial sectors – especially automotive manufacturing – feeding a policy of import-substitution industrialization. In the decades following the First World War, the development of a national steel industry became a fundamental concern of nationalists and of the armed forces. Witnessing industrialized and mechanized warfare in Europe, those nationalists and officers came to believe that Brazil could only persevere in a military conflict if it possessed an industrial capacity capable of waging that kind of war. This set of approaches – economic developmentalism, nationalism, and national security thought – combined to shape a distinctive trajectory for developing Brazil's steel industry. This trajectory favored a strong hand for the state, limits to foreign firms, and a heavy role for the armed forces.

This chapter focuses on the intersection between nationalist ideology and state policy around the creation of Brazil's domestic steel industry. It explores the perceptions that shaped industrial policy and defined the trajectory for the development of Brazil's complex of large steel mills, first by stalling the entrance of foreign investment and later by pursuing a state-controlled project heavily shaped by military officers and their emerging thinking about national security.

Werner Baer and the question of the Brazilian steel industry

The idea that the national expression of the development of the steel industry in Brazil needed to be understood within its specific historical, political and economic context formed the basis of Werner Baer's approach to *The Development of the Brazilian Steel Industry*, published in 1969. Baer's study interlaced thick readings of Brazilian history and of the technical and engineering dimensions of steel manufacturing in order to interpret the experience with economic development as one that is locally grounded and dependent on a convergence of historical, political, economic and technological factors.

Baer's approach opened new interpretive directions. He considered the role of nationalist thought and ideology in framing the perceptions of opportunities and constraints that shaped the emergence of Brazil's steel sector. As Baer argued, "the Brazilian experience in establishing a steel industry should make it clear that the usual condescending cliché about the wastefulness of implanting a heavy industry in a developing country has no universality."[2] In making this case, he challenged critics of nationalist economic policymaking such as economist Harry Johnson, who argued that "Nationalism tends to emphasize investment in visible symbols of development – large irrigation projects rather than individual wells, large new modern factories rather than improvements to old factories – in preference to less visible but frequently more socially profitable types of investment."[3]

In *The Development of the Brazilian Steel Industry*, Baer challenged this view by bringing the politics of industrial development into dialogue with a set of factors that ranged form the requirements for different kinds of steel production techniques employed in the early twentieth century, to the raw material requirements and their Brazilian context, and the limits to the demand for steel in a country that still had an agrarian economy. He emphasized the significance of changes in Brazil's changing political culture, which in the 1930s overcame the reluctance to have the state finance and lead the development of the steel industry. In doing this, Baer pursued a context-driven approach to economics that guided his subsequent work and frames the studies in this volume.

For Baer, there were questions that "can only be answered by individual industry studies." Seeking to understand industrialization in rural economies, he asked: "How fast do factors of production adapt to new technology? How fast can costs be brought down to competitive levels? How long does the new industry have to be protected? To what extent is the dearth of skilled manpower and managerial personnel a bottleneck for new industries?"[4] What he found is that in the Brazilian case, small-scale experience with steel production had prepared a sufficient labor force of technicians to pursue the development of a national steel industry; the context of the Second World War created the opportunity to import technology and for the state to finance the development of the industry; and the availability of coal, iron ore and other minerals close to Brazil's major industrial cities and ports, all facilitated the development of an efficient and effective steel industry. Baer also found the timing of the development of the industry fortuitous because it allowed for the "early vertical integration of Brazil's industrial complex, that is, the creation of a whole contingent of heavier industries accompanying the development of consumer-goods industries."[5]

Nationalism and Steel in the trajectory of Edmundo de Macedo Soares

This chapter explores the confluence of nationalist ideology and planning that sparked the state intervention in Brazil's industrialization that Werner Baer analyzed. This nationalist ideology incorporated influences ranging from the thinking of jurist Alberto Torres (1865–1917), who advocated for the creation of a strong central state capable of implementing solutions to perceived national problems; the influence of European and, more specifically, French nationalism in the aftermath of the First World War in conceptualizing the integration of industries; and the strain of nationalism and regionalism among Brazilian political leaders who were wary of foreign ownership of mineral resources and major industries. The chapter especially focuses on the thinking of Edmundo de Macedo Soares, the central actor in the planning and development of Brazil's state-owned complex called the National Steel Company – Companhia Siderúrgica Nacional, or CSN.

Macedo Soares (1901–1989) was an army officer who studied metallurgy in the 1920s. After Getúlio Vargas came to power in Brazil in 1930, Macedo Soares returned and participated in a succession of commissions studying the potential for the development of a steel industry in Brazil. The opportunity for doing this came through the terms by which Vargas negotiated Brazil's alliance with the United States in the Second World War. In return for land leases for airbases, and the deployment of Brazilian troops alongside the US 5th Army in Italy, the US government provided financing and technical expertise for building a national steel complex. Macedo Soares became technical director of the US-financed steel complex being built in Volta Redonda and oversaw its construction.[6]

After the armed forces deposed Vargas in 1945, Macedo Soares served as federal Minister of Transportation and Public Works and was appointed governor of Rio de Janeiro state, where the Volta Redonda CSN complex was located. He became director of a new state-owned motor factory, a critical piece of Brazil's nascent automotive industry. After he retired from active duty in 1952, General Macedo Soares circulated through the boards of directors of the diversifying array state companies and multinational firms that formed part of Brazil's growing steel industry and heavy manufacturing. He participated in planning commissions and took on his first private sector role as vice-president of Mercedes-Benz of Brazil, a pioneer in domestic truck manufacturing.[7]

Macedo Soares supported the 1964 coup and under military rule continued to shape the realm of planning commissions, state-owned enterprises, private corporations and associations of industrialists that defined Brazil's industrial sector. He headed the powerful Industrial Federation of São Paulo and the National Confederation of Industry. Later he served as Minister of Industry and Commerce from 1967 to 1969, the years in which the military regime extended its rule indefinitely and suppressed civil liberties. In 1969, Macedo Soares returned to the private sector, becoming president of Mercedes Benz of Brazil. For the remainder of his career, he would serve on the boards of some of the largest manufacturers in Brazil, ranging from Mercedes to General Electric and Volkswagen. During the decades after the Second World War in which Brazilian industrialization accelerated and in which the steel industry became a hub of that process, no one was a more central figure in either public or private industrial enterprise.

Macedo-Soares' trajectory from the armed forces into a succession of roles directing and coordinating Brazil's steel industry and Baer's "contingent of heavier industries accompanying the development of consumer-goods industries," originated in a spark of nationalism that gripped junior military officers in 1920s Brazil.[8] Beginning with the centenary of Brazil's independence in 1922, a succession of revolts were carried out by junior military officers, known as the Tenente ("Lieutenant") Revolts. The Tenentistas, as the rebels were known, were nationalists who decried the condition of Brazil and demanded strong state intervention in areas ranging from political reforms fighting corruption, instituting the secret ballot and protections for freedom of the press, to efforts to transform the decentralized government into a stronger force for national development, especially in public education. The longtime leader of Brazil's Communist Party, Luis Carlos Prestes, emerged from the Tenente Revolt, as did many major figures of the Getúlio Vargas regime after 1930.

Twenty-one year old Lieutenant Macedo Soares took part in the first of these revolts. Describing his mindset and that of his peers, he explained: "The military youth to which I belonged as a lieutenant… suffered with the ruinous decadence that was scandalously witnessed by Brazilians… No one thought about changing the regime, but in remodeling it – 'republicanizing the Republic'… [Our] ideal was to create a grand cohort of technicians and seek to change the economic structure of the country."[9] After participating in the first revolt in 1922, Macedo Soares was jailed and served a prison sentence at the penal colony on Ilha Grande, an island near the city of Rio de Janeiro which he escaped from in a canoe in 1925. His family sent him to France, where he studied metallurgy.

In France, Macedo Soares was exposed to the psychological, economic and political effects of the First World War. He visited the battlefield of Verdun, and had classmates who were veterans. During his time in France, he was struck by the discourse of André Tardieu, a politician who was Minister of Commerce, who spoke of the need for industrial renewal after the war, calling France's factories "the factors that make a country." For Macedo Soares, "that reinforced what I already thought in regards to Brazil, meaning, the need for industrialization."[10]

Nationalist restrictions on mining and the steel industry in the 1920s

Brazilian President Artur Bernardes (1922–1926), against whose government the Tenentes had revolted in 1922, brought an early nationalist resistance to the development of a steel industry by foreign firms. Bernardes' approach was evocative of the kinds of federal policies the Tenentes decried: he stalled industrialization using foreign capital without pursuing a mechanism, such as state financing or a state firm, which would induce development. His stance had been developed in his previous tenure as President (Governor) of the state of Minas Gerais, where much of Brazil's iron ore was concentrated. He had challenged the rights to steel production of the Itabira Iron Ore Co., owned by a foreigner and railroad tycoon, Percival Farquhar, who was from the United States. Bernardes' opposition to the Itabira project had to do with Farquhar's model that relied on heavy exports of iron ore to defray investment in constructing the Itabira steel mill and the importation of coal. Macedo Soares also believed that part of Bernardes' opposition stemmed from a further regionalist resentment that the Farquhar plan called for the Itabira mill to be built in Três Rios, Rio de Janeiro rather than in Minas Gerais, where the ore and Bernardes' political base were located.[11]

In 1922, as President of Brazil, Bernardes blocked Farquhar's project by imposing a tax on the export of iron ore. In 1926 he enacted a revision of Brazil's constitution that prohibited foreign ownership of subsoil mineral rights. The clause of the revised constitution read: "Mines and mineral deposits that are necessary for national security and defense, and the lands where they exist may not be transferred to foreigners."[12] Brazil's 1891 Constitution was a liberal document that took pains not to place limits on private property or foreign ownership. Bernardes' revision was deliberately illiberal. He argued: "The equality of rights of foreigners and citizens could not have the absolute character that the letter of the Constitution prescribes... [that] would act fatally against the Country's security and against the very future of the nation... The ownership and exploitation of mines is a grave and preeminent problem, since their products, in the majority of cases, are of interest to national defense. Their exploitation, without supervision from the national government, can present a serious risk to prosperity."[13]

Bernardes' concern with subsoil mineral rights reflected both nationalist and regionalist tendencies. The opposition to foreign firms dated to Bernardes' tenure as state president, when he envisioned local, state-centered development of the steel industry. But the question of domestic rather than foreign ownership of subsoil mineral rights was an idea that had gained currency in Latin America since the First World War. Mexico's 1917 Constitution included that prohibition, and its application led to the nationalization of the Standard Oil wells and refineries that created the state oil monopoly PEMEX in 1938. This was followed by Venezuela's 1943 Hydrocarbons Law, which transferred 50 percent of the profits from the Rockefeller family's Creole Petroleum.

The 1953 creation of the Brazilian oil monopoly Petrobrás reflected not only the ongoing resonance of the question of mineral rights in Brazil, but the configuration of Petrobrás and the oil sector in Brazil further reflected the paradigms that guided the formation of the steel industry: a state firm controlled the major development of the industry (for oil, this was extraction and most refining), while private firms, many foreign-owned operated on a smaller scale in specialized areas (for oil, this meant refining and distribution).[14]

What Bernardes' restrictions had the effect of doing was to prevent foreign firms from constructing large steel mills in Brazil in the 1920s. As an agrarian society, Brazil consumed limited amounts of steel, and Brazilian firms generally lacked the capital and did not possess the technology for developing large, modern mills. Foreign firms like Itabira Iron Ore could build mills (and steel manufacturing made sense for Farquhar, since his railroad construction in Brazil consumed large amounts of steel), but depended upon the export of iron ore to finance the construction and operation of the mill. Whether he realized it or not, Bernardes created conditions in which only the state would have the legal capacity and the access to capital necessary to construct a steel mill of the scale established at Volta Redonda.

Nationalist thought: Alberto Torres and Macedo Soares

Jurist Alberto Torres was one of the major intellectual architects of Brazil's First Republic (1889–1930) and a prominent abolitionist. He had served as Minister of Justice, helping institute the liberal constitution of 1891, and later was governor of Rio de Janeiro and a justice of the Supreme Court. But Torres ended his life a disaffected critic of that regime. Between 1911 and 1914, Torres published a series of essays decrying the failures of the regime and of Brazil's elites in meeting national needs. He advocated for the creation of a strong state and a deepened nationalist consciousness. He disdained the kind of political self-dealing and insularity of political leaders of the republican regime, figures like the Artur Bernardes the Tenentes defied.

Torres described Brazil's politics as "a flowery game of theories laid out over a field of miserable realities."[15] Torres reached the conclusion that: "We have been a country that lacks: economic organization and education, capital, credit, an organized workforce, politics adapted to the means and ways of the population: in sum [we are] an ungoverned country."[16] While not pining for a return to slavery – Torres had been an abolitionist – he was nonetheless dismayed with the economic and political stagnation that followed: "Slavery was one of the few things by way of organization that this country has ever possessed... Socially and economically, slavery gave us, for many years, all of the labor and all of the order that we possessed, and is the basis of all of the material production that we still have." In its absence, "having destroyed the rudiments of organization we once had, we've set off on bad ground, nothing has worked out, and the façade of our civilization conceals a reality of total disorder."[17]

With regard to industrialization, one of Torres' main interpreters, Barbosa Lima Sobrinho declared: "In an underdeveloped or undeveloped country, only state initiative can lay the foundations for an independent economic structure. But for that to happen, it is necessary for the underdeveloped to begin an effort of liberation, clearing the path of doctrines created for others, in the tailor-shops of the supposed economic sciences, sciences conditioned to the social and economic context for which they are intended, as are all political sciences."[18] Torres rejected laissez-faire liberalism as a doctrine created by and serving the interests of others, particularly in Europe, and called on Brazilians to chart their own course of national development through state intervention.

After Torres' death in 1917, his critique of the Republican regime became the ideological meeting point for a generation of nationalists including many of the Tenentistas. A network of reading circles called the Society of Friends of Alberto Torres, whose participants gathered to discuss Torres' ideas and relate them to national problems and state policy. Macedo Soares cited Torres' influence over his own thinking on different occasions. He explained "Some nationalist thinkers had great influence over my generation. Alberto Torres, for example. I have all his books here at home. Another was Oliveira Vianna [a disciple of Alberto Torres, though he diverged from his mentor by holding openly racist views]; we read all his books. Both influenced that generation a great deal, especially in the armed forces."[19]

Macedo Soares' reflections on industrialization and political consciousness closely echoed those of Torres. In 1964, he declared "the industrialization of a country means the formation of a [national] consciousness. The history of industrial development shows us that. It can be accelerated by action from the top, carried out by 'elites,' in countries where free initiative prevails, or through government action, where the influence of the State predominates. In the first case, the government also acts, given that it is composed in large part of the dominant classes."[20]

Reflecting in 1983 at his career trajectory in the armed forces and in industry, Macedo Soares spoke of what he saw as Brazil's needs. He echoed Torres almost verbatim in his critique of Brazil's First Republic: "the country was stagnated in time, since the abolition of slavery and the proclamation of the First Republic. You couldn't feel the pulse of statesmen capable of the foresight to bring Brazil out the prostrate apathy it wallowed in... Eminent men emerged, but none saw Brazil as a state capable of progress in a manner similar to Europe or even Argentina. 'Brazil was just essentially agrarian' they said."[21]

This discussion, about the difference between countries that had the capacity for autonomous industrialization driven by free enterprise and countries that did not, echoed the Marxist dependency theory that many economists and intellectuals in mid-century Brazil employed to diagnose the country's economic state and prescribe steps for accelerating industrialization. Macedo Soares' line of thought resembled the Marxist interpretation of Brazilian history by Caio Prado, Jr., whose 1942 *Formação do Brasil Contemporâneo – Colônia* made the case that Brazil's economy had always been organized around a colonial model of production for export that inhibited the formation of internal markets.[22] As a result, Macedo Soares argued, "Brazilian industrialization was retarded and we did not have the leap of progress that the United States experienced."[23] Macedo Soares elaborated:

> The concern with economic development, and the succession of problems that must be overcome to achieve it, has generated debate within undeveloped countries about the right limits for the participation of the State in the process of accelerating that development. The debate, when rationally conducted,

certainly concludes in favor of accepting a greater degree of intervention than would be acceptable for countries where the process occurs automatically. And, assuredly, the right criterion for delimiting public and private activity should be the greatest functional efficiency with a mind to economic development, but reserving exclusively to the State, for obvious reasons, the area related to national security. In countries with an economic stage and structure like Brazil, State intervention can be accepted for the reason that its economic development is induced and not autonomous.[24]

Macedo Soares' emphasis on the national security implications of state-induced development departed from the line of thought pursued by dependency theorists. It returned to the kinds of reasoning that Alberto Torres had laid out. Torres had envisioned an "organic" relationship between the state and segments of society, closely aligned around national goals.

For Macedo Soares, the central role of a strong state was related to his belief that a close connection between industry and the armed forces was a necessity: "National Security depends fundamentally on the support of a civilian industry capable of equipping and supplying the Armed Forces, and these in turn are more conscious of their role in national life the more intimately they are connected to industry. It is the responsibility of the industrial leadership to maintain an intimate coexistence with the national military complex."[25] His emphasis on the link between industrialization and national security also reflected the mindset within the members of Macedo Soares' generation in Brazil's officer corps. It was this generation which seized national power in the 1964 military coup that ushered in both the longest military dictatorship in South America. And this generation and regime launched a cycle of accelerated economic growth characterized by intensified state planning and state participation in business, industry and finance, which depended increasingly on foreign loans and resulted ultimately in Brazil's worst economic collapse, the debt crisis of the 1980s.

Nationalism and Brazilian steel

We can trace three specific strains of nationalism influencing the formation of Brazil's steel industry. The first is what we could call, somewhat ironically, regionalist nationalism, reflected in the actions and rhetoric of Artur Bernardes. Both as president of Minas Gerais and President of Brazil, he resisted any model of steel development that entailed the export of the iron ore deposits in his home state. This strain of nationalism had two consequences: first, it delayed the development of the steel industry by substantially eliminating foreign firms and investors from participating in steel mill construction; and second, as a result, the remaining options for developing a steel industry relied on state investment and state ownership, neither of which were possibilities for the largely laissez-faire and highly decentralized regime of the First Republic.

Two other strains of nationalism converged to make the construction of Brazil's first major steel mill complex possible: the nationalist strain that emerged from

Alberto Torres' thought, and called for a strong hand of a centralizing state to accomplish national objectives that had eluded Brazil; and its corollary nationalism within the armed forces which linked those goals to strengthening national security. Macedo Soares recalled opposing that first strain of regionalist nationalism when he was a Tenente opposed to Bernardes. With regard to the question of foreign ownership, "we were divided. There were those who were opposed to foreign capital, but I was not one of them. I already had the sense that this kind of capital was necessary for development."[26] Nonetheless, in the wake of the policies of Bernardes and other political leaders of Brazil's first republic, the possibilities which remained were Torres' statist nationalism and the armed forces' security nationalism, both of which were compatible with the worldview of Macedo Soares, and more significantly, became the foundations of the Vargas regime.

In 1930, Getúlio Vargas was brought to power in a military coup known as the Revolution of 1930. He held the support of liberal elites disaffected with the concentration of political power in the hands of the Republican Parties of Minas Gerais and São Paulo. That political coalition's concern with accelerating economic development was not well developed in 1930. But over the course of the next 15 years of increasingly authoritarian power, culminating in the Estado Novo dictatorship of 1937 to 1945, the Vargas regime absorbed and applied many of the nationalist and strong-state ideals coined by Torres and espoused by his disciples. Alberto Torres had not defined accelerated industrialization as a priority: he focused his attention on more rational and intense engagement in agriculture. But among his followers, especially in the armed forces, accelerated development, focusing on heavy industries capable of sustaining a war effort, became an increasingly focused goal.

Many former Tenentistas were drawn into government. Among them was Edmundo de Macedo Soares, who was called upon to serve on a series of commissions intended to make plans for an eventual steel mill complex, as well as the infrastructure necessary to support it. In addition he taught metallurgy at the Army School of Engineering. The industrial limits to Brazil's military capacity were at odds with what junior officers perceived to be Brazil's needs in the aftermath of the First World War, which placed the importance of heavy industry in support of the war efforts of each belligerent nation on full display. Macedo Soares observed that:

> The Army always had a great interest in developing steel. We thought that a country that did not have iron could not have agriculture, because machines were needed to work the fields, and it could not have armaments; we specifically focused on the manufacture of machines and armaments, so much so that I participated in the commission that organized the munitions factory of Andaraí, in Rio… One of the goals of the Army School of Engineering was to have a faculty chair in armaments, based on my chair in metallurgy. In the Army, we believed that Brazil, even if it did not face war, should be adequately supplying its own arms, in order to not fall into dependency on other countries.

As the Latin phrase goes: *"Si vis pacem, para bellum,"* in other words, "If you want peace, prepare for war."[27]

The consequence of the Army's focus on steel and industrialization is that when the opportunity to build Brazil's first large mill presented itself, it was the accumulated capacity of the Army, personified in the experience of Macedo Soares, that gave shape to the mill.

In the late 1930s, it was this combination of military planning, increased centralization of the authoritarian Estado Novo state, and the looming Second World War which converged to make the construction of Brazil's first large steel mill possible. In the late 1930s, Macedo Soares traveled extensively in Europe and the United States to study steel complexes in different countries. He spent time in Nazi Germany, and was interested in the combination of refining technology and use of hydroelectric power he saw in Sweden. He also saw the potential for working with the US, both the US government as well as with US steel conglomerates, to finance the importation of equipment, the development of the steel complex, and the technical expertise necessary to bring it into operation.

In the geopolitical environment created by the looming war, the fascistic appearance of Vargas' Estado Novo, along with entreaties from Germany, prompted the US government to pursue a wartime alliance with Brazil that would give the United States access to Brazilian raw materials as well as the possibility to establish air bases in the Brazilian northeast and to use Brazilian ports for Atlantic naval patrols. This alliance deepened diplomatically and militarily as the US entered the war, defining a role for Brazil as a guarantor of an alliance between other Latin American nations and the United States as well as a combat role for the Brazilian Army alongside the US Army in Europe.

The wartime alliance created the conditions under which the US Export-Import bank financed the Brazilian purchase of the equipment needed to build a steel mill complex as well as the support of US steel companies in providing equipment and technical assistance. The other component of the project to develop the mill entailed the domestic political conditions for the project in Brazil. Macedo Soares recalled Vargas' thinking on the political context in Brazil: "Getúlio always said that it was necessary to resolve everything that big steel called for without Congress functioning [it had been dissolved by the 1937 Estado Novo constitution], because with the deputies and senators in action, there would be an immediate struggle over the site for the mill, the size of the mill, in the end nothing would happen."[28] This logic, like Vargas' Estado Novo regime, served as a bridge connecting the implicitly authoritarian critique that Alberto Torres made of Brazil's political system, with the later experience of authoritarian rule at the hands of the armed forces – including Macedo Soares – between 1964 and 1985.

With financing in place and equipment on order for the construction of Brazil's first large steel mill, the Vargas regime settled on the site of Volta Redonda, in Rio de Janeiro near the borders with São Paulo and Minas Gerais, as the location for constructing a state-owned Companhia Siderúrgica Nacional. As construction got underway, Macedo Soares hailed the achievement in: "Brazil will soon have a great steel mill with metallurgical coke. The negotiations carried out to good effect in the United States guarantee us the amount in dollars necessary for acquiring the equipment destined to executing the first phase of the operation... We must first stress that the mill will be built and operated by a Brazilian company, with Brazilian capital... The fact that it is a Brazilian company is a great conquest. Base industries must be oriented toward exclusively national objectives. The association of alien capital in its formation can often result in conflicts and misunderstanding."[29] The motor force for the construction of Volta Redonda had been nationalism – both in its political form expressed in the authoritarian Estado Novo and in its military form expressed as a means of advancing national security.

The CSN's location at Volta Redonda, the networks of infrastructure such as rail lines connecting coal reserves in southern Brazil and ore in Minas, the training of workers, and technical questions such as the importation scrap metal needed in the milling process, were all aided by the planning that had taken place in the Army over the preceding decade. Macedo Soares became the technical director overseeing the construction of the mill at Volta Redonda. He oversaw a process through which converging nationalist objectives and a specific political culture created the conditions for building Volta Redonda as a state-owned firm. As Baer observed:

> The pressure throughout the 1930s for the establishment of a large, integrated steel mill which finally resulted in the creation of Volta Redonda shows that those elements of Brazilian society that believed in the long-run future of Brazil as an industrial country thought of the steel industry as a natural element in a growing industrial complex... the Brazilian government only reluctantly came into the picture when it became clear that private foreign capital would not finance the establishment of large, integrated mills. The steel industry's example thus provides a clear case of a situation wherein the natural resource endowment and the market (given the general industrialization process) made the creation of large-scale steel establishments a viable undertaking, but where the socioeconomic development of the country was still such that private institutions did not exist to assemble the needed capital and provide the organization necessary for such an undertaking.[30]

It was Macedo Soares who played the central role in this process. After overseeing Volta Redonda's construction, he would be appointed Minister of Transportation and Public Works and then Governor of the State of Rio de Janeiro, positions that allowed him to attend to the state infrastructure needs of the project. He retired from the Army at the rank of general in 1952. From this point on, he circulated through the directorships of state, national and multinational companies that would turn the steel produced at Volta Redonda into intermediate and finished goods. This trajectory began at the state-owned National Motor Factory, and continued to Mercedes Benz and other firms.

Conclusion

According to Macedo Soares, "in 1949, the Brazilian federal government held 30 companies… State governments held another 34. In 1978, the number of state firms was 584, of which 186 belonged to the federal government… These state firms hold tremendous importance in mining, steel, chemical and petrochemical products, and dominate energy production, transportation and telecommunications." Macedo Soares was not unaware of the irony that "state intervention in the Brazilian economy grew strongly after 1964, the period in which the architects of policy were great advocates of the free market." Macedo Soares credited this to the need to right the economy after the coup. Though no less significant in fact was the mindset of the armed forces, which was consistently nationalist and quick to reach for solutions involving the state.[31]

It is no coincidence that the longest military dictatorship in Latin America occurred in Brazil, or that the leaders of this regime pursued economic development and industrialization as national security goals. The armed forces, which had repeatedly intervened in politics before 1964 held a nationalist mindset that ultimately led to the belief that only they could solve national problems. It is also no coincidence that this dictatorship was a regime built by the generation that became politically and ideologically aware amid the Tenente Revolts of the 1920s. This was Macedo Soares' generation, and he was an integral part of not just the thinking that led to military rule, but also its consolidation and administration. As Minister of Industry in 1968, Macedo Soares was a signator of Institutional Act 5, which suspended most civil liberties and gave the military regime broad authoritarian powers. This was the context in which Werner Baer wrote his study of the Brazilian steel industry and wrote it with an emphasis on the idea that the political and historical contexts mattered.

In the case of the steel industry, that context was one that incorporated a profound shift in political culture that intensely affected the armed forces. The question of developing steel responded not only to economic circumstances, but also and more immediately to a nationalist critique first articulated by Alberto Torres and taken up by disciples such as Macedo Soares. Writing in 1983, during the end of the cycle of military rule, and reflecting on the previous moment of authoritarian state building under Getúlio Vargas, brought to power in the Revolution of 1930, Macedo Soares reflected on Brazil's industrial development since that Vargas regime within which he coordinated the construction of the CSN: "All of that great transformation was the consequence of the Revolution of 1930. It was worth it."[32]

Macedo Soares' technocratic vision of industrial advance carried out by skilled technicians working in an authoritarian context resonated with the era of military rule in which he spoke; he acknowledged its role in the context of Vargas' Estado Novo, and it had its roots at the beginning of the twentieth century in the nationalist critique made by Alberto Torres. In the end, though, like any authoritarian vision, Macedo Soares' was limited in scope to technical achievements and blind to the cost of the political contexts that permitted them, and the harsh social costs that military rule entailed.

Notes

1 Edmundo de Macedo Soares, "O momento e a missão da indústria," discurso de posse, 7 de julho de 1964. CPDOC/FGV, EMS pi Soares, E. 1964.12.07.
2 Werner Baer, *The Development of the Brazilian Steel Industry*. (Nashville: Vanderbilt University Press, 1969), p. 164.
3 Baer, p. 164, fn. 1.
4 Baer, p. 4.
5 Baer, p. 165.
6 See Oliver Dinius, *Brazil's Steel City: Developmentalism, Strategic Power, and Industrial Relations in Volta Redonda, 1941–1964*. Stanford: Stanford University Press, 2010.
7 "Edmundo de Macedo Soares," in *Diccionário Histórico-Biográfico Brasileiro, Pós-1930*. 2 ed. Alzira Alves de Abreu, Israel Bloch, Fernando Lattman-Weltmann and Sérgio Tadeu Niemeyer Lamarão, eds. Rio de Janeiro: Editora FGV, 2001, vol. V, pp. 5511–5516.
8 Baer, p. 165.
9 Edmundo de Macedo Soares, "A Revolução de 1930: A razão do seu desencadeamento, exemplo da nova orientação na formação técnica do povo," *Revista do Instituto Histórico e Geográfico Brasileiro*, No. 34 (October–December, 1983), pp. 78–79.
10 Edmundo de Macedo Soares, *Um construtor de nosso tempo: depoimento ao CPDOC*. Lúcia Hippolito and Ignez Cordeiro de Farias, org. Rio de Janeiro: Fundação CSN, 1998, p. 47.
11 Macedo Soares, *Constructor*, p. 57.
12 Article 72, Paragraph 17, Constitutional Revision of September 3, 1926. Brazilian Chamber of Deputies, http://www2.camara.leg.br/legin/fed/emecon_sn/1920-1929/emendaconstitucional-35085-3-setembro-1926-532729-publicacaooriginal-15088-pl.html
13 Alexandre Barbosa Lima Sobrinho, *A presença de Alberto Torres*. Rio de Janeiro: Civilização Brasileira, 1968), p. 491.
14 Baer, p. 165.
15 Alberto Torres, *O Problema Nacional Brasileiro*. Rio de Janeiro: Imprensa Nacional, 1914, p. 11.
16 Torres, p. 146.
17 Torres, pp. 11, 28.
18 Barbosa Lima Sobrinho, p. 380.
19 Macedo Soares, *Construtor*, p. 31.
20 Edmundo de Macedo Soares, "Etapa Vencida. Nova Etapa," *Boletim do Instituto Brasileiro de Siderurgia*. No. 2, 1964, CPDOC/FGV, EMS pi Soares, E 1964.03.06.
21 Edmundo Macedo Soares, "A Revolução de 1930: A razão do seu desencadeamento, exemplo da nova orientação na formação técnica do povo," *Revista do Instituto Histórico e Geográfico Brasileiro*, No. 34 (October-December, 1983), p. 73.
22 Caio Prado Jr. *Formação do Brasil Contemporâneo - Colônia*. São Paulo: Editora Martins, 1942.
23 Edmundo de Macedo Soares, "Etapa Vencida. Nova Etapa," *Boletim do Instituto Brasileiro de Siderurgia*. No. 2, 1964, CPDOC/FGV, EMS pi Soares, E 1964.03.06.
24 Edmundo de Macedo Soares, "A empresa pública e a empresa privada no desenvolvimento econômico," CPDOC/FGV, EMS pi Soares, E 1964.11.27.
25 Edmundo de Macedo Soares, "A empresa pública e a empresa privada no desenvolvimento econômico," CPDOC/FGV, EMS pi Soares, E 1964.11.27.
26 Macedo Soares, *Construtor*, p. 28.
27 Macedo Soares, *Construtor*, p. 58.
28 Macedo Soares, *Construtor*, p. 98.

29 Edmundo de Macedo Soares, "Editorial para o Boletim do C.T.M." October, 1940. CPDOC/FGV EMS pi Soares, e. 40.10.01.
30 Baer, p. 165.
31 Edmundo de Macedo Soares, "Intervencionismo Estatal" 1a reunião plenária da indústria do Estado do Rio de Janeiro," CPDOC/FGV, EMS div 1980.06.02.
32 Edmundo Macedo Soares, "A Revolução de 1930: A razão do seu desencadeamento, exemplo da nova orientação na formação técnica do povo," *Revista do Instituto Histórico e Geográfico Brasileiro*, No. 34 (October–December, 1983), p. 94.

References

Amaral, Afrânio do. *Siderurgia e o planejamento econômico do Brasil*. São Paulo: Brasiliense, 1946.

Avelar, André de Sá. "Educação técnica e engenharia no pensamento do General Edmundo de Macedo Soares," *Revista Tecnologia e Sociedade* Vol. 3, No. 4 (2007) 205–227.

Baer, Werner. *The Development of the Brazilian Steel Industry*. Nashville: Vanderbilt, 1969.

Bastos, Humberto. *A conquista siderúrgica no Brasil*. São Paulo: Martins, 1959.

Dinius, Oliver. *Brazil's Steel City: Developmentalism, Strategic Power, and Industrial Relations in Volta Redonda, 1941–1964*. Palo Alto: Stanford, 2011.

Gentil, Alcides. *As idéias de Alberto Torres*. São Paulo: Editora Nacional, 1938.

Lima, Medeiros. *Petróleo, energia elétrica, siderúrgia: A luta pela emancipação*. São Paulo: Paz e Terra, 1975.

Lima Sobrinho, Alexandre José Barbosa. *A Presença de Alberto Torres (Sua Vida e Pensamento)*. Rio de Janeiro: Civilização Brasileira, 1968.

Marson, Adalberto, *A ideologia nacionalista em Alberto Torres*. São Paulo: Duas Cidades, 1979.

Pimenta, Dermeval José. *O minério de ferro na economia nacional*. Rio de Janeiro: Aurora, 1950.

Prado Jr., Caio. *Formação do Brasil Contemporâneo – Colônia*. São Paulo: Editora Martins, 1942.

Soares, Edmundo de Macedo. "A revolucão de 1930: A razão do seu desencadeamento, exemplo da nova orientação na formação técnica do povo." *Revista do Instituto Histórico e Geográfico Brasileiro*. 341 Outurbro–Dezembro, 1983, pp. 77–95.

Soares, Edmundo de Macedo. *Um construtor de nosso tempo: depoimento ao CPDOC*. Lúcia Hippolito and Ignez Cordeiro de Farias, org. Rio de Janeiro: Fundação CSN, 1998.

Torres, Alberto, *O Problema Nacional Brasileiro*. Rio de Janeiro: Imprensa Nacional, 1911.

Torres, Alberto, *A Organização Nacional*. Rio de Janeiro: Imprensa Nacional, 1914.

Wirth, John D. *Minas Gerais in the Brazilian Federation, 1889–1937*. Palo Alto: Stanford, 1977.

Index

Page numbers in **bold** refer to figures, page numbers in *italic* refer to tables.